A Common Market

Episodes in the evolution of the European Union

Jeremy Taylor

With a light-hearted look at the future by Dean Swift

Years 2005 - 2010

DEDICATION

*Jeremy Taylor was married to a Spanish lady and has three adult children.
He has lived and worked in Britain, France, Spain, Germany, the United
States and South America.
After working as a soldier, salesman, artistic controller of a UK national
theatre, teacher of English, French and History, he has retired to the
Canary Islands where he has lived on and off since 1971.*

PREFACE

The European Economic Community was established in 1958, following the Treaties of Rome in 1957. The concept was then known as 'The Common Market' because that was the idea. After the horrors of the Second War, most countries in Europe wanted a kind of customs union, with a common external tariff and a common market available to all with the removal of barriers to trade among its members. In addition there were to be a number of common policies, among which the most important would be the agricultural policy, which would also be common.

There would be common policies for fisheries, regional development, industrial intervention and guidance for economic for economic and social affairs. A European Monetary System would be set up to regulate exchange rate movements among member states' currencies – but this would be superseded in 1998 by the European Monetary Union.

IN 1986, THE SINGLE EUROPEAN ACT WAS PASSED, PERMITTING COMPLETION OF A PROCESS OF MAKING A COMMON MARKET WITHIN THE EUROPEAN COMMUNITY, BY THE BEGINNING OF 1993.

"Bullshit!" said the future Lord Braden of Ham to the farm's security officer. But the guard, who was armed with an empty Kalashnikov, was adamant. "This 'ere farm's running with minks, ferrets, brown rats and . . .ermine. . .wh'ever tha'is. The Law's the Law. No untin. Can't go untin ermine if you can't go untin foxes canyer? Stay away! Can't you read or somepin?" Like everybody else, the guard spoke with the N.R.P. (New Received Pronunciation). He pointed to a printed notice which announced: *'No trespassin. No unting. No awkers or circulars. No himmigrants. No children. No domestic animals. No jernallists. **By order of the UE.***'

"What you want ermine for anyways?" demanded the guard. "'Snow business of yourn," said the future Lord Braden of Ham, but I'll tell you though, right!" (Thirty years of forging a career in the trade unions had made of him a passable orator). "Lords, I'll ave you know," he said, "lords ave to ave ermine on their back when they sit in the House of Lords; I aint go'it. Gotta ave ermine. Some gink tole me there's ermine on this farm. I wannit." This seemed clear enough. Only active members of important trade unions could now be ennobled. Things had changed since there was a Common Market, or the European Commission, or the European Parliament, Union or Congress or whatever it was called this week. What will they be up to next? There were no real lords now, mused the guard, who was a thoughtful sort of fellow when not in the grip of alcohol. Now the Duke of Norfolk, *he* sells fruit and veg at Norwich market; Duke of Northumberland failed and upped it to New Zealand. Marquess of Bath cut off all his hair and joined the auxiliary fire service. The guard read the newspaper – there was only one because of a recent EU Law banning all newspapers in each UE country, except for one. And now er was this old mucker asking to hunt ermine. *The idea*!

The guard raised his Kalashnikov. The future Lord Braden scoffed: "No use pointin that thing at me," he warned, "and besides, it aint got no bullets. Britain can't afford them. I saw it! It's in the newspaper!"

"True enough sport," said the guard, dropping the weapon. They had known each other for years. "Owz that girl of yourn, the sporty one, plays rugby and things?" he asked. Braden snorted, "She's off to join the women's SAS. Good luck to 'er. And your boy?" "My youngest? *He* went to the University! *He* got a whatsit – a degree it's called, in Electoral Engineering. *Now* he's signed on in the Gay Marines. There'll be a war somewhere I suppose." "Always a war somewhere," agreed Braden. The guard nodded, thought for a moment, eyed his old friend, and asked, with a wink, "Suppose I let you in, then, *ow much*!" "Don't be daft!" laughed his future lordship, "you know well as I do there's a tax on bribes!" "*And sex*!" muttered the guard sadly; "*and* using your car for pleasure." agreed Braden; "*and* goin on oliday in Britain instead of abroad! And keeping grey'ounds!" added the guard. But with all things considered he uttered the magic words, "Oh come on in then, get your ermine and I ope it bites you before you strangle yerself wivvit rarnd yer neck". And with these amiable words ringing in his ears, the future Lord Braden of Ham went happily in search of ermine.

Dean Swift

2005

21ST JANUARY

Unemployment in Europe

According to Eurostat (European Office of Statistics), Poland, Slovakia and Spain stand at the top of the list of the twenty-five nations which comprise the European Union – for unemployment that is. The Spanish figure for able and/or qualified people out of work is 10.5%. Here at last is a really positive achievement for the socialist government which won the March 14 election last year. The overall average out-of-work figure over the twenty-five is 8.9%, as of last November. The figure rose a little during the Christmas period, as it always does, and will probably now recover during the early months of 2005. European money men are pleased that the euro remains stable against the dollar, in some accountable months much stronger.

Lowest unemployment figures are found in the Republic of Eire (Ireland) – 4.3%. It is a generally known fact that Ireland is doing well in the economic stakes, along with other countries not in the EU such as India. Luxembourg is up there too, with 4.4% unemployed in her workforce. Austria can boast 4.5%. But it is poor suffering Poland which drags the averages up, with her 18.4%, followed by Slovakia (17.3%), Spain (10.5%) and Germany (9.9%). A quick look at the whole group of nations that make up the European Union shows (counting only those nations where such figures are made available) that ten have rising unemployment, while thirteen can prove a decrease.

Holland, Cyprus, Luxemburg and Hungary are showing a slightly alarming tendency to increase unemployment; though their annual figures are good, they have been better. Also figuring in this list are Lithuania, Estonia and Malta, each of which have had better figures. Over the Eurozone (countries whose currency is the euro) as a whole, unemployment among men stays relatively stable at 7.9%. Women out of work reduced from 10.3% just before the recent addition of new UE members, to 10.1%. Eurostat informs us that the countries within the European Zone that use the euro registered 12.6 million out-of-work citizens in November last year, but among the full twenty-five, that figure rises to 19.1 million.

Those erotic drawings by Turner were not burned after all

Art history is full of mysterious cases of 'lost' or 'missing believed burnt' pictures turning up again. The occurrence is usually singular in both senses, but the very recent re-appearance of 145 drawings by J.M.W. Turner (1774-1851) has solved a deep mystery that had lasted since the death of art critic and wit John Ruskin (1819 – 1900). Art students have always been taught that a huge collection of erotic drawings and paintings by the master of land and seascapes was burnt on discovery by Ruskin, probably in 1848. Why Ruskin should have destroyed works of art by a master painter must be explained by psychologists, but Ian Warrell, art specialist at the Tate Gallery in London has announced that the Turner erotic's were never burned by Ruskin or anyone else. Warrell reached this conclusion after a minute inspection of thousands of Turner originals. Warrell says that the 145 erotic drawings that Ruskin confessed to having 'burned', were actually hidden by him in an archive with a classification system designed to confuse. The motive, according to Warrell, was that Ruskin feared publication of the drawings might 'emotionally disturb the British people'. So, he 'burned them for the greater good of Britain'.

Here it should be added that a Parliamentary Commission of 1851, three years after the supposed burning, had 'expressed their fear that the Turner drawings might be shown to the public', indicating that art experts were suspicious of Ruskin's avowal that he had burned them. It is a fact that John Ruskin was more than a little mad in the last years of his life. He was a great admirer of Turner, making his actions difficult to believe. In a letter to the National Gallery, Ruskin said; ' I am satisfied that these works have been burnt, just as well for the reputation of Turner as for his interior peace, and I am pleased to have been witness to the burning.'

4TH JANUARY

Focus on Britain and Spain in Europe

In precisely the same way as his equal in Spain, Mr. Tony Blair has, since 1997, contrived to hide the fact that he values power for its own sake. Both Zapatero and Blair *like* being Premier – the Number One voice. Both like smaller voices at their elbow, so long as they do not offer differing opinions. Zapatero has his Miguel Sebastian; Blair has his Jack Straw. Both Blair and Zapatero also have deadly enemies, disguised as allies; Gordon Brown and José Bono respectively. Now both governments seek to tear up the constitutional map traditionally known by their countrymen, and re-design it to suit themselves and their Socialist parties. The excuse for this is 'modernisation'. In the case of Britain, one of these modernising moves was Devolution. It has not worked and has led to near economic ruin in Scotland, and boredom and apathy in Wales. It has also led to outstanding injustices, such as the fact that Scottish MPs sit and vote in the British Government in London, whereas not one single English MP has a seat in Edinburgh.

Blair's reform of the House of Lords has descended to farce. He expelled the hereditary peers from the Upper Chamber to replace them with toadies who would allow his absolute majority in the Lower House to rule Britain how he wishes. But that hasn't worked either, because the 'toadies', once the ermine is on, turn traitor and thrown out his bills! The whole affair has been mismanaged: there is talk of simply returning to the happier old days of ancient and modern inherited aristocracies acting as a Senate under no kind of influence from cabinet ministers. But we must wait for a Tory Government to make *that* reform. I doubt it will.

On taking power in Spain Zapatero promptly chose eight women and eight men as his Cabinet; each one also loves being a Minister, but what do they *do*? If you read the papers you will find they don't appear to *do* anything, except squabble, and 'rectify' what another Minister has just said. Only two, Pedro Solbes at the Treasury and José Bono at Defence *do* anything worthwhile, but they too are constantly correcting each other, their Leader, and their colleagues. In both Britain and Spain the same wily process of destruction of the opposition by any means available has been employed, by Blair since 1997 against the remains of the Tory Party, and Zapatero, Rubalcaba *et al* since March 2004 against the Popular Party. The latter is led by a charming, witty *Gallego* called Rajoy. But Rajoy has no *teeth*. His late boss José María Aznar had a lot of very sharp teeth beneath that awful moustache. Rare indeed was the occasion in the *Cortes* when any member of the then Opposition could master Aznar. No-one ever did. But still the PSOE, following the magnificent example set by the Labour Party in UK, is heavily involved in a media-led assault on the Popular Party. It is easier for Zapatero, Caldera and Blanco to orchestrate this, because the chief financier of the PSOE is a multi-billionaire communications boss called (of all the misnomers), *Jesús* Polanco. All Polanco's resources are at Zapatero's call. If he wants to doubt a good reputation, spoil a career, cause the ruin of a once popular figure, all he has to do is call on Mr Polanco's vast network of newspapers, magazines, TV and radio stations etc. gathered together under the name *Grupo Prisa* – and Bob's your uncle. In Britain Mr Blair's 'useful uncle' had, until recently, been Mr Rupert Murdoch, but 'Rupe' seems to be changing his tune these days, and Mr Blair cannot expect unqualified support today in his newspapers. Mr Murdoch and his group care more about the death agonies of their Twentieth Century Fox film company.

Now, the latest bitter pill the British people must swallow is the obvious decrease in the popularity of the Crown. Mr Blair's government is in the stealthy process of introducing questions on monarchy's rôle in Modern Britain, in order to promote more control of the country by the Labour Party.

18TH FEBRUARY

No hypocrisy like British hypocrisy: Prince Hal gets it in the silly neck

There is no news like stale news, but since a vulgar newspaper like the *Sun* still fills space with 'comment' and 'personal interest' muck about young Prince Harry, I thought I might as well add my ha'porth. British hypocrisy is of course the best known in Europe, though Americans are pretty good at it too. *Time Magazine* and *Newsweek* were always at it. But the *Sun* and *News of the World* are past masters at the art. Let's see what Somerset Maugham had to say about it: 'hypocrisy is the most difficult and nerve-wracking vice that any man can pursue; it needs an unceasing vigilance and a rare detachment of spirit. It cannot, like adultery or gluttony, be practised at spare moments; it is a whole-time job'. Historian Macaulay puts it better: 'we know no spectacle as ridiculous as the British public in one of its periodical fits of morality'.

No more perfect example can be found than the inaptly named Dickie Arbiter, I believe this to be his real name, using a radio programme to rant about the 'atrocious actions' of a 20-year old male. As no-one is expected to attack anyone *young* these days, I assumed it must be a member of the royal family. Anyone can assault *them*. It is so easy. What happened was this. A young man went to a young people's fancy dress party dressed as a member of the Afrika Korps. He was badly advised by his tailor, because the 'uniform' included an armband with a swastika on it. Historically speaking, this is an error because very few, if any members of the Afrika Corps were members of the National Socialist Party. Their leader, Rommel, was not only *not* a Nazi, he was persuaded to take a lethal dose of poison by Hitler's messengers after they inaccurately connected him with the July 20, 1944 conspiracy to blow up the Fuehrer.

Someone, no friend to Prince Harry, took a picture of him in his fancy dress, and sold it to the yellow press. The *Sun*, among others, exploded in perfect frenzy. Out it flowed, pomposity, class hatred, a bullying tone, assumed outrage and other examples of Blair's Britain. The object of all this venom was the Prince of Wales' younger son. It was said, among other things, that Harry's guilt was doubled because of the proximity of the anniversary of the liberation of Auschwitz. Oh dear, as if we were ever going to be allowed to consign German concentration camps, the Second World War, the horror of it all to History, where it belongs. *The odd thing is that Stalin's Gulag is hardly ever gets a mention.* There is certainly not any trumpeted anniversary every year to remember the twenty-four million or more, exterminated in the Communist camps. If young Harry had gone to the party dressed up as a member of the NKVD I suppose no-one would have cared. But it is not only the vulgar press that smells of hypocrisy. China, a communist country, organises the biggest system of slave labour in history, but you never hear a squeak from any British Labour MP about US or British spending taxpayers' money there in unheard of quantities. How could they? They spend all their time condemning a likeable boy who, like his father, has *always* been badly advised. No doubt the same Labour MPs who scream at the British royal family go to Chinese tourist resorts, which if they only knew are but a few miles from the gulags, where prisoners are daily worked to death. How strange it is that while we are satiated with reminders about Hitler's atrocities, those of Mao Tse-tung never get a look in. Worthy French historians have already estimated that the victims of Communism already reach the sixty million mark; the process has never stopped in China.

But back to Prince Harry; why should he choose the uniform of a storm trooper in the Africa Korps? He could have gone as Dracula, or Frankenstein's Monster, or the Terminator. The reason is that he is probably not interested in politics or history, like virtually every other young person of his generation. I doubt if he confesses any ideology, but like all young men, he does like a good time, a laugh, girls, fast driving and a drink or three. So what's new, Doc? He has abundant energy, and he's going to need it in a few weeks' time when he goes to Sandhurst.

4ᵀᴴ MARCH

The redundancy of Left and Right

I'll bet during all your life you have heard the ordinary expression for direction, 'left' or 'right' used as a cant mode for denoting someone's political position. Are they conservative, or labour? Is she a 'leftie'? Is he that nonsensical 'a little to the right of Ghengis Khan'? Perhaps this use of left and right must be re-valued. An example springs to mind; Fidel Castro. Now is Fidel left and right? He shoots gays, smashes trade unions, doesn't permit democratic elections, locks up anyone who fails to agree with him, has billions of dollars stashed away in the hated United States (waiting for what I wonder?), and has introduced a positively royal system of accession to the Cuban throne. Anyone who has been to Cuba knows this last expression is not far from the truth. Castro making a visit to a hospital, say, is worth seeing. 40 bodyguards, armed to their Miami-fixed teeth; doctors and administrators bowing and knuckling the forehead – now, is Castro left-wing or right-wing? You decide.

We are told by the history books that it all started in that chamber of horrors the French Revolution. It was the French who taught us to think 'right' or 'left'. It was a not very clever notion that was used to replace rational debate with an easy division into two rival gangs who exercised hate for each other. Ever since then we have been doomed with this 'left', 'right', quick march to the wall, guillotine, prison cell or lunatic asylum. But this is cretinous. It has strangled political philosophy. Many writers agree that this rubbish can only be stopped when someone arrives on the scene with *both* political stances so marked that all our ordinary, every-day political reasoning will be thrown into confusion and we will be forced to think it out again.

But first we had better ask ourselves a few pertinent questions: Is it logical, for instance, to think of communism as 'left-wing'? Communism has invariably led to total rule by a tiny group in government that has everything the 'elite' always used to have. All communist countries are neatly divided into the 'Haves' and the 'Have-nots'. The former enjoy private dachas with flocks of servants; private boxes at the theatre, uniformed footmen holding trays. Anyone who has travelled in Soviet Russia or any of her satellites before the fall of the Wall will remember the sumptuous palaces, hundreds of eager secretaries, the best food available. Outside those palaces the people, in whose name the Revolution was invoked, queued or starved. Was the Soviet government left-wing or right-wing?

'He is a little to the right of Attila the Hun, or Ghengis Khan'. What does this mean? Were these two horde-leaders 'right-wing' because they were cruel? Joseph Stalin was crueller still 'in the name of the people', naturally. We are told that 'the right believe in economic freedom, and the left in personal freedom' If this is so, why has the 'left-wing' government of Mr Blair spent the last eight years restricting the freedoms of the British people; is there anything left in Britain that you are actually allowed to do. Check it first, because a new Statute may have been passed yesterday making you a criminal if you do it. If the movement of a citizen within his or her own country is controlled by the possession of an ID card, is that person free? Is the government that introduced the card 'left-wing' or 'right-wing'? Is it left-wing or right-wing to hate capitalism, by the way? Both Hitler and Lenin and many previous South African pro-apartheid regimes hated capitalism too. But Hitler was a millionaire before 1933 via his association with capitalists.

What about our attitudes towards 'the weak' and 'the strong'? Can we take it as read that the 'left' will protect the 'weak'? Equally, must we assume that the 'right' will only protect the 'strong'? Good examples of weak and strong would be an unborn but perfectly formed baby inside its mother, and a healthy, adult murderer of pregnant women. Is it all right to use government power to make abortion not only legal but recommended, and at the same time pass laws that will protect the life of the assassin?

18TH MARCH

The Queen, her son, and his new marriage

Now was it right for the Queen of Great Britain (and Canada) to refuse to attend the marriage (in a civil ceremony) of her son the Prince of Wales? Was this boycott necessary? Could anyone in the anti-royalist Britain of today really care? Who imagines that Charles will ever be King, or indeed his eldest son William either? The Queen shows every sign of enjoying the same long life as her mother. If she does live that long - the Prince of Wales will be well over seventy when he ascends to the throne – if there is still a throne. Is it not obvious to the British that Mr Blair intends to be the Prime Minister who supervised the gradual elimination by stealth of the British royal family. After all, Mr Blair has prohibited practically everything else, destroyed the House of Lords, banned hunting, stopped you smoking (or tried to), ridiculed the House of Commons, and fully expects the British people to give him a third term to complete the process. Completion of Mr Blair's plans must include the end of the royal family. The excuse will be its *'uselessness'*, its *'antiquated image*? And 'its *cost'*.

But back to that ceremony at the Windsor Guildhall; should the Queen sally down from the Castle to a registry office to watch her always badly advised, always obstinate son go through a second marriage, to his mistress of thirty years? Why not? The Queen goes there frequently, the last time in 2002. Anti-royalists will say that there is plenty of precedent for monarchs not attending the marriages of offspring. In 1863 Queen Victoria, for example, refused to attend the wedding of her wayward son Edward (future Edward VII) to a real princess (Alexandra of Denmark), but then Victoria was in mourning for her recently dead husband Albert, and in Victorian times it would have been unseemly for a queen to attend a (supposedly) enjoyable occasion.

Chief adviser to the Queen in everything, not just royal marriages, is her Prime Minister. To date it is difficult to think of a worse adviser than Tony Blair – perhaps our Ken the mayor of London? But can we expect sound advice from a man determined to end the whole caboodle anyway? One supposes that Blair now claims the news of the imminent wedding of Mrs Parker-Bowles with the Prince of Wales took him by surprise, and he hasn't had enough time to consult Cherie? Surely the British press has been intimating rather loudly since the year 2000 that such an occasion will be inevitable. Mind you, there are laws about these things: the Marriage Act (1836) prevented members of the royal family marrying in a civil ceremony, and the 1949 Marriage Act made civil marriages available to everyone – *except* members of the royal family. '*Nothing in this Act shall affect any law or custom relating to the marriage of members of the royal family*'.

Why does the Government hesitate in this matter? They do what they like anyway. They have torn up eight hundred years of legal history by suspending Habeas Corpus in the new Prevention of Terrorism bill. They have closed the book on hunting foxes on horseback, effectively ending eleven hundred years of historical and agricultural tradition. Farmers declare that stopping the hunt will upset a natural balance of Nature, and besides, foxes must be kept down somehow; if by shooting, those against hunting on horseback haven't thought about the agonising consequence of a shotgun blast that only wounds the wild animal. Not finished off, a fox will make its way to its home, where it may have to bite off a leg. Which is less cruel, ask the experts, allowing hounds to kill in less than five seconds, or making a wounded creature live out the remainder of its life in pain? The main problem with do-gooders and liberals is that they are braindead.

The answer is so simple, that no-one except about five hundred journalists have thought of it. As this Government can do anything – lie, cheat, abuse, prohibit, ban, change for the sake of change etc., why can't they pass a new Bill. It will clarify that although a previous Law stated that if Windsor Castle were to be used as the site for a civil wedding, it would have to be made available to any ordinary member of the public to get married in for the next three years – a wedding between Camilla Parker Bowles and the Prince of Wales would be exempt from this obligation: and, two, that from the passing of the new Bill onwards, members of the British royal family should be able to get married in a civil ceremony. The problem is, or was, that the Marriage Act of 1836 barred members of the royal family from getting hitched in such a ceremony. This Government can do everything *else* with impunity; why can't they do *this*?

1ST APRIL

'For Valour' – after twenty-three years, another Victoria Cross

The last time the VC was awarded in Britain to a serving member of the armed forces was in 1982, posthumously, to the families of Ian John MacKay and Herbert Jones, two British soldiers who died in the Falkland Islands. Before that, a Victoria Cross was won in 1965. In all, only eleven of the most prestigious military medal the British monarch can bestow has been given either to the hero personally, or their family.

I once met a VC – Sergeant Vic Speakman, who had rallied the last of his regiment's men, all officers and other NCOs killed, in the trenches of the Korean War, fighting desperately against overwhelming Chinese forces. He was a legend of course, partly for his valour, but also for his constant rise and fall in rank in the British Army due to a tendency to raise the elbow. I asked him about Korea. Spectacularly brave people never talk about their own exploits unless the questioner is very persuasive– though sometimes they will write about them. Speakman said, 'we didn't have anything left to shoot with, the ammo ran out a long time before. We had plenty of bottles and cans of beer though, so we kept them by our side until the Chinks were near enough, and then we threw the bottles and tins at them.' At no time did Speakman use any other pronoun but 'we'. Another famous VC was the leader of a group of young men who should have *all* won the medal. These were the 'dam busters', pilots and crew of Lancaster bombers who destroyed a number of crucially important dams during World War II, crippling (if only for a while) the Rühr Valley's heavy industry. He was Squadron Leader Guy Gibson, who survived these amazingly dangerous bombing raids made in the very teeth of accurate enemy artillery, but did not survive the War.

Now, for once the news from Iraq is not about murdered hostages or civilians, shockingly withdrawn troops, or the snail-slow process of change that might lead to democracy. The news concerns a young man of 25 who serves with the first battalion of the Royal Princess of Wales' Regiment called Johnson Beharry. He has been awarded the Victoria Cross for saving the lives of thirty companions-in-arms at Al Amarah. Wounded in the head after a murderous rocket attack conducted by the 'Resistance' against soldiers in trucks, driver Beharry managed to crawl out of his nearly destroyed vehicle. Under fire, he then returned again and again to drag the surviving members of his company out of the wreckage into cover. He was badly wounded in the head, again, only six weeks later, when once again the truck he was driving was attacked with rocket fire. Noting that his commander and companions were not in any position after the explosion to help themselves, and in spite of his wound, Beharry again found the strength to assist his friends towards adequate cover. Having done this, and only when he had finished, Beharry fainted, and remained in coma for some time, before recovering in a military hospital. When the full story of his exploits reached the High Command, the soldier was immediately recommended for the Victoria Cross, a rarely awarded medal originally cast from the remains of two Russian cannons captured in the Crimean War. Before long, the young man born in the Caribbean island of Grenada was told he would be given the medal 'for his repeated extreme gallantry and unquestionable valour', as part of the citation read. Another paragraph says 'he was valiant despite suffering direct attacks, his own serious wounds, and the damage done to his vehicle by the enemy, and it is this that makes him deserving of the highest award for valour.' Beharry's answers to the hundreds of questions directed at him after the recent award ceremony were brief in the extreme. 'Perhaps I was, eh, valiant. I don't know. I think anyone in my, that position would have done the same. I was just doing my job, and you don't really have much time to think about things in that sort of situation.'

15TH APRIL

Another comic budget?

By the time you are reading this Mr. Gordon Brown will have delivered the news kept so far as a half-open secret in his black dispatch case. His ninth annual Budget since Labour election in 1997 was more or less common knowledge any way, according to the papers. Mr. Brown told us that Britain has a robust economy; sound, healthy, not obese but well-fed. It is expected to grow by 3 to 3.5% this year We might have high inflation, low productivity and growing unemployment, a public sector growing like mad, as it takes on more and more thousands of uncivil servants; it may be that public spending is so high no country's economy could sustain it, but everybody seems to run two or more cars and take their holidays thrice a year in Playa de las Américas. So that's all right then.

Mr. Brown is borrowing money so fast Britain will need fifty years to pay it back, but his creative accounting will think of ways to cruise round corners and keep smiling. Take Network Rail as a good example, a splendid loser, but, as it is described as a private company, any cash shoved towards its emptying coffers cannot be defined as public spending.

The public pension scheme is a doddle too. The papers tell us it would require an intake of about seven hundred billion pounds to 'put the account in order', but I doubt if Mr. Brown will make mention of this in his Budget speech. This kind of glossing over is hardly new – I remember Mr. Howe invented 'negative public expenditure', a splendidly conservative manner of cooking the books. Mind you, compared to Brown, Howe is no champion at this sport. Brown's method is loud delivery with plenty of accentuated, no-nonsense, Scots accountant speaks, holes stopped up, holes left open, and plenty of emphasis on popular causes; local municipal tax cuts, free public transport for pensioners, double-paid maternity leave for new mothers over one years, a million new child-care places, stamp duty on buying property starting at £120,000, money for British science research, money for British film studios (are there any?). Mr Michael Howard branded the measures a "vote now, pay later budget". He said, 'the simple fact is that if Labour get in again, taxes will go up again'.

It is sad to think that the one seriously hopeful reform that Mr. Brown *could* introduce in his Budget speech is the one he *won't* mention: this is the flat tax system, in which everyone pays the same rate of tax, usually between ten and twelve percent. As it is, rates become progressively higher on incomes as they rise – which leads to stronger tax evasion and less revenue at the end of the day. The gains made by using a flat tax rate are tremendous, as has been found by the few brave countries that now employ it – Jersey, Hong Kong, Estonia (26% but about to be reduced to 20%), Lithuania, Latvia, Russia (12%), where revenues *doubled* after its introduction, Serbia, the Ukraine, Slovakia, Georgia, Romania and Poland (18%).

Germany, in severe financial trouble, is responding by an imminent presentation of a flat 30% rate on corporate and personal income, though the Opposition there proposes an even flatter system, much simplified. One of the advantages of a flat rate system is the abolition of national insurance, which is of course yet another form of direct taxation, and whose administration costs more than it earns.

In modern Britain, the people in the top fifth of income earners pay a little less tax. But if you come within the bottom fifth you pay not far off 40% in direct and indirect taxes, local town hall taxes, income tax etc. One state in America, New Hampshire, has had no income tax at all since the Second World War. The tough guys from New England believe a worker should receive his or her whole income untouched; the tax comes on anything and everything *he or she chooses to buy,* from a house to a tube of toothpaste. In New Labour Britain, after eight years of New Labour government, it is the poorest in society who are still bashed for more tax than the richest. This is what has been called 'Mr. Brown's progressive consensus'.

*It is well known that the Blair/Brown acme of political economy has been the quite enormous increase in the creation of public sector jobs. A million new jobs have been added to the public sector bill since 1997. From the middle of 2002 to the same time in 2003, the British state added 162,000 workers to the state payroll, while the private sector managed only 98,000. There are now nearly seven million public sector workers, not to mention their dependants (or voting age), not forgetting the gigantic army of contractors, lawyers, suppliers and consultants who must depend on the generosity of the public sector for their living. There are 94,000 workers in the Department for Work and Pensions alone. Am I politically naïve? Not me, and most certainly not Messrs. Blair and Brown, for they have given a huge chunk of the total British workforce the best reason of all to vote Labour in the forthcoming election - their job depends on it. The Conservatives have promised to *start* (if they should by some miracle win the election) by excising 225,000 public sector jobs as irrelevant and money-wasting.

Gordon Brown will (at last) have to admit that public money cannot continue to nourish the levels of spending to which Blair's government is committed. In order to do this the Budget will have to raise taxes in infinitely more noticeable ways – and that *would* be politically naïve! In 1979, the Labour government had to admit to employing 7,449,000 public sector workers. *Tsunamis* of disgust at this kind of fat-cattery aroused Britain's voters from their usual torpor, and an election brought Margaret Thatcher in as Prime Minister. This will not happen in the imminent general election (May 5th), but unless Mr Brown has some razor-sharp cuts up his sleeve (excuse the mixed metaphor); it will happen at the next.

Two more heads of state die

At the time of writing (morning of 6 April), Prince Rainier of Monaco has died after being *in extremis* for some time. The Pope, as tough as ever, held on longer than any of the Vatican's doctors ever expected. Fighting to the last, he died on April 2nd. By the time you read this there will have been an overflowing abundance of tributes to this fearless man; One remembers Pope John-Paul's first words when he moved from Cracow in 1978 to become Pontiff of the Roman Catholic Church. He said: "Do not be afraid". I don't believe he has ever been afraid in his life, not of dangerous sports like ski-ing, at which he was expert, or of assassins (having survived a murderous attempt on his life, he went and prayed with the young man sent to kill him, in a prison cell). Far from being afraid of the mighty Soviet Union, he set out to destroy it, and with the tumbling of the Berlin Wall, he achieved his wish. Carol Woyjtyla faced down every adversity, illness, wars, internecine squabbling in his own Church, doubts, injustice, immorality. There have been many popes before him. There certainly will not be another like him.

The Prince of Monaco also had a tenacious hold on life. His life was not happy until he married Grace Kelly, and has not been happy after her early and mysterious death. Rarely has he been 'a darling of the Press'. The papers have already started making un-called for remarks about Prince Albert's future as the Prince of Monaco, not forgetting to mention the doubtful past life, reputation and bad example of Albert's two sisters.

When Prince Rainier married Grace Kelly the TV commentators around the world made jokes about banana principalities. Rainier ignored this and set about making Monaco the real jewel of the Mediterranean.

17TH APRIL

The demise of MG/Rover

It does seem peculiar. The British car industry appears to have crashed on the rocks, sunk with all hands. When I was a young man a double-page spread of the magazine *The Motor* was filled with columns of entirely British motor cars, classified under HP and price. Within fifty years they have vanished. Morris, Austin, Standard, Hillman, Sunbeam, Singer, Riley, Jowett, Armstrong Siddeley, Wolseley, Triumph, Healey vanished; Rolls-Royce and Bentley gone to the Germans; Vauxhall to the Americans. Of the famous solely British companies I believe only dear Morgan of Malvern still battles on. Now MG and Rover, *marques* embodying everything that was best in British motoring, have gone up the spout. How difficult it is to understand. In Madrid, a new shop has opened in the Calle Zurbano selling new Aston Martins. My brother-in-law lives almost next door to the showroom. He says these seriously expensive cars are selling like the proverbial hot cakes in the capital of Spain, and that the owner of the concessionaire has told him they are about to open a branch in Barcelona. Who can afford the insurance? Aston-Martin is owned by Ford*.

The newly defunct Rover 75 and 45 were both excellent, prize-winning cars, selling well in Europe and the States. Perhaps some economist can explain. Why do auto factories go bust when they have products selling well? The British owners of MG/Rover, called Phoenix Venture Holdings, have made the measly offer of €71.5 million to try to keep the company afloat, though production has stopped. It is said Phoenix awaits a substantial offer from China (Shanghai Automotive). I'll believe that when I see it. What SAIC wait for is *total* bankruptcy in the hope they'll pick up the essential machinery and technology cheap, before shipping it to China. Phoenix bought the Rover Group from German BMW in 2000, for a

nominal ten quid (€14.5). Now, in addition to the afore-mentioned sum, they offer MG/Rover the Victorian castle of Studeley, near Warwick, presumably to see what they can get for this splendid house and gardens. But *Price water house coopers*, who have directed the company since its forced cessation of production, say that none of this proposed injection of capital is enough. Meanwhile the British Government has come up with the super-small sum of €9.4 million (out of an annual budget that runs into tens of billions) to help pay salaries until the end of the month; and Brussels, always ready to help Europe's least favourite daughter (Britain), has reminded Brown and Blair that any financial help potentially heading for MG/Rover must count on the appropriate permission from Our Lords at the European Union. You can always rely on Brussels to stand by with the coffin nails and hammer, especially if the corpse is British.
*But not for long . . .

Mr Blair's part in the royal wedding

Since the post of Prime Minister began, the men (and one woman) who have held this post have inherited from each other the duty to advise, and protect if necessary Britain's kings and queens. This sometimes irksome task (for both parties) is taken on in order to maintain both the dignity and the continuity of the British crown and our constitution. Oddly enough, this good solid relationship has applied with both the Labour Party and the Conservatives, even if the Queen's subtlest and probably warmest relationships were with two Labour PMs, Wilson and Callaghan. Much has been written about the cordial, but cold relations the Queen maintained with Margaret Thatcher, and the avuncular ones practised with skill and decorum by Winston Churchill and 'Uncle' Harold Macmillan.

On the subject of the recent marriage of the Duke and Duchess of Cornwall however, things have broken down. First came the much publicised cutting-dead of the Prince of Wales and Mrs Parker-Bowles by Cherie Blair in Westminster Cathedral, following sweet Cherie's refusal to curtsey to the Queen. Recently, Mr Blair has made reference to 'my armed forces' while on a visit to Kosovo, which caused some raising of eyebrows. Perhaps Mr Blair does not know that Britain's armed forces owe their allegiance to the Monarch, not to the Prime Minister, precisely to avoid *coups d'état,* popular in banana republics. Indeed, I tremble when I think about the positively dangerous consequences of the military giving their allegiance to a political party. We are told by the newspapers that Mr Jack Straw makes regular reference to Mr Blair as 'Head of State'. Only three years ago No. 10 Downing Street made a serious attempt to enlarge its role at the lying-in-state of the Queen Mother. Of course I know that New Labour and its leaders dislike the Monarchy because it occupies too much space in the area they believe should be theirs alone. But nothing demonstrates Mr Blair's contempt for the constitution and his part in it than his preparations for the royal wedding.

As soon as news of the Pope's death came through, it was known that the Vatican funeral would take place on the same Friday as that chosen for Prince Charles' nuptials. While Charles and his advisers (including his parents) were trying to work out how best to react and what to do, Downing Street remained silent. Then without any consultation with anyone, Downing Street announced that Tony Blair would attend the Pope's funeral in Rome rather than take up his already officially accepted invitation to Windsor. The PM and Mrs Blair chose to ignore the wedding ceremony without prior notice, or consultation. Some might see this as simple bad manners. But it is odder than that. No British PM has ever attended a papal funeral before, for Britain is actually *not* a Roman Catholic country. More, the papacy stands for certain autocratic principles and a liking for antique dogma supposedly alien to the British state. For the British Prime Minister to abandon his duties towards the future Head of the Church of England and rush off to the Vatican instead is to say the least questionable and distinctly odd.

On the other hand, one must remember Mr Blair is first and foremost a politician. At the Vatican there will be photo-calls with world leaders, including 'both Bushes and a Clinton'. At the Windsor service Mr Blair and especially his wife would be unnoticed – at a wedding already written-off by the British press as 'a farce'. The British Prime Minister's duty is to advise the Monarch. He should have talked urgently with the Queen about timing and constitutional implications. He didn't. Worse, the timing of the wedding itself was suspect. No-one believes the PM was unaware of his own plans to hold the next general election only a few weeks after the ceremony. Any pre-election period is always full of media coverage, and an examination by the Opposition of the Government's record. The wedding would however cover at least a week, in which both electorate and the press could concentrate instead on Camilla and Charles. Politics, especially of the damaging kind to New Labour, would effectively be suppressed for a week. The date was, however, proposed by Downing Street, and the advice taken by the Monarch. Then, following the Pope's death, Mr Blair opted for the Vatican on Friday. This is characteristic of the man. It doesn't matter that the wedding was then put forward to Saturday. The damage to the constitutional relationship between Monarch and PM had already been done. New Labour has allowed enormous rises in stealth taxes, increased public sector jobs by 850,000, debased both Houses of Parliament, introduced the most divisive Law (the anti-Hunting Bill) seen in Britain since Cromwell, attacked the judges and their courts, lost the reputation of the secret services, reduced the Army to a couple of colour sergeants with halberds, ruined the transport system, abused its own organ (the BBC), fouled up the Civil Service, lied consistently, and lost its integrity. But New Labour will win again, of course, unless the EU does something positive for a change, like insisting on a turn-out of more than 50% at the polls for results of a General Election to be legal.

27TH MAY

What a surprise! Labour wins again, and again, and again . . .

In what must be the most easily predictable general election for a hundred years, the reliable British public returned New Labour, Tony Blair, Gordon Brown, old Uncle Jack Straw and all to power, for the third time. No one in their right senses could have thought Michael Howard and his 'nasties' might win. Blair himself stole the Centre-Right position from the Conservatives in 1997, and since then the Tories have been a Party looking for a political position. Having said that, one must hope that Mr Howard does not really mean to resign; he is not that old (62), his training as a lawyer stood him in good stead, and if only he were to stay and not give up the good fight, promise to continue demanding smaller government, deregulation, an end to stealth taxes, tougher discipline in schools, and overall reformation of the NHS, there will eventually be a change. For him to go now would mean the end of the Conservative Party. John Major's demise was the result of his own feeling of superiority. William Hague was an excellent debater who constantly thrashed Blair at Prime Minister's Question Time. But he decided to go, arrogantly, and peevishly, after the defeat in 2001. What was left in the Tory party after that was a sad vacuum and trauma, instead of intelligent reflection. It was at this time that internal conflict became commonplace among Conservatives. Blair had divided – and thus rules.

However, to be a little ruthless myself, I can only hope that if Mr Howard does resign, he will be replaced by one of the Young Turks in the Party, someone cunning and ruthless, such as David Davis or David Cameron – more partisan than whom you cannot get. A third consecutive defeat has not happened to Mr Howard's party since 1910. But even then the newly elected Liberals could only govern with the aid of the Irish Nationalists, which must have made Mr Asquith feel a little reduced. And a little later the Kaiser's international ambitions caused an urgent need for a coalition government anyway. There are extraordinary anomalies afoot. The British public has just voted yet again for an entirely discredited Prime Minister, an originally rather charismatic young man who has surrounded himself with cronies, and lied himself out of every crisis. I believe he has believed all the lies himself. In this startling notion there can be little doubt Blair has been much helped by his wife Cherie.

Those Britons who thought the end had come at last for Mr Blair must be heart-broken. Let us look at it this way: in the next five years there really is a chance for the Conservatives to 'get their act together', whoever their leader is. They must be brave, and stick to their belief in stricter immigration control, before it is too late. They will be supported in this by the British press being less politically correct. They will be helped also by those British ethnic minorities who themselves are frightened of breakdowns in race relations if this colossal immigration stays out of control. Surely, stalwart Conservatives hope, there must be someone, somewhere who believes in strong border controls. Or will the British just give up and head for Tuscany or the Canary Islands. If the latter should prove to be the choice, they had better sell up quickly and get on the 'plane with the family aspidistra, because stronger border controls in the Canary Islands are the 'in thing' right now.

Future Opposition leaders must stick to the belief that is wrong for hospitals to kill people, and wrong for young men to kill old ladies for their handbag. Mr Straw and his police chiefs never seem mind very much. The Conservatives still believe that teachers should not feel they must go armed to work, and must continue to insist this is as 'incorrect'. No-one wants to see caning re-introduced, especially teachers, but something has to be done about rowdy classrooms and dangerous school corridors, no failures allowed in examinations, and illiteracy and innumeracy across the board. Mr Blair, Mr Brown and a whole succession of 'Education Ministers' have achieved precisely nothing in this respect, except win elections. That is what New Labour is there for – to win elections. No-one said anything about governing afterwards.

Meanwhile, what of the immediate future? Mr Blair will probably step down, and Mr Brown will step up. He was responsible for creating 850,000 new functionaries who depend on the continuance in power of a Labour Government. The salaries and perks of these 850,000 are paid by everyone in Britain, not just those who vote Labour. In modern Britain those with jobs work for the Government from January 1st to the 1st July every year. He has spent all Britain's hard-earned cash and reserves, but the Chancellor will still become a thoroughly Scottish Prime Minister. It is said he intends to turn Britain into a kind of Sweden, whatever that means. Now, will the British people want to become Swedes? Not that there is anything shaming about being a Swede. Lots of people already are. The question is, should Europe have two Swedens?

How very odd

In passing, I found a singular fact in a motoring magazine that I must mention. It should be interesting even for those not moved by prices, or automobiles for that matter. Compare two brand new cars, both to be found in the very highest echelons of quality motoring. The Bentley Continental Flying Spur is to be launched in July. It is powered by an engine of 12 cylinders and nearly 6000 CCs, producing 560 HP. The price of this, the fastest (312kph) 5-seater saloon car in the world, is to be €184,320. The Ferrari 612 Scaglietti has two occasional seats at the back suitable for Yorkshire Terrier puppies. It is also 12-cylindered, producing 540 HP. It will do 320 kph. Owners will probably need to take out a couple of mortgages just to pay the annual insurance. *The price is €244,207.* I have to ask myself, as a good European, what is the difference between these two dreamboats that leads to a price disparity of €59,887? It can't be the name, as Bentley and Ferrari are equal in prestige, history and class. Why should a Ferrari cost more than a Bentley? Can someone explain?

12TH AUGUST

Money for jam in Brussels

I am grateful to a good friend for drawing my attention to the international news section of a serious London daily. It would be madness to believe anything you read in the juvenile gossip columns invented in Mr Murdoch's *The Sun*, but the truth quotient percentage in the *Telegraph* is at least in double figures, whereas the same figure in the *Sun* or the new format *Daily Mail* hardly makes it to single figures. Justin Stares in Brussels gravely informs us that civil servants 'on the Brussels gravy train' now earn £70,000 a year after tax. It seems the European Commission, not always eager to talk about its own perks and allowances, has now been forced to open its mouth and answer some pertinent questions put by a Czech member of the European Parliament.

There are around 20,000 'officials' droning about the Commission. They are entitled to seven separate allowances 'over and above their pay', plus a generous pension scheme 'after just 10 years' service'. Stares goes on: 'The average take-home pay of seventy thousand is based on the income of an "A" grade Eurocrat – one who can draft new laws for example – married with two children and in the middle of his or her career'. Why do I shudder when I read the phrase 'one who can draft new laws . . .?'

A prominent MEP has described the figure as obscenely high. Chris Heaton-Harris said, "they get paid too much for doing too little and most of it is done badly. They take Friday afternoons off and they get all the Belgian bank holidays. And what is more, they get extra money for having children." So now the Brussels authorities have owned up to permitting the following family staff perks:

'(1) Household allowance: 2% of basic salary plus £100 a month. (2) Dependent child allowance: £185 a month per child. (3) Pre-education allowance £22 a month. (4) School fees: reimbursement of up to £150 a month "doubled in certain cases". Eurocrats are also eligible for other allowances: (1) Expatriation allowance: 16% of the total sum of basic salary, household allowance and dependent child allowance. (2) Secretarial allowances of between £77 and £120 a month.'

The article explains that bureaucrats posted outside Brussels and Luxembourg are also eligible for an promising allowance called a 'correction coefficient'. This compensates officials posted to cities with a high cost of living, and it also 'rounds down salaries where life is cheaper than in Brussels or Luxembourg'. Ah, I thought, *that* little idea will produce all-round smiles, and I was right! As a result, 'expatriate officials posted to Britain are entitled to a further 42% on top of their basic deal'. If you thought the perks stopped there you are mistaken. When these civil servants lucky enough to have climbed on the EU gravy train reach the end of their luxurious career, as pensioners they can expect £3,681 per month for the rest of their life. This cost the taxpayer £303 million last year. I wish the European Commission had been invented during my youth, when I worked in the UK. I could have worked for the Commission, and would now be a pensioner getting almost exactly twenty times the pension I actually receive.

26TH AUGUST

Drink, drink and be drunk, says the Brutish Government

The penultimate word in this sub-title should be 'British' of course: some Europeans might say the mistaken adjective is more appropriate. This Government and its Cabinet have spectacularly reduced freedom, nannied everyone into a state of nervous disorder, decided to cover the whole of South-East England with roads, housing and factories but no adequate water supply, destroyed the effective political power of Britain's democratic senate - the House of Lords; introduced top-up fees at the universities, decimated the armed forces, made accountability in the NHS, the police force and the school system so convoluted not even Einstein would have understood it; done nothing to alleviate the looming pensions crisis, supervised the killing of millions upon millions of bovines after a false plague scare, privatised the railways and then denounced and dismembered its own invented rail transport companies, done away with *Habeus Corpus*, made ordinary farmers and other citizens feel like criminals because they need, or simply like to hunt foxes on horseback; refused to admit a connection between 7/7 and Iraq, permitted noted Irish Republican terrorists a seat in the Commons, tried to explain away the police murder of an innocent Brazilian on the underground with dishonest excuses that wouldn't fool a five-year- old, introduced a Bill allowing twenty-four drinking, lied to the press and people over non-existent WMD in Iraq, and grossly mis-informed the people about the reasons for the death of David Kelly – their own expert. After showing pride in this magnificent record, they were re-elected in Scotland and Wales (not in England), leaving half the population stunned.

Individual ministers have come and gone like summer flies; one of these is 35-year old 'Licensing Minister' James Purnell, who recently stated flatly that the Government has decided to ignore police and judicial protests about the 24-hour opening laws. Purnell says that after November 24, when the Bill becomes Law, the police will have new powers to 'deal with problems caused by binge drinking'. Now this really *is* odd. I thought the concept of permitting people to drink all day and night in pubs was precisely designed to prevent 'binge drinking', which in case you didn't know means mostly young people drinking themselves stupid in pubs during the original restricted opening hours. Purnell rejects the claim made by circuit judges that the new Law would lead to an inevitable explosion in alcohol-fuelled violence. He has however promised a government re-think of the new licensing regime. 'If there are any problems, we will of course act on that,' he said; of course. Not that anyone should think, he paused to remark, 'that the Government is in any way preparing itself for a U-turn'. Naturally not, this Government has distinguished itself by being Right, whereas anyone who disagrees is Wrong.

Mr Purnell became a Minister after the recent general election. He was speaking in reply to an assault by Mr Michael Howard (still leader of the shadow cabinet), the judges and quite a lot of senior policemen, who are clamouring for an entire re-think. Mr Purnell has said 'the Government is trying to get rid of the "double madness" of people being forced to binge drink in pubs until the normal closing hour of 11 pm, and then being able to go on drinking afterwards in late-license clubs' When the new Act becomes Law, all pubs and clubs can apply to their local authority for a permit to stay open as long as they want. Polls taken among pub-owners and brewery chiefs suggest that 90% of city and large town pubs wish to stay open an hour or two extra at weekends. Purnell says; 'At the moment, if there are problems with a pub, the only real option is closure. But that's a nuclear option (sic), and people are reluctant to do it because it means taking away someone's livelihood. That's why only 0.2% of pubs and bars fail to get their licences renewed.'

23RD SEPTEMBER

Stability Pact in the Ukraine, game-shooting in the UK, and M. Chirac in hospital

President of the Ukraine Viktor Yushchenko has placed a virtual ultimatum before his own parliament. He wants the various elected parties to coo together like doves, instead of shouting imprecations. The problem in this young democracy is the usual one: corruption on a massive scale. The mess is so troublesome it has already caused the destitution of the female Prime Minister, Yulia Timoshenko. On 9 September Yushchenhko spent all day talking with eleven of the *thirteen* political parties with representation in the single Ukrainian parliament ('Supreme Rada'). Ukraine has no Senate, or Upper Chamber, yet. The President with the raddled face (the reader will remember how a political opponent did his best to poison the boss immediately after the last election, leaving Yushchenko looking like something out of a Hollywood make-up department) is pleading for an 'efficient collaboration' between the temporary premier, Yuri Yejanurov, and the rather numerous parties with representation in the Rada. This means the formation of a new Cabinet at top speed, because the Ukraine seems to be showing all the signs of wishing for a peaceful but impossible return to the now defunct Soviet regime that governed the state for so long.

The two groups not bothering to turn up for these talks were the Ukraine Region Party, and the Social Democratic Party (both communist). It is no coincidence that these two rogue parties were those who supported the President's rival in the recent elections – Viktor Yanukovich – suspected by many of having a lot to do with changing Yushchenko's facial appearance. "The only way out of this vicious circle," said the defeated presidential candidate Yanukovich, "is to introduce a total reform of our Ukrainian political system. This will prevent the assumption of power by forces that represent no-one but themselves." By this he means a constitutional reform that will restrict the powers of the Head of State, and greatly increase those of the Prime Minister.

Meanwhile, the deposed Prime Minister, Yulia Timoshenko (removed from the premiership 8th September) has blamed the entourage of Viktor Yushchenko for her sacking. "This wasn't the President's idea," she loyally told a radio station in Kiev; "my removal was engineered by those who surround him," she announced. This confusing concept was made even more confusing by the fact that Yulia accused Piotro Poroshenko of being the ring-leader in the plot to get rid of her. Poroshenko used to be Head of Security, but he got fired too. No-one seems to know quite what is going on in this former Soviet satellite, an applicant to join the European Union. Javier Solana, a Spanish politician who has the EU portfolio for Foreign Relations and Security, said in a speech on 9 September that it is most essential for Ukrainian leaders to stick to the rules (and promises) of democracy, reform and 'Europeanisation' declared by them before and during the 'Orange Revolution' that brought Yushchenko to the presidency.

Game shooting is the next target

Since their success in getting on to the Statute Books an unenforceable law against chasing vermin on horseback, the animal rights lads and lassies can now concentrate on an all-out attack on game-shooting. They will be helped in the new campaign by the RSPCA itself, that once-amiable and efficient association that used to ask children to be kind to feather and fur, and did so much to reduce the horror of maltreatment to animals. Director-General of the RSPCA J. Ballard (an ex-Liberal Democrat MP), who along with her Board takes pride in the part they played in the banning of fox hunting, has recently pronounced: "shooting is horrible and nasty; we will get round to try to end this." How very Blairite that sounds.

Ted Heath

Sir Edward Heath died in July. The English politician known cruelly by *Private Eye* as 'Grocer Heath' died peacefully in his beautiful Georgian home in The Close at Salisbury, after a lifetime of causing fury, or, conversely, deep pleasure in those who associated with him, or merely watched his political life unfold in the Press. He was almost eighty-nine years old, old enough to have been an MP in the late Thirties, when his anti-appeasement stance made him unpopular in Conservative circles anxious to prop up Chamberlain and dislodge Anthony Eden. His greatest rival in the Conservative Party was naturally Margaret Thatcher, though he admitted he had given her much help on the tortuous climb upwards. When she replaced him after his four-year saga as Prime Minister, he declared Thatcher 'treacherous'. He wrote, "the reason for our enmity is her, and her alone . . . I made her career by appointing her to the shadow cabinet, and later having her appointed to the Cabinet itself." Heath described Thatcher's manoeuvres during the 1975 leadership challenge as a 'betrayal'.

Edward Heath was one of the original 'mandarins for Europe'. His belief in the unity of Europe was undistinguishable, and still was when he died. 'I see Europe as the means by which the nations of Europe can join together rather than fight each other. This is a view which may seem unpopular at present.' But when did holding 'unpopular' views stop Sir Edward? I never knew him as a politician, only as the owner of a beautiful racing yacht he kept on the Hamble. She was called *Passing Cloud,* or was that a Wills cigarette? He was quite fearless as a yachtsman, often taking risks during ocean races, shooting tides, zipping over breaking waves on the broadest beam you ever saw, all sails sheeted in taut, the hull at an angle of 45°. These were his happiest times. He would sing lustily at the wheel, with the same enthusiasm as when he conducted Elgar or Mahler. It is just a pity that his leadership of a fractious and often openly rebellious cabinet was never as smooth and controlled as his orchestral conducting. Heath was the son of an in-between-maid and a carpenter, which gives one an idea of how possible it was, if never *easy*, for a lower middle class grammar school boy in England to shoot upwards to the dizzy height of being Prime Minister. His was the oiliest, most unctuous speaking voice I have ever heard. He always claimed his crowning achievement was the 1973 Common Market accession. But he also felt the 1975 referendum was another betrayal, though he realised it at last consolidated and legitimised what came to be known as the European Community.

Blair's 'balance between security and liberty'

After the 'amateur' bomb attacks on the Underground, important persons have lined up to say the silliest thing they can think of at the time. On TV we has a 'consultant' who said that shooting people in the head (like the police mistakenly did to Brazilian de Menezes) does not mean you intend to kill them. Then a lady on a 'think-tank' programme declared the bombings were 'clearly a major incident'. While we were in floods at these acute examples of modern British thought, a suggestion came on *News night*, from a former anti-terrorist police officer, that the police forces should immediately be permitted to detain anyone they liked, without charge, for three months. This, explained the former expert, was because 'they needed time to allow Muslim suspects to pray'.

Now you can always rely on TV and radio programmes, and newspapers and magazines, to make statements that would seem to qualify them for the nearest bin, but this last proposal is too sinister to raise a laugh. What the officer was proposing was a bare-faced power grab, pretending to be a piece of religious consideration. It is probably the best example of the British Government's exhilarating new post-July 7 campaign to turn the country into a nightmare not even George Orwell could have foreseen. The proposal will perhaps become Law in a week or two, after it has been formally sanctioned by some association of police chief officers and the secret service bosses (none of whom are elected to their posts by the poor old public). When everything is tidied up, it will be passed to the boring old Houses of Parliament (both Houses) for their seal of approval. That is the way things are done today. Thus, by November or thereabouts, we will be able to enjoy in Britain a 'significant extension' of detention without trial rather like Dr. Verwoerd used to employ in his 'apart-hate' South Africa not very long ago. It will become, as we already know, a criminal offence to 'condone terrorism' anywhere on the planet. *Hush, hush, whisper who dares; Cherie and Tony are coming downstairs*, and they've both got a recording machine. Another example under the new Law might be Zimbabwe, where anyone who contradicts Dr. Mugabe is described by him as a 'terrorist'. So let no Englishman good and true support or protect any dissidents in the former Rhodesia, or a big policeman in blue may come for you in your home at Welwyn Garden City.

It is worth noting in passing that, as so often happens with this Administration, none of these proposals have been made after a consultation with the senior man at the Home Office, Mr Charles Clarke. Nor have there been any meetings with members of Her Majesty's Opposition, still ably led by Mr Howard. As always, the British learn of what is going to happen to them by a series of leaked articles that appear in the popular press. Now where was that system used with such conspicuous success before, surely I can remember, ah yes, Dr. Goebbels was jolly good at it in the Nineteen Thirties.

Following the British electorate's decision to keep Mr Blair and his wife to themselves for a good few more years, it is also interesting to see that the Great British Public eagerly approves these new laws, as detailed in Mr Blair's 12-point plan. For instance, we have abolished Habeus Corpus, after eleven hundred years, because of a successful terrorist attack which killed around fifty people. Habeus Corpus was a particularly famous cornerstone of British liberty, copied and revered throughout the world, so it of course it had to go. It has *not* gone in the United States however, where there was an infinitely more atrocious terrorist attack. Why I wonder is it so immensely popular in Britain to welcome repression? Is it because we are afraid? No-one wants to be blown up as they go to work or shopping, and the threat Britons live under now is serious, but surely things must be kept in proportion. Our old enemies the IRA killed rather more than fifty of us during an open conflict of more than forty years, but no mandarins proposed curtailing our hard-won freedom because of it. Indeed, leading Irish terrorists have now become suited and waist-coated Members of Parliament.

English as she is spoke

The European Commission has just published some statistics connected with languages spoken within the EU. In each case the percentage figure given includes those (in each country) who speak a language as a mother tongue – principal language spoken at home or used at school etc. – plus a language learned. English is the most used language in the European Union, known and used by 47% of the EU population. Of this sum, 13% use it as mother tongue, and 34% use it as a learned or adopted tongue; German is next, with a total percentage of 30. French (which used to be the diplomatic language *par excellence),* is third with 23%. Fourth is Italian, at 15% (only 2% have learned it), and Spanish comes fifth at 14%; a rather better 5% of EU citizens have learned it. After these come Polish (10%), Dutch (6%), Russian (6%, but again 5% of Russian speakers in the EU have learned the language, which is not easy and uses a different alphabet).

As an average, only one in every three Spaniards is able to conduct a conversation in any other language, a terrible indictment of the hordes of Ministers of Education and Culture who have inhabited the Ministry in Madrid since the beginning of democracy. One of the problems is that none of these distinguished ladies and gents have been able to make up their mind, or produce a coherent education system – and languages have suffered from this uncertainty as much as mathematics – or more. In the rest of the founding nations that make up the Union, one out of every two is perfectly able to carry on a conversation in one other language or more. Most Scandinavians, for example, manage German as well as near perfect English, and Dutch people at every level have English as a second tongue. It is the same with German/Swiss, though this is *not* the case with French or Italian/Swiss.

The Commission's report shows that, contrary to what you might have believed, it is the smaller nations, Estonia and Luxembourg for example, where moist citizens manage another language as very nearly their mother tongue. Luxembourg 99%, and Letonia 93%. As the pole opposite of this, 72% of Hungarians questioned declared they knew nothing more than Hungarian, while seven out of every ten Britons admitted to knowing nothing but English, and judging by the correspondence received either by mail or by e-mail, very few of these can write English either. This is a proven fact, and all newspapers have the proof on file should the need for proof arise. It should also be pointed out that in the recent ten additions to the Community made last May, the percentage of citizens who cannot express themselves in any language but their own is considerably higher than the average in the older members of the Community.

Everything is relative however, and one positive result of the recent inquiry launched by the EU has shown that whereas in the year 2001 a similar investigation took place, it was found that only 47% of all Europeans could converse in another language, the figure has now risen to 50%, which is most encouraging, though the Spanish figure of only one in three is a disgrace, given that educational laws decree an English class in every scholar's day at school, or more. The Spanish have shot themselves in the foot, so to speak, in this context, by bravely insisting on the employment of *native* teachers of English. By the nature of things, these teachers are young or in their early middle-age, and this means they themselves have been taught no grammar or alphabet, Latin or Greek, decent literature, or the arts of composition and discussion at their places of education in Britain, because various Ministers of Education have decided these disciplines are simply unnecessary. How therefore can a Spanish child learn English from an English person who himself hardly knows correct English?

European enlargement has meant the incorporation of Polish and Russian, in sixth and seventh places respectively, among the languages most spoken within the Union. In addition, now that the EU consists of 25 nations and not fifteen, German has displaced French from its number two position, where it stood before 2001, simply because most of the ten new member states enjoy a distinct Germanic influence in everyday speech, and commerce.

21ST OCTOBER

Mr Blair goes to see M. Chirac in Paris

It is often observed these days that both Great Britain and France wish by to preserve harmony in Europe. Tony Blair and Jacques Chirac know the melody all right, but will they be able to sell the tune? Blair is doing his six-month stint at the moment, as president of the European Union, and it was while he wore this well-fitting hat that he travelled to Paris, where he began a series of talks with *monsieur* Chirac, Head of the French State. In 'frank and open' discussions in their respective languages, the two leaders set about preparing for the forthcoming 'informal' summit meeting to be held in the majestic surroundings of Hampton Court palace. Mr Blair intends to launch a debate at that summit with the subject of the European Social Model high on the agenda. He and Chirac were discussing how the ESM fits inside the ongoing, perhaps rampant globalisation that so disturbs liberal thinkers and defenders of the eco-system. Both Blair and Chirac have enquiring minds on this, but their respective answers seem to be poles apart. At a mutual press conference held outside the Palace after the talks, M. Chirac said: "Both of us are determined to create a force for Harmony in the Europe of tomorrow, instead of allowing for divisions between member states." Mr Blair , however, seemed to base his statement on what he described as 'the inevitable differences on one side and the other.' From the beginning of his half-yearly presidency of the EU, Blair has said his task is to extract Europe from what appears to be a deadening paralysis. With the impending summit coming up on 27 and 28 October, he pronounced in Paris his determination to enforce the general reflection over 'the manner in which we in Europe are going to face up to, and deal with, the challenge of globalisation'.

One of the problems facing the French President is the difficulty of judging exactly where Mr Blair stands, experienced by everyone of whatever political persuasion in the UK, and (because of globalisation) in the European Union, too. As a labour Prime Minister, Blair has never been anything but an ultra-conservative, even stronger in conviction than Margaret Thatcher. The man is a riddle wrapped in a mystery inside an enigma to paraphrase Mr Churchill's thoughts about Stalin and the Soviet Union. Ever since he became the Prime Minister chosen by the people, Tony Blair has emphasised the importance of freedom for modern Man, freedom of choice, liberty of the individual and so on. Yet his administration has been instrumental in ruthlessly reducing every segment, every aspect of that liberty Britons used to enjoy and take pride in as his natural inheritance. The New Labour government has been responsible for promoting and passing the most divisive Acts in the political history of Britain. There is absolutely nothing of the dedicated socialist about Tony Blair. For that one must turn to Gordon Brown, Blair's natural, but by no means guaranteed successor. In modern European terms one supposes that Blair is a social-democrat, and that his main objective should be to disencumber the economic mechanism in an attempt to save what is left of social well-being and the Welfare State, before the Union sinks under the weight. Chirac however, allegedly from 'the forces of the Right', is the one who will do everything in his power to overload the mechanism of the State, and its bullying and interfering power over the individual.

In Paris, it gradually became obvious that Mr Blair was hard at work tunnelling under M. Chirac's defences. For example, Chirac is at present locking horns with the President of the European Commission, Manuel Barroso. In addition, no-one knows yet who will take up the seat for Germany at the Hampton Court summit. Will it be Angela Merkel, or will it not? And where does she stand on globalisation? If on the other hand Hampton Court is graced by Herr Schröder, most of us know where *he* stands, and Schöder's intransigence will hardly aid the atmosphere. It is during the week in which I write these lines that the Merker/Schröder dilemma will be settled by the German voters. In a coalition, who actually becomes Chancellor is obviously of vital importance, but how is such a matter decided?

Schröder is much more socially democratic then Blair, and up till now he and his unnatural ally Chirac have mutually supported each other in defence of policies which, socially speaking, are tasty and tempting, but which hardly serve in the re-activation of the half-asleep economies of their respective countries. Should Angela Merkel represent Germany at Hampton Court, it is clear that she will more likely back Blair's theses than those of M. Chirac.

Spain is one of those states which has demanded that the approaching summit should not merely serve to reflect and discuss theories, but promote the possibility of making positive reforms, especially those of financial perspective. Good intentions tend, by the way, to be dropped by the side of the road in European conventions. Maybe our political representatives lose them in the ministerial jet.

24TH OCTOBER

Tony Blair has something to say

At the end of October, British Prime Minister Blair will open the 'informal' summit meeting which marks the most momentous part of his presidency of the European Union. In an equally informal interview with Ana Romero of the Madrid newspaper *El Mundo*, Mr Blair spoke frankly about the Union and its 25 members. He is a young fifty-three, and a lawyer, though he has not practised recently because he has won three consecutive general elections as leader of the 'New Labour' Party. He was educated at Fettes, a Scottish public school. He once belonged to a pop group, and still plays the guitar as a hobby. He is married to a thriving barrister, Cherie, and the couple has four children. The summit meeting is at Hampton Court, a palace built by the ill-fated Cardinal Wolsey, and then removed from it by Tudor King Henry the Eighth, an absolute monarch, who ruled absolutely, when Kings were able to. The interview between Romero and Blair lasted a little less than an hour, possibly because Mr Blair seemed tired – hardly surprising when one considers his average working day, and the fact that his usual brilliance (outside Parliament) when dealing with the UK and his own political party has been considerably dulled by contact with so many premiers of the twenty-five members of the Union, with whom he has consorted during the last four months. Nevertheless, give Blair a camera opportunity, and an affable interviewer, and a little of the old brilliance will always shine through the clouds.

"The most important thing in the forthcoming summit is to see what one has achieved as (temporary) President of the Union. I have established the objectives we decided on in our meetings, all of which were ambitious, but whether or not we have reached an agreement is another question. I do see it as important that we reach one however, over what directions we should take in the immediate and long term future.

"The fund for globalization, presented by Barroso, of which I approve, does not exacerbate the distancing between the British and the rest of the Union, or become yet another obstacle, as some say; quite the opposite. The fund is there is not to protect jobs, but the employees. If companies have to accommodate some re-structuring, they will have to do it. What we must do is make it easier for workers to find jobs, anywhere in Europe, and if necessary learn new skills. In Britain, we are already doing it. We have funds for the re-structuring of the work force, like for example what we did for those suddenly unemployed at MG/Rover.

"What we have tried to do since June is work with the Commission on proposals made about the consequences of globalization. If you examine the documented work of the Commission, you will find that we wish to stimulate investigation and development, make the European universities more competitive, and create more contact between corporations and the universities, because this is how the modern world has to function. At the same time, the Commission proposes, and I am generally speaking in agreement, that we come to a financial agreement in which directly, as well as via essential changes in the structure of funds, one third of the European budget should be dedicated to what is called the new area, which included research and development. Finally, we must learn how to manage immigration so as to obtain benefits from it. We have to use the Hampton Court summit to reach agreement on these essentials, and others. The 'others' include working hours, and the development of the service industries.

"I should say that in the long term, the European budget has to be reformed. I do not say this provocatively – it is obvious that this must come about. Obviously this cannot come about suddenly, but is clear that the budget must reflect economic growth."

22ᴺᴰ NOVEMBER

This violence may be good for France

As I write these words many large cities in France are still woken up by the traditional church bells, to hellish chaotic view of charred cars, now only fit for insurance claims. While Jacques Chirac agonises, Dominique de Villepin begs, and Nicholas Sarkozy threatens, gangs of French youths express themselves with home-made firebombs and Molotov cocktails. Youth will have its fling, it is said, but what is *not* said is that these young people are poor, Muslim immigrants, or children or grandchildren of same. The dreaded word Islam is heard neither in Britain or Spain on the news; it can be found, with difficulty, in the newspapers. A restraining hand has been laid on the media. It is only on the Internet that you will see the forbidden words. Why? Why do European governments show such fear of a religion that is still in a small minority in each of them – though that minority is growing at a stupendous rate?

The situation in today's France is like awakening in a brothel you don't remember visiting, alone, on a dirty bed, with used syringes on the grubby floor. How did you get there? What have you done wrong? Whose fault is it? Wise people now propose that perhaps this convulsion in France may be the best thing that could happen. The same people reckon Germany could do with a few thousand burnt cars too. It seems that both these great countries need a short, sharp shock to awaken them for the torpor that not even reformers like M. de Villepin (in France) or the newly almost elected Angela Merkel (in Germany) can budge. No-one wants mindless destruction of private property, but surely France can see that there must be a palpable reason for young, mostly lower middle class students, who happen to be Muslim, to take to the streets, get hurt by zero tolerance; or as has already happened, die.

There *are* commentators who try to link the French disorders with international terrorism – and it would be easy to do so. But people who think with their brain know that the burnt-out cars reflect sadness and disillusion, not al-Qu'eda's orders and planning. It is a general feeling of national economic failure spreading across France, not the stirring words of some mullah that has caused this revolution – for revolution it is. It is in the immigrants' suburbs, ghettoes all that French despair and melancholy have merged, like two streams forming a swift and dangerous river. If children see nothing but bleak dissatisfaction on their parents' faces at breakfast, day after day; if there is the barest minimum to eat; if the same children feel segregated at school from kids of another religion – when they are big enough they will demonstrate how they feel, almost certainly with violence. And they will express themselves *outside* the ghetto in their adopted country. This fact, and this alone, might make the French people accept at last that there is something rotten about their vast and beautiful country which has nothing to do with the fabled towns, the best food in Europe, or the unequalled Alpes Maritimes. In Germany, unhappy young immigrants have yet to imitate their French cousins. If Merkel does indeed become Chancellor (by no means a certain bet), and shows herself as weak and complaisant as all recent administrations, Berlin, Munich and Frankfort may get its share of wrecked and incinerated cars too. Perhaps a sense of imminent disaster may push Germany to do away with her entirely self-invented, stifling and restrictive economical corset, enabling her to breathe and use that remarkable energy that the German race has always shown, especially during the period of her economic miracle immediately post-War, enduring until the mid-Eighties.

9TH DECEMBER

The way we are now:

in *Berlin*;

There is so much stuff to get our teeth into in Europe these days it is hard to know where to start. Angela Merkel became the first female Chancellor of Germany, but I fear she will not last long, as she is popular with the people, but anathema to other politicians. Staying in Germany for a moment, a German company has just sacked one of its employees (with a £19,000 job) for smoking a cigarette, *at home.* How George Orwell would have smirked. Sandro Beier lost his job with the Berlin printing company Laserline after a private detective hired by the company photographed Beier having a quick fag in his garden. When asked about this, a director of the company said it runs a health and fitness programme for the staff (compulsory of course) for the hundred members of staff, and Beier had promised not to smoke. For this he had been awarded an extra payment of £68. Babett Deuse, an 'operations and risk management supervisor' at Laserline said quite ruthlessly, 'Tip-offs from his fellow workers led us to believe Mr Beier was not sticking to the rules, so we sent a detective to find out the truth. He was smoking in the garden at home. If someone steals from their company, it is normal that they are punished.'

Beier had worked for Laserline six years. When interviewed, he said that he suspected the company had used these no-smoking rules as a way around Germany's over-strong rules against dismissal. Mr Terhedebrügge, his lawyer, said, 'it is extraordinary that in modern Germany it is possible for your employer to spy on you at home.' Babett Deuse, who sounds like a real tartar, replied, 'we had no choice but to sack him.' Beier can take comfort in the notion that at least they did not put him against a factory wall and shoot him.

And in *London*;

On 6 December David Cameron (39) in Britain became the new leader of the Conservative Party. A taken among Tory Party members beforehand showed Cameron with 63% of Tory voters behind him, as against 33% who would prefer another David - Davis (56) to face Tony Blair as Opposition leader. The result of the ballot of 253,689 members of the Conservative Party was announced at 3 pm by the Chairman of the 1922 Committee of Conservative MPs. Cameron, an Old Etonian and Oxonian, started preparing for his baptism of fire, an encounter with Tony Blair during Prime Minister's Questions on the following day. By the night of 8 December Cameron completed the task of selecting his back-up team, the shadow cabinet. Expected old faces, some new faces, and more women, with an average age of 46 (that of Blair is 54) accepted jobs instantly. Among these are Theresa Villiers (37), a Eurosceptic MP; another Theresa, May, moves from culture to be shadow Commons leader; Caroline Spelman will now shadow the irascible Prescott, and Cheryl Gillan now deals with the Welsh; David Davis supporter David Willets becomes the new shadow Education Secretary; Christopher Grayling the new shadow Transport Secretary; Alan Duncan moves to trade and industry; Hugo Swire is shadow Culture Spokesman. Surprise absences were John Redwood, and Boris Johnson, editor of The Spectator.

Prime Minister's Question Time had Tony Blair made nervous by a friendly, companionable Cameron offering to get 'the good bits of (Blair's) education reforms through the House of Commons and into Law'. More accustomed to the naked animosity of Michael Howard, it seemed for a moment that Blair was put off his stride by this offer to help. But if anyone thought that David Cameron is soft they must have changed their mind as he drew Blair into making mistakes, reminding some of William Hague, who used to push Blair into making a wreckage of his own case.

CHRISTMAS, 2005

As we don't all have 'instant recall', let us take a look at each month of the year 2005, and try to remember the important, or at least thought-provoking things that happened:-

January: In Britain, the Director of Public Prosecutions assured Britons that it would be OK if we defended our home and hearth and killed a burglar, as long is the killing was done 'honestly and instinctively'. The Director did not clarify how investigating police officers would be able to ascertain degrees of honesty and instinct in a householder at the time he killed the intruder. In Bucharest, a Mrs Iliescu, (67), gave birth to a baby girl. After a series of tidal waves attacked coasts around the Indian Ocean, Mr Tony Blair stayed on holiday in Egypt. He said, "at first it seemed a terrible disaster, but I think as the days have gone on, people have recognised it as a global disaster." Mr Viktor Yushchenko was elected President of Ukraine.

February: In Ireland, the IRA murdered Mr R. McCartney, a Roman Catholic, in a Belfast pub. His sisters protested, and were supported at mass meetings by thousands of people. In Germany, some Humboldt penguins said to be gay, were encouraged to mate with Swedish female penguins from Sweden. In Britain, the Attorney General allegedly warned ministers that the Home Secretary's plan to put suspected terrorists under house arrest would be contested and ruled illegal by the courts. Meanwhile, Mr Clarke (Home Secretary), invented a points system, by which skills could be measured to determine which immigrants from outside the E.C. could be permitted permanent settlement in Britain.

March: Immediately after hunting foxes with dogs was made illegal in England, around two hundred hunt clubs met. Something called The Food Standards Agency learned that more than 400 products on shop shelves contained a dye used in floor polish, which may cause cancer. The Prevention of Terrorism Bill was passed in the British Parliament, providing for house arrest for suspected terrorists. Lord Callaghan, a former PM, died one day before his 93rd birthday. HSBC announced annual profits of £9 billion, the largest sum ever made by a British-based bank. The Blair government passed a law obliging all horses and donkeys to be issued with passports, in case unsuitable examples of either race should be eaten. Russia signed an agreement with Iran to supply nuclear fuel for a reactor, which will produce electricity. The used fuel, which could be employed in the production of nuclear weapons, will of course be returned to Russia.

April: The Pope died after a long illness, aged 84. Cardinal Ratzinger (78) was elected as Benedict XVI. The Prince of Wales married Mrs Parker-Bowles, who is to be known as the Duchess of Cornwall. The car company Rover/MG was declared bankrupt, and 5000 lost their job. Twenty-two black immigrants died when their hotel in Paris burned down. Prince Rainier of Monaco died aged 81. Mr Blair said a General Election would be held on 5 May. A court found six Labour councillors in Birmingham guilty of electoral fraud in a council election. A High Court judge said that this episode 'would disgrace a banana republic; short of writing "steal me" on the envelopes, it would be hard to see what more could be done to ensure that postal ballots fell into the wrong hands.'

May: New Labour won the election with 9,556,183 votes, 35.2% of the total, thus gaining 356 seats, against the Conservatives' 197. In England more people voted for the Tories than for Labour. The already disgraced Mr Blunkett re-joined the Government. A surprise referendum held in France had nearly 55% of the population voting against a European Constitution. A woman in Norfolk was struck by lightning as she was doing the washing-up; she was saved because she wore rubber-soled trainers and gloves. Postmen in Britain were awarded a £1000 bonus after the Royal Mail made a profit of nearly £600 million by stopping morning deliveries. In France, workers stayed at home on Whit Monday, which had been cancelled as a holiday by the Government, in order to save money.

2006

22ND JANUARY

Another soldier speaks his mind, and gets into serious trouble

The warning signs are there, if anyone in power wants to see them. First there was General Mena, speaking as the Spanish say 'without any hairs on his tongue'. Now it is Capt. Roberto González, in command of a company in the Spanish Legion based at Melilla. He has been arrested by senior officers after expressing his thoughts in a letter sent to the *Melilla Hoy* newspaper. In the letter, which has been published, the captain speaks of 'bad feelings and disquiet that exist inside, and outside, the Armed Forces'. He also makes mention of 'the demolition men in charge of the political and social situation in Spain.' The letter also talks of 'a gradual building-up of circumstances, including the dismemberment of the Nation, and its anti-terrorist strategies, which,' (in the opinion of the writer) 'provide more rights for the executioners than their victims.' The captain said that after a longish period of studying his own conscience, he preferred sending this letter to a newspaper to actually presenting himself *at the head of his company* in the Ministry of Defence, with the intention of giving it personally to Ministry of Defence, José Bono. For that we are grateful, because that would represent an act of defiance even more dangerous to national security and peaceful co-existence than the writing of the letter.

In the letter, Captain González explains that he was inspired to write it after watching several programmes on television in which the President of the Government, and his Minister of Defence Bono had scoffed at declarations made by Lieutenant General Mena, who only the week before had made some startling and provocative statements in a speech made at an important ceremony – with the result that he had was now under house arrest, pending his immediate expulsion from his post as commander of land forces in the Spanish Army. The captain had heard the President of the Government claim that he was certain very few other officers held the same opinions as General Mena, especially on the subject of the forthcoming acceptance by the Government of the new Catalan Statutes (about which daily Spanish newspapers are using up so many of their pages). He therefore thought it might be as well to inform the President of the Government that he might well be mistaken, and that many officers and men in all three armed forces were in severe doubt as to the Administration's handling of the pretended reforms to the Statutes, as well as the sudden softening of official attitudes towards ETA and the officially illegalised Batasuna Party, also in the Basque Country. 'Well, *señor Presidente,*' writes González in the published letter, addressing his president of the government, 'what your advisers have told you is not correct, or your interpretation of what they have told you is not correct. Of course there is unrest, both within and without the armed forces. Unrest because we can see how you are in the process of dismembering Spain; unrest because people are permitted to burn the Spanish flag with impunity in public at organised public ceremonies; unrest when we see the manifestation of public acts organised by illegal terrorist groups or political parties ; unrest because we have to stand by and watch while a generation grows up without recognising Spain as their Nation; unrest when we see the appearance of any military uniform on any programme in every one of the television stations, private or of the State, being used as an excuse for mockery; unrest because no-one can wear any kind of national emblem in certain Spanish regions without the risk of being mocked or assaulted' Captain González continues in this vein for several more paragraphs. The thrust of this professional soldier's rather desperate letter is that he believes he and many other members of the armed forces are profoundly disturbed by what they see as a violent dismantling of their country as a Nation/State. He and the others believe that the Catalan Statutes (already approved by the Catalan Government) when finally approved by Madrid, will prove a challenge, if not an actual threat, to the Spanish Constitution *as it stands*. They believe that recognition of the new Statutes will lead to a re-writing of the Constitution, dictated not by the beliefs and needs of the whole Spanish nation, but by those of the leaders of the minority groups who maintain the PSOE in their seats in Cataluña and Madrid.

17TH FEBRUARY

Looking around us

It is not always easy to focus on Europe, rather specially now that the idea of a united Europe, if not the geographical and physical components of which it is made, seems to be splitting into precisely what it was designed to prevent – the Haves, and the Have-nots. The best possible move made by the Union was allowing former communist states into the newly formed Twenty-Five. This was a good thing; now the Estonians and the Slovakians can cuddle in the warm and democratic embrace of Mother Brussels. What is more, most people think it a good idea that Britain opened her borders to Eastern European workers on First of May, 2004.

What we can proudly call the New Europeans have proved to be hard-working, highly educated, well-mannered on the whole, and so perfectly adapted to integrate easily into the British background, they will become as British as you or me in a generation or two. Some choose to change their surname, more do not. I found myself recently in distinguished company, a professor at Law, and another of the *lengua* – Spanish. The conversation swung here and there; points of ethics in broadcasting and journalism, essential differences between slander and libel – and the question of surnames and their significance. In Tenerife, for instance, many English and Irish settlers chose to translate their name literally, to fit in with Spanish life and customs. Brooke became *Arroyo,* Dr. White became *el doctor Blanco*, while others, such as the Scottish Hamiltons, decided against it, and here they are, generations later, Spanish people called Hamilton. This might not be so easy if you come from Eastern Europe - an ex-Soviet satellite for example. Following Anthony Powell's splendid argument, what do you do if your name is Karamazov? And there are two of you – The Brothers Karamazov, in fact. The Serbian royal house was called Karageorgevitch, founded by *un tal* 'Black George'. '*kara'* means black in Turkish too, and the Russian for 'grease' is '*maz*', as in '*to* smear' or 'oil' something. Indeed, the Russian for swarthy is *chernomazy*. Thus a pair of Ukrainian brothers arriving to work in Britain might called themselves 'The Brothers Blackvarnish', or 'The Blacklacquer Brothers', or even, as Powell suggested, 'The Linseed Brothers'.

Personally I am all for Poles and Hungarians and Estonians etc. coming to Britain. These countries have had a rough time for hundreds of years, mostly from Russia, the Ottoman Empire & Austria/Germany. They will lose their fatalism, and Britain will gain from their enthusiasm and sheer enjoyment of everyday life. But (there is always a 'but'), immigration does not only concern quality, manners, education and so on. It is about numbers. The British Home Office said that something between 5000 and 13,000 would report for duty in Britain after the borders opened. The latest count is around 293,000 – and this is certainly an underestimate. An English weekly newspaper quotes the Association of Labour Providers (representing recruitment agencies) as having calculated twice that number.

Our New Europeans are by no means confined to London or any of the huge cities. Three thousand Poles have settled down in Crewe, which itself has a population of 48,000. Crewe's schools are gradually filling up with thin, intelligent, enthusiastic, soccer-*playing* Poles, which makes a bit of a change from the obese, intellectually dull, apathetic, English soccer *fans* in the same classroom. Two other EU countries, Ireland and Sweden opened borders at the same moment – May, 2004. Ireland has a population of four million, and has already accepted more than 160,000 Eastern Europeans in two years. 21,800 settled in Sweden during the first year. Holland was tougher, or thought it was going to be; the Dutch organised a quota – 20,000 work permits for Eastern Europeans, but they received 24,728 applications in the first twelve months.

4ᵀᴴ MARCH

Half Term Exams

Very nearly two years have passed since the first 'family' photograph of the new socialist cabinet and Spain's leader was taken on the steps of the Moncloa Palace in Madrid. This is sufficient time to enable us to examine some of the sixteen ministers (eight of each sex). Valuation of this administration is made with care and precision every 3 months, via a poll conducted by the *Centro de Investigaciones Sociológicas (CIS)*. The poll shows what the general public thinks, but a Spanish weekly magazine has managed to penetrate a little farther, by questioning different advisers actually working within the confines of the Moncloa itself. It is plain that opinions of citizens, and the criteria of experts within the administration do not necessarily coincide. For example, the minister María Antonia Trujillo, who never seems to do very well in the opinion of the public, is in fact highly esteemed by the experts closest to the President of the Government. On the other hand, Labour Minister Jesús Caldera never does badly in the people's estimation, but is hardly popular with the Moncloa professionals.

The magazine makes it clear that those it calls 'the plumbers' have wished to remain anonymous for obvious reasons, and their wishes have been complied with. The experts have divided the sixteen ministers into five separate groups for the purposes of analysis: the 'polemicals', the 'best', the 'managers', the 'wild-cards or old reliables', and the 'autonomous or independents'. Among the polemicals or potential problem people is Caldera; the weekly says 'he expected to be made vice-president after the general election, and he wasn't, and as a result he feels a bit dislocated'; this despite the fact that the majority of those star initiatives put forward by the administration are within his orbit - the Law against Domestic Violence, the rise in the minimum salary, the rise in basic pensions, new laws concerning paternity, and the Dependency Law etc. The making of the last-named is taken as a good example of the peculiarities of Caldera's department. After Zapatero announced in public that the new Law would shortly be approved, the Ministry of Labour called for a copy of the new act for examination, in order to examine it before it was placed before the Council of Ministers for approbation. The document apparently caused some perplexity at the Ministry, as some of its clauses 'were seemingly unconstitutional'. Minister Solbes refused to countenance it, saying that technically speaking, the proposed new law was weak. In order to get the thing sorted, cabinet chief José Serrano called a special crisis meeting which set to work during five days on the text. According to the experts consulted, the Dependency Law arrived unfinished before the Council of Ministers. If the press had learnt this, it would have erupted. Another critical point about Caldera's running of his ministry is apparently his problematical relation with the trade unions. These complain that he takes very little notice of them. The unions consider that a Minister of Labour should spend at least 80% of his time working in and with the labour market. In spite of these criticisms, the experts find that Caldera is one of the closest to the President of the Government, and has been since their days in Opposition. They are certain that even if a government re-shuffle takes place shortly, as is rumoured, Caldera will not be left without a job.

Minister for Culture Carmen Calvo is, in the eyes of the plumbers, very clever, 'but won't listen'. This results in the provocation of conflicts in all sectors of culture, and this is important for a Party such as the PSOE. There are those who think Carmen Calvo is a little played out, that she has been too much involved in quarrels with the film-makers, with publishers of educational books, with the direction at the Reina Sofía Museum etc. At the Ministry itself it has been admitted that the Minister offered her resignation last September, after a crisis with the film-makers during the San Sebastián film festival. The resignation was not accepted. Another potential problem, the third, is said to be María Jesús San Segundo, appointed to *Educación* more or less personally by ZP himself. The experts consider that she has not 'come up to expectations. Technically, she comes out better, but politically she has been found wanting. It is certain that her work at the Ministry of Education has not been what was expected of her, especially as education as such was given such prominence in the 2004 election campaign. Though she has managed to go ahead with the always polemical *Ley Orgánica de Educación (LOE)*, and is making progress with the *Ley de Universidades (LOU)*, the future of María Jesús is uncertain within the Executive. Among the 'best', as perceived by the experts, in the present administration is the rather frightening woman María Teresa Fernández de la Vega, senior vice-president, seen by all as Zapatero's 'right-hand'. She has consolidated her close position immediately with him, and regularly replaces him inside and outside the Congress during his frequent trips abroad. The experts have now been convinced by her, though many admit that at first they looked at her a little askance. She has worked on both her image and her political acumen, and seems to have passed *sobresaliente.* Her new-found popularity does not prevent her, however, from being accused of a certain tendency towards interference in the work of other ministers. Nor has it prevented her from a very definite tendency towards that which the socialists always accuse the Popular Party of – *soberbia,* or an impression of lofty superiority. In a recent session in Parliament, after a vehement, but perfectly acceptable parliamentary attack on the President, Fernández de la Vega got to her feet trembling with rage, and said the following words, impressive if not puzzling to any true democrat – "*I* shall not tolerate, nor shall *we* tolerate, any attack on this President of the Government!" One must assume this means she would prefer there to be no Opposition, or, if there had to be, one that would *not* include the same kind of relentless political and personal assault on the Popular Party's President as was made by the PSOE during its eight years in opposition.

Others in the 'best' group include Vice-President Pedro Solbes (Economy, and one of the traditional barons of the PSOE), a man almost as popular in the ranks of the Popular Party as in his own; José Antonio Alonso as Interior Minister, and the newcomer from Las Palmas, Juan Fernando López Aguilar. Solbes is popular though he is responsible for controlling any excesses in spending among his colleagues, and equally hard when it comes to 'tightening the belt'. Pedro Solbes has calmed the Market, quietened the financiers and bankers, and ensured that the Spanish economy grows spectacularly, just as it did during the Popular Party's terms in office. The experts find that near-perfect cohesion and empathy exist between Solbes and ZP. Indeed, they think that Solbes will remain in the cabinet until *he* chooses to leave it. The Minister of the Interior, Alonso, is another politician highly valued by the President himself, not only as a result of the close friendship he has always had with him, but because of his success in this difficult job; according to the experts: 'Alonso is doing well at Interior ever since he stopped making public reflections and learnt how to defend the goodies and attack the baddies'. López Aguilar at Justice is also assessed highly by the plumbers, despite the *Canario*'s 'occasional verbal incontinence'. We will presume that among the latter was Aguilar's reference to 'certain Spanish autonomous communities where political corruption is rampant . . . and most rampant of all in the Canaries.' The experts say that Aguilar is 'technically most astute, and directing well that most conservative sector in Spain, which is the judiciary.' It is Aguilar who has led from the front in certain socialist initiatives, such as the Law of Homosexual Marriage, and reforms to the divorce laws.

Among the 'managers' is Elena Espinosa (Agriculture and Fishing), 'doesn't create big problems.' She is one of those valued more by the experts than by the public, according to the polls. In this category can also be found María Antonio Trujillo (Housing), and Miguel Ángel Moratinos (Foreign Minister), both of whom are 'good managers'; neither are revolutionary, spectacular or problematical. Trujillo has not managed to do what the socialists promised, which was to put the brake on the truly extraordinary rise in property and land values, which continues unabated . . . but she is popular with the experts and the Cabinet. Moratinos is popular as a diplomat with the President, who relies on him a great deal.

When journalists ask if the possibility might arise that Javier Solana might replace Moratinos in the future at the Foreign Office, the experts are derisive. 'Do you think that we would have withdrawn our troops from Iraq if Solana had been Minister? Only the 'Atlanticists' want him, like Carlos Solchaga, and some sections of the Prisa Group'. The Development Minister *(Fomento)* Magdalena Álvarez is also considered an efficient manager; but the experts cannot restrain their condemnation of her 'unbearable character; proof of this is the fact that she has had no less than four Cabinet secretaries'. Elena Salgado, Minister of Health is seen as 'a revelation' by the shadowy barons at the Moncloa. Everyone appreciates the 'great work she is doing', especially her dependability shown during the putting-through of the anti-tobacco Laws promised during the pre-election campaign. In addition, coming under the protection of the all-powerful Spokesman for the *Grupo Parlamentario Socialista,* Alfredo Pérez de Rubalcaba does little to hinder her career. Three *'comodines'* (old reliables) are versatile, and in the case of cabinet changes could comfortably assume other mantles. These are Cristina Narbona (Environment, 'most capable'); Jordi Sevilla (Public Administration, 'popular in the Cabinet, good reputation, but not as effective as we would have liked in respect of the Catalan Statute,' again, Sevilla is not halted in his ascent by enjoying a sound working relationship and friendship with Solbes; and the Industry Minister José Montilla, 'a good manager, but doesn't spend enough time at his own ministry'; Montilla has been ferocious with the Opposition over the Cataluña Statute, as befits the First Secretary of the PSC, an arduous post which occupies, according to the experts, 'perhaps too much of his attention'; finally the almost unclassifiable – José Bono, who can only be called 'independent'; also a bit of a loose cannon. This eminently presentable and able politician is the Defence Minister, and was placed in this supremely important place by Zapatero himself, some say so that he could keep him on a tight rein. No-one believes that Bono will ever accept that he will not become, one day,

President of the Government. Nor that he thinks that *he* should have become General Secretary of his Party, not Zapatero; The experts claim that Bono himself does not understand that the PSOE is notorious for its treatment of 'losers', probably because his pride could never allow him to see himself as a loser. Bono has been heavily criticised in the Party for his own criticism of fellow socialist Maragall in Cataluña; nor for those regular bombshells of his that might perhaps have been better left unsaid. As head of Defence, Bono has not been left unscathed by the declarations of General José Mena and others.

20TH MARCH

No French leave for M. de Villepin

At this moment two thirds of the eighty-four universities in France are either closed by order of the tutorial board, have their entrances and exits blocked by rioting students. This situation is exacerbated by worrying local authorities. It all reminds one of 1968. I am also reminded of Gore Vidal's truism, when he said there was no such thing as a 'student' in Europe. There are rioting students, disgruntled, disguised or drunk students yes, but it is hardly feasible to be a real student. One of the reasons for this state of affairs, especially in France and Britain, is that the vital position of Minister of Education in both these countries is usually occupied by a simple politician, whose knowledge of Education might be nil. He or she is there for political reasons, often to shut a grumbling mouth, or satisfy someone's insufferable ambition. This tendency is often noticeable in Spain too.

In Paris, however, students' unions and workers' unions threaten Prime Minister Domenique de Villepin with a 'General Strike', if he does not withdraw his proposed Contract of First Employment Act (CPE). The new contract has nothing to do with classes, courses or examinations in the colleges, but everything to do with what happens to students after they leave the hallowed walls, looking for a job.

According to the European press, 71% of French people think that 'the anti-CPE mobilization is a reflection of the profound social crisis, which can only get worse . . .' Not very optimistic. M. de Villepin's reaction does not surprise: He is 'prepared to improve the terms' of the first job contract – but is not prepared to abandon it.

Young M. Tristan Rouquier, president of the *Fédération Indépendente et Democratique Lycéene* has this to say: 'Everything is in our favour; we shall remain mobilized until the CPE is withdrawn. If the government does not withdraw it immediately we will organize strike after strike, including general strikes across the country, and we shall start by holding students' demos this weekend!' And they did. Television news programmes showed us the usual horror of cops dressed like Darth Vader smashing big batons on the heads, shoulders and legs of students armed with cell-phones and paving stones ripped from the streets. A permanent moan of sirens rose above the *arrendissements.* Young Rouquier was joined by crowds of students from their national Unions, reader to use violent or non-violent measures to combat the CPE. As per usual, ordinary workers' unions joined in the happy throng, and were gassed, or shot with rubber bullets for their pains. Everything for the *cause démocratique.* Three of the biggest unions, CGT, CFDT and FO are studying the best way to organise general strikes. At least *they* are studying something. M. Jean-Claude Mailly, general-secretary of the FO (wonder what FO stands for?) said: 'Villepin behaves like a pyromaniac! He is just like a person who sets fire to a valley and then climbs a mountain to watch.' Other, furious because not everyone agrees with them, shout louder.

The Prime Minister has invited leaders of the students' unions to meet him and talk. He has also invited leaders of the workers' unions, but have refused the invitation. The general public looks on with horror as things worsen day by day. Some of them remember 1968, when violence, fear and violence blackened Paris, and France neared revolution again.

2ND APRIL

Infants of the Autumn:
some not very reassuring statistics about Europe's birth-rate

How intelligent we Europeans are! With the exception of some of the youngest members of the political family called the European Union, the leading states are prosperous enough to have passed laws that separate childbearing from sexual congress; the latter bored people by making giving birth an unpopular labour among women, and was often the result of a bit of physical fun between a male and a female. Everybody is too busy making money by one means or another to start large families; there are plenty of biographies around which tell awful stories about being one of seven or eight in a family. Now people are encouraged to have just one child. The newly-born might have a test tube for a father. Legal abortion deals with unwanted babies.

The birth rate in each of the leading European countries has dropped well below replacement level, while the actual population of each gets larger and larger, because of immigration. The British, French, German and Dutch have started the long slide towards national extinction. One weekly publication with a big readership recently claimed that the last real European will die in 2960. In the same article, we learn that the world population stands now at around 6.5 billion, though in several European states the reduction in population is actually producing alarm. Depopulation is prominent in Scotland, Latvia and Slovakia. Experts predict that the world's supply of really French people will peak within eight years and then drop. In another fifty years the Ukraine will have its population halved. Russia's will be down by one-fifth.

Probably the same experts predict that after only forty years more, there will not be any housing problem in Great Britain. Whole villages and large zones of towns will be empty. This is already happening all over rural

Spain and Portugal, where entire villages are still there but have no inhabitants. Everyone has headed for the cities, where there *is* a housing shortage.

One of the hundreds of European Community committees – the European Commission – had presented a report that examines population trends up to 2050. Severe problems with the aged catching up with an ever-dwindling working population are just around the corner. There will be 'severe financing problems for social welfare systems' i.e. our pensions – private or state. We are forced by governments to finance them directly from our incomes throughout our working life, and we trust these governments to give us a pension when we retire. But today, we are informed, four workers with jobs support each pensioner. Countries with severe unemployment are therefore the worst affected.

Something will have to be done; the elderly, instead of happily gardening in Surbiton, for example, and taking their holidays some foreign shore, will have to go back to the factory. Equally, it is likely that the current massive influx of immigrants will decide to behave like their 'hosts' and not have any children. All of this gloom is quite the opposite to the hysteria of the 1970s when a different kind of apocalypse was predicted. We were told that the world's population was becoming too big to feed it. In 1977 the World Bank warned that over-population was 'the gravest threat next to a nuclear war'.

One of the results of the sexual revolution of the Sixties was treated at the time as a revelation. It was The Pill, which would change women's lives for ever. From the moment contraception became cheap and easy, couples started having less children. None of this applies in the good old United States, where women have lots of babies, at a rate not seen in Britain since the end of the 2nd War. But hold on: this population boom only happens in Hispanic, bible belt or black areas. Washington D.C. has worse fertility rates than Italy. California has as many gay marriages (barren) per month than male/female marriages. Everybody's happy then, no babies = no problems. And by the year 3000, no California either.

The European public cares little for scary reports from committees. The present wealth, or near wealth will continue. Not having babies is a result of the cost of living imposed by greedy governments of course. Everything will flow along just as smoothly as it always has, with a few hiccups like World Wars One and Two getting in the way, but not for long.

16TH APRIL

Becoming resigned to Bono's resignation

The analysts have been busy at work this last week, though the discrepancies between them, following creed, political philosophy, instinct or even pay check, have been remarkable. The papers, all of them, have been trying to untangle the strings. Why did José Bono resign? Was he fired? If he did resign, why did he resign at that precise moment; if he was fired, why? The papers owned by master spider Jesús de Polanco all opt for the simple resignation, due to family reasons, exhaustion etc. The papers independent of him (there *are* a few) are sceptical, as one would expect. Anyway, and notwithstanding, the issue is not at all clear, and such are the plots and stratagems woven in the Moncloa, we may never know the truth. Bono himself, never known for dishonesty, has said that he sent his letter of resignation at least three months ago to Mr Rodríguez Zapatero. What happened to this letter is not known, but no action was taken. The letter emphasised Bono's strong desire to quit, for personal reasons. The question in the mind of the sceptics – those who dare – concerns the timing. Why should Bono's resignation, presented three months ago, be accepted precisely now? Why not twelve weeks ago? The papers suggest a possible answer: The President of the Government needed, immediately after the announcement of ETA's offer to cease firing, a man absolutely in his camp, in his tent with him in fact, in the immediate area of the *Centro Nacional de Inteligencia*. This man needed to be Minister of Defence, head of the ministry that controls the Intelligence Centre. Bono did not fit the bill, as had made it perfectly clear in public that he was not sure of the legitimacy of the present Government's desire to negotiate with a dangerous band of murderers. Mr Zapatero has decided that his desire is indeed to negotiate with ETA, because (if successful) it will be an enormous and merited feather in his cap, and that of his Party, if these thirty or forty years of assassinations and extortions are brought to an end – by the PSOE and its leader. But first, Bono had to go. That is the prognosis put forward by many analysts, and it bears close examination: If Zapatero was prepared to jettison one of the finest men in his cabinet, a spectacularly successful President of Castilla/La Mancha for many years before he rose to the Ministry of Defence, he must go the whole hog and replace him with someone so close to him that it is difficult to find them apart – Antonio Alonso must leave Interior and enter Defence, ready to do what he is told without question, which is what good old friends are for. But is this presumption correct? Maybe, but there are many buts; beyond doubt, there are strange, unsettling things about this pretty kettle of fish, a feeling of emergency, panic almost, of improvisation at the last minute, to a certain extent relieved by the apparent resignation of José Bono. Sighs of contentment all round, except perhaps, from the direction of the few prickly, difficult barons left around, like Guerra, Rodríguez Ibarra and Felipe González. You see, the Bono eruption took place just a few hours before a Cabinet Meeting, at which it was planned to discuss at length and in detail the imminent negotiations with the terrorists. We are told that a long discussion took place between Bono and his President and leader, so long that the President could not physically attend the Cabinet Meeting. It was inevitable that commentators surmised that a political 'accident' had occurred, the consequences of which had to be rapidly dealt with, in the President's customary, quick-thinking, perhaps ruthless manner. Supposing Bono had clarified that he wanted no part of any negotiations with ETA, and the President had discovered an enemy close at hand. We shall never know. The PSOE moves, like God, in mysterious ways, and the Party's spokesmen are masters, like Tony Blair, of the art of revealing absolutely nothing during an apparently cogent and acceptable speech. Incidentally, the *maestro de maestros* of this art himself, Alfredo Pérez de Rubalcaba, now finds himself Ministry of the Interior, which must surely have plenty of members of the Popular Party shivering in their boots.

26TH MAY

Italy, Russia and France

On the tenth of May Italy elected an ex-Communist who fought against *Il Duce* as the new President. The Quirinale, traditionally home of the country's presidents, is now to be occupied by an 80-year old sonnet writer called Giorgio Napolitano. He spent fifty years of his life in the Italian Communist Party, and then moved a little to the Right by joining the democrats of the Left Party. He was elected after four scrutinies of the ballots, backed only by parties on the left. Some parties in the right and centre were against him, but had used only blank voting sheets. Napolitano is the eleventh President of the Republic, the first to be a militant member of the Communist Party.

He is not known as an eloquent orator, indeed his thank-you speech was "Thanks, everyone!". His name was on 543 of the papers, exceeding the quorum of 505 required for the Presidency. Those who voted for him were 540 members of the Centre/Left Coalition led by Romani Prodi, and Marco Follini, ex-President of the Christian Democratic Party (UDC), and Giulio Andreotti, failed candidate for the Senate. 460 members of the coalition led by Silvio Berlusconi respected party discipline by refraining from voting against Napolitano. Nor did they abstain. Here were the blank sheets. I am not certain how to take this peculiar gesture, but it certainly won the octogenarian the Presidency. It has been reported that Prodi had tried to persuade *everyone* to vote for the old gentleman, regardless of their political pòsition, but in the matter of the famous blank sheets, he failed.

When the results were proclaimed, Prodi referred to Napolitano as 'President of all the Italians', which was at least conciliatory. He said, 'this process has now closed a period of unnatural divisions,' by which he meant that he thought it unnatural that a centre/right coalition approved of a chap with fifty years of determined Communism under his belt becoming president of Italy. Silvio Berlusconi wished Napolitano the best of luck and added that he prayed he would carry out his tasks impartially . . . He added that he notes that after the elections of 10/11 April *all* the highest positions in the land had gone to the Left.

There was ecstatic acclaim from the Left benches, and catcalls and booing from those of the Right. If he does not die before the month is out, Romani Prodi becomes the new Prime Minister, and will form an entirely left-wing government.

In Russia, President Putin mentioned the frightening decline in the birth-rate, as part of his speech during the debate on the State of the Nation. He also mentioned the strengthening of Russia's defences, and her proposed entry into international markets and economies, plus his determination to stamp out mafias. He warned his country that her population drops by 700,000 annually, though he admits the fault lies largely with his own government, where bureaucracy and inefficiency is preventing the right moves being made to stop the drooping birth-rate. He will introduce a series of economic measures that will encourage couples to have more children. In January next year a Plan to Support Maternity will start, and remain for ten years, while mothers will receive grants of between 700 and 1500 roubles per month for a first child, and 300 roubles for a second. An additional grant will be given to mothers of two or more amounting to an extra 250,000 roubles per annum. Parents must get down to serious work for their country.

In France, the Sarkozy Scandal marches on; President Chirac had broken his usual mournful silence (very similar to de Gaulle's) to accuse the French press of organizing a plot to defame both Prime Minister de Villepin and himself, suggesting it was their idea to investigate some supposedly secret bank accounts in Sarkozy's name. 'This republic is not the republic of dictatorial rumours!' thundered the normally calm Chirac, from his palatial offices in the Elysées Palace, following a council of ministers. He did not actually mention the words 'The Clearstream Case' in his speech to the country, but few had doubts about what he referred to. Now we will see if the President is firm enough in his presidency to maintain M. de Villepin in office as Premier. This will not be child's play, as the Socialists have already programmed a Motion of Censure to be presented on 16 May. It is plain that many of de Villepin's colleagues consider that he has tried to discredit Sarkozy using false information supplied by the vice-president of an arms conglomerate, a monsieur Jean-Louis Gregorian. This gentleman has already resigned from his job in order properly to defend himself from accusations of involvement in Byzantine plots.

Blair must go (but will he?) Brown grits his teeth (but can he beat the Blairites?) and what of Mr J. Reid?

Scotchmen seem intent on governing England (from London, not Edinburgh). But as Scottish tradition demands, they are at each other's throat. Tradition must be respected. They have always been fighters siding usually with the French, though they are confused sometimes about what, or whom, they are fighting *for*. If the great clans could have shown a united front to the Georges, instead of chasing each other round the lochs, they would have got their independence centuries ago. Our Mr Blair (a sort of Scot himself) would not now be giving the Scots everything except their own King. They have their own Parliament in Edinburgh, a fitting place. Many Scots have a seat in Parliament in London as well, though no bloody Sassenach has one in Edinburgh.

Mr Brown was outgunned in the battle to become Leader of the Labour Party in 1994. Three years later Mr Blair became PM. Brown gnashed his teeth and was told he must wait. Since then Brown has been observant, seeing who his most likely opponents might be, then blowing them out of the water with a series of Machievelian 'leaks'. Alan Milburn, Charles Clarke and David Blunkett have been Macbeth'd out of the way. Now they sit on the back benches looking like something out of Hogarth. Only one of Brown's competitors has survived, remained perky, and is likely to challenge Brown in his own way when the inevitable changeover occurs. This is John Reid, a Scot.

Reid is *all there* all right. He has become this month's Home Secretary; He doesn't do interviews: If asked about the leadership crisis in the Labour Party, he smiles but won't mention 'a smooth transition from Blair to Brown'. He insists on a proper election, and is preparing to fight it. Some people say Reid is the only one in the Cabinet not afraid of Mr Brown. And what of Tony Blair? There is failure in his expression. He is sickened by the sudden collapse of popular Blairism, and angry at being found out by the British public. His 'New Labour' is being gutted by the few remaining Blairites who once wanted him to serve a magical third term; now they seem to whisper, 'In the name of God, go!'*

However, the odds against Brown not becoming PM seem poor, though Reid, who is cynical enough to refer to himself as 'the current Home Secretary', is the only member of the Cabinet with the guts to face the powerful Chancellor of the Exchequer (and self-appointed Dauphin). Reid is not one of those who endlessly repeat the lie that it was Brown who brought about Britain's strong economy. He knows that Brown *inherited* it. All Brown has to do is to tax it.

John Reid does not hide his Communist past. Keeping the hammer and sickle on his sleeve, he said at the last Labour Conference, 'working people are as much entitled to choice as the well-heeled. The State should be the servant of the individual, and be taken off the people's backs. If it is purity and impotence you want, join a convent!' What is the difference between Reid and Brown? Reid is genuine working-class, and Brown is a product of selective state education and the son of a minister of the Kirk. What could be more damning! Reid talks with people as if he believed he was simply one of them, whereas Brown's head has been high above the clouds for years. Any knowledge he might have had of how ordinary people breathe, think, work, earn money and behave in a reasonable manner has vanished. Reid is married to a hard-working Brazilian film-producer, who is not only politically articulate, but very easy to look at. This brings Reid *glamour.* Brown has as much glamour as a ragged sporran. His mumblings on future problems with China and India don't stand up well against a glamorous wife.

Mr Brown recently modestly admitted that he could run the Home Office just as well as he runs the economy. Probably at the same time too. One wonders why David Cameron does not question him on this. As we said before, Brown does not run the economy – he taxes it. He takes the country's pensions savings to use on other matters. He has created 800,000 government jobs, thus buying 800,000 votes for himself and his party. He has chased away private insurance schemes, but does not guarantee ordinary state pensioners their monthly cheque. He has, notwithstanding, the labour unions in his deep pocket, and it is *that* which will win him the leadership contest.

Will he destroy Reid as he did away with Blunkett and Co.? It is certain he will try. Or perhaps he will agree to come to terms with him, which is what he fatally did with Tony Blair. The latter told him he would stay for one term only, and then stayed in Downing Street for nine years. I cannot help but tremble a little about the thought of Brown as Prime Minister; he is known to hate England and all she has ever stood for. Yet Brown will probably become Britain's next PM! Palmerston, Disraeli, Wellington and Churchill must be sleeping badly in their grave.

Leo Amery, Hansard, 7 May 1940

21ST JULY

London remembers

On a Friday in the first week of July, at noon, the whole of London simply stopped in its tracks and stood in silence. And not only in London, all over the United Kingdom people stood in silence for two minutes in remembrance of the dead and injured of the seventh of July, 2005. There had been a bomb attack on a bus and several Underground stations in the capital. Some reporters from other countries who were said the silence was 'thunderous'. Others said 'A tiny piece, infinitesimal, but solid enough, of the Blitz showed again in the spirit of the British people'. Such mayhem had not been seen in Britain for over sixty years. Four young persons who had been born and brought up in Britain *because they were British*, had been persuaded by a devil to kill both themselves and fifty-two other innocent people. It was done in the name of Religion.

The 'persuader' or 'persuaders' are unknown, and may be living in the reader's own street. Dear God, how politicians crave the photographer's flashlight! Two prominent examples of the breed arrived at King's Cross station to leave wreathes, just at the place where the four conspirators met before going off on their murderous enterprise. They were Messrs. Jowell and Livingstone, minister of culture and mayor of London respectively. Most Londoners, as well as the people of Birmingham, Bristol, Manchester and other huge cities stayed self-contained, but thoughtful. The Londoners had been attacked without warning, but they did not rush off to the polls to change the government, as has happened in excitable Spain. A Scotland Yard chief said that this kind of occurrence may be repeated anywhere, and just as suddenly and inexplicably. It may be your husband, wife, sister or fiancé who says goodbye to you one morning but you never see them alive again. The police officer stressed that those responsible may come from far-away countries, or have been living next door since they were born. He reminded us that the four suicides were official residents of the United Kingdom, not casual visitors, just as the seven terrorists who murdered one hundred and ninety-two people in Madrid on 11 March, 2004 were citizens of Spain. They, it was said at the time, chose to blow themselves up instead of facing arrest. That is what we were told, anyway.

The Arabist TV station *Al Jazeera* tried to show an amateur video of one of the London Four reading his own last will and testament, but failed because the authorities disallowed the broadcast. To all extents and purposes, the Muslim population of Britain is not living through a happy period. It is an unquiet time for them, because employment is scarce, and might become impossible to get because of the stigma this atrocity has forced on them. This is unfair and unnatural, because there can be little worse than blaming an entire community for the foul actions of the few. But the British people have every right to organise memorial days like the one on the seventh. Barbarous acts should *not* be forgotten. We must not allow a centralized European hatred for Islam, seeing it as the enemy within. If the British, the New Yorkers or the Spanish allow themselves to do this, they will be doing everything possible to make it come true.

24TH JULY

Portrait of (another) disturbing week

First: A youngish man with greying hair and his exceptionally attractive young woman are on trial in a specially constructed glass booth for the murder of Miguel Angel Blanco (PP) and Fernando Múgica (PSOE). An unnamed source not unrelated to the illegal Basque separatist party Batasuna has told the newspapers that this man known as *Txapote* may well upset the attempts presently being made by Zapatero and his friends to *negotiate* with ETA round a table, accompanied by water carafes, microphones, and translators. The trouble is *Txapote*'s attitude to his trial. He refuses to accept the legality of the court; he is openly contemptuous of the leading judge, the prosecutor, even his own counsel; his beautiful girlfriend, on trial with him, smiles at the cameras, and enjoys visual jokes with members of their respective families, who come along, as is their right, to enjoy the fun. It seems that *Txapote* feels that he is a freedom-fighter and thus, a hero in Basque eyes. His cold-blooded murders only form part of his role as defender of Basque liberty and independence. He was not disturbed by one of Múgica's sons facing him in Court, though he was, allegedly, the person who shot Miguel Angel Blanco, unarmed of course, and bound, in the head as well as planning and executing the assassination of Múgica. This trial must be vexatious to Mr Zapatero, who does not need proud cold-eyed assassins challenging the authority of a court to judge them for their sins, just at the time when negotiations with the ETA leadership and Mr Otegi of Batasuna are nearing. Of course officially Batasuna has no voice, because it is still illegal, but few doubt that by the end of Autumn this year the party will be legalised again, despite all efforts by the Popular Party, Mariano Rajoy, and the various Associations of ETA's victims to prevent it.

Second: Poor Miguel Angel Moratinos, the Foreign Minister is having a terrible time as a result of the rather wayward foreign policy philosophies of his Leader: the President of the Government managed to appear for a photograph, grinning widely, with a pro-Palestine handkerchief round his neck, just after Israel launched a ground and air attack on both the Gaza and Beirut, following kidnapping and killing of Israeli soldiers, and a lethal rain of Arab missiles on Israeli cities. One supposes Mr Zapatero was making his sympathies clear, which is absolutely his right, but such a photo-call does not help his Minister for Foreign Affairs, who is trying, mostly in vain, to keep a friendly relationship going between the Governments of Spain and Israel. At a banquet given in Spain to congratulate prominent businessmen from both countries involved in business together, an Israeli businessman didn't help matters by accentuating what he saw as Mr Zapatero's rather obvious anti-Semitism. Moratinos was the first to rise when the time came for speeches (he was present at the banquet), and treated the Jew to another example of this Government's superiority complex. Moratinos quivered with rage as he told his guest that no-one, *no-one* would be permitted to call The President of the Government an anti-Semite. Later other members of the PSOE, such as the lady Vice-President of the Government, rose in other places to castigate the businessman, or the Popular Party, for daring to criticise the Leader, a crime infinitely worse than blasphemy. As everyone knows by now, the PSOE is teaching us to accept that the Popular Party is responsible for all ills in Spain, past, present and future, in or out of actual power. Only when the PP has been removed from the political map will the PSOE be able to rule without criticism (or opposition). The Third Republic is just around the corner. We must remain on our knees praying that it will be more successful and less inhumane than the First or Second.

Third: Talking about the *Partido Popular* for a moment, Mariano Rajoy announced this week that his Party would be taking an appeal to the *Tribunal Constitucional* following acceptance by Congress of the Catalan Statutes. Rajoy is not giving up. He thinks that the Statutes, if they finally become law, will create a separate state in Cataluña, a nation within a nation, and he reckons that at least half of the population of Spain thinks alike. He may be right. He also demands the immediate appearance of the President of the Government in parliament to explain why he seems so determined to divide Spain into separate states, and at the same time explain why his Government is sworn to reinstate what Rajoy (and the historians) insist on calling 'The Two Spains'. This pungent old expression simply means the monarchy, nobles, rich and the Church on one side - and honest, simple, ordinary, atheist, hard-working people on the other – in other words, how Spain was for centuries before the frightful carnage of the

Civil War, the uneasy forty years of Franco, and finally the marvellous reality of the 1978 Constitution, which was designed to do away with the ogre of 'The Two Spains', and had done, until the insistence of the PSOE in dragging it all back.

Fourth: 36 kilometres from Madrid, on the road to Toledo, on the dusty plain described so acutely by Cervantes in *Don Quixote,* a kind of Las Vegas is rising like a modern Phoenix from the rocky, waterless sand. This town designed for a population of fifty thousand, with more than 13,508 homes, is the dream-coming-true of one Francisco Hernando, known as *El Pocero.* Right now this development in the desert is the grandest speculation ever seen in Castilla/La Mancha. Permissions were sought and rapidly gained during the reign of José Bono as President of the region. One year was all that was needed, and on the 6 May, 2003, the Provincial Commission of Toledo gave the glad eye to the project, with some reservations added with caution. A little later an extraordinary session at the Seseña town hall approved everything, just in time for local elections, which the Socialist Party lost, but by now the colossal project was in motion. Very soon the bulldozers of *El Pocero* were hard at work clearing the Hípica Almenara, a *finca* belonging to the family of José Bono, future Minister of Defence in Mr Zapatero's cabinet. This coincidence was later investigated by the *Fiscalía Anticorrupción* for a presumed 'favour' awarded to the developer by the government of Castilla/ La Mancha (President, José Bono). Permission was granted to Francisco Hernando to build 13,508 residences, in so far as the Law said that half of these must come under official protection (which means each would cost less than if sold as a private deal). In 2004 the construction was well away, having built the first phase of *viviendas.* Now, no-one seems to know if there will be an adequate water supply for fifty thousand residents, only 10,000 less than the population of the city of Toledo. No-one seems to know if there will be places of education, clinics, hospitals, or any other essential parts of the infrastructure. In the middle of this Phoenix arising from arid rock, there is an enormous and most decorative lake, with a high-flying fountain in the middle. How was this possible? Difficult to say, but the company that controls the Isabel II Canal has denounced the theft of thousands of litres of water from Aranjuez, using motorised water-cisterns. The lake is there, and its fountain, and will help a lot in the sale of homes. Three councillors in the *Grupo Municipal Socialista* at Seseña appear to have maintained excellent relations with the developer. The daughter of one of these is responsible for the sale of homes at *El Quiñon,* as the urbanisation is called. Another is chief of building operations for ONDE 2000 (proprietor, *El Pocero*), and the third works in administration for the same corporation. Yet another councillor, this time in the PP, has a brother-in-law who sold land needed for the urbanisation.

Fifth: Razor-toothed Eduardo Zaplana, official spokesman for the PP in Congress, awarded *El Pocero,* a special medal (Labour Medal of Merit) while he was Minister of Works and Social Services. The nomination of this medal has been made the subject of a denouncement made by *Izquierda Unida.* An attempt to build 500 houses in the Madrid suburb of Villaviciosa de Odón in 1992 was made by the same developer, Hernando, but the attempt was thwarted by the combined forces of PP, PSOE and IU. One can only assume that this much larger development in the desert has progressed so far because it was supported and encouraged by the PSOE government of José Bono, then President of Castilla/La Mancha. Until recently, Bono was Zapatero's Minister of Defence, but there was a falling-out, and he has now disappeared, perhaps to write his memoirs. It was Bono who recently murmured that to commemorate the seventieth anniversary of the end of the Second Republic was absurd, especially when the Spanish did not bother with any such celebration on its fiftieth anniversary. Bono has obviously been plotted out of the small congregation of very left-wing socialists led by Mr Zapatero, whose intention is to somehow fight the civil war again, by any means, and any methods – though this time with a clear intention of winning it.

Fairy tale at St. Paul's

I am not among them but some people would like this fairy tale to be called *Beauty and the Beast.* The fact remains that the heir to the British throne married Lady Diana Spencer in St. Paul's Cathedral on 29 July, 1981. The British are good at this kind of ceremonial, and the wedding was as splendid as the British expected. It seems like a Hollywood dream now, that royal wedding, followed by years of bitterness and anguish.

If the world thought they watched on their television screens a Romantic Fairy Tale, with *The End* at the end, they were to an extent right, for fairy tales are nothing more than a myth, and the marriage between the Prince of Wales and Lady Diana was no more than a gossamer thread, easily broken with a single twitch. We have watched the same thing happen to other fairy tales, like Father Christmas or St. George and his Dragon. The myth of Diana started with her wedding in London because no-one knew much about her before Prince Charles announced his forthcoming marriage in March, 1981. She was a daughter of a much-married Earl burdened with addiction to the bottle. Diana had a step-mother whose ambitions had made her Mrs Gerald Legge, then the Viscountess Lewisham, and now Earl Spencer's Countess. Upwardly mobile, indeed. Diana's real mother was alive and living in Argentina. Columnists knew that Lady D. was good with children, and had a job working with them at which she excelled.

Charles Prince of Wales was born in 1948, first-born of very famous parents, and his every move had been recorded by the world's press since he was born. As the British Empire shrank, Charles' popularity grew; as a small boy with his grandmother's taste in children's overcoats, as an unhappy small boy at Cheam Prep. As an even more unhappy junior, then senior prefect at Gordonstoun. There could not have been a worse choice of school, as young Charles was a sensitive, thoughtful youth, whereas his father Prince Philip (who chose his old school for his son) had been a wild, sporting, bundle of mischief, preferring his own little sailing dinghy to studies. The two could not have been more different. Charles did his stint in all three British armed forces, and picked up a useful pilot's licence on the way. The more racy papers told us about Charles' loves, when he was old enough to have them. Millions of words were published about the man, mostly wishful thinking, or plain lies.

Myths last, of course, which is why they are myths. Some make you comfortable, some uneasy. The myths surrounding Diana, Princess of Wales since her marriage, bearing of two fine boys, and horrible death in a barely lighted Paris street tunnel on 31 August 1997 have lasted and still grow. You can put a picture of her on the cover of your fruity magazine and sell double the normal circulation. She was a character straight out of Hemingway – the 'doomed heroine'. Conspiracy theories surround her death as they still do around President Kennedy's. The Diana Myth was so strong that when she was dead and Charles married his girl-friend of thirty years she could only be Duchess of Cornwall because Charles is the Duke. We shall have to wait and see if she becomes Queen Consort.

One is doubtful about the British people's acceptance of Camilla as the future Queen, if Charles finally reaches the throne. She might be 'Queen Consort', or 'Consort Royal', in the same way as Princess Anne is Princess Royal. Lady Elizabeth Bowes-Lyon became Queen, so did Mary of Teck and Alexandra of Denmark. These last two were doubtless told before marriage that their future husbands came from a dynasty whose male members liked a lot of womanizing. They would have to make a decision: become Queen of Great Britain (with all that that means), and ignore the philandering – or *not become Queen.*

The oddest thing about Diana is that she accepted a Windsor as husband, and was later bewildered when he carried on relations with his mistress, whom he had known since his teens. Diana could not bring herself to accept the inevitable. What is sauce for the goose is sauce for the gander.

She did a bit of philandering herself, but could not prevent the world's press from crowing about it. She took up with Mark Hewitt, but that didn't work so she took on a son of one of the nastiest men in Europe, so nasty the Foreign Office would not give him a British passport. Then came the tunnel and Diana's awful death, with Dodi at her side and his French employee drunk at the wheel. At the funeral service (a masterly piece of theatre orchestrated by King of Spin Blair and his ghillies), Diana's brother was evil-mannered to the royal family and spoiled whatever reputation he might have had. Blair read the Bible as if directed by Michael Winner. Verdi's Requiem soared above politics. The myths continue.

Stephen Frears makes *The Queen*

The extreme tension between Queen Elizabeth II and her prime minister Tony Blair following the fatal accident in Paris in which Diana, Princess of Wales, her friend and the chauffeur died has now been filmed by director Stephen Frears. British actress Helen Mirren gives a remarkably deep performance as the queen who has to make overwhelming efforts to overcome her natural reserve, given her severe upbringing. The audience wonders if the Queen can do it. Will she show emotion after learning that her oldest son's wife, possibly the future queen, has been killed? Meanwhile we are reminded of the disturbing, perhaps insane grief which exploded among most of the British population when the news broke.

Helen Mirren has already played Elizabeth I on the screen, and Ann Boleyn too. Now she 'becomes' Elizabeth II with her (few) bad points and (many) good points exposed. Michael Sheen is Blair to the life, the 'man with a thousand faces', a consummate actor himself, and Sheen never allows the tension to drop. Mrs Blair is shown as a disagreeable woman from every angle possible, and members of the (huge) cinema audiences must wonder why Blair married her. Prince Philip is masterfully portrayed by Canadian actor Richard Cromwell. The only disappointment is the actor playing Prince Charles, who never convinces us for a moment that he is anything else but an actor playing a part, even with this marvellously defined character to play.

The thrust of the film is the relation of Prime Minister and Monarch, given that the official palace reaction to the accident was one of indifference after the royal divorce, and not much more before it. Very few courtiers made any effort to like the girl. The public adored her and the press knew a good thing when they saw it.

Helen Mirren says, "the Queen is a most genuine person; she refuses to be artificial. She is firm, sincere, honest and very British." The film takes place mainly in the castle at Balmoral, where the tragic news was first heard. Later Blair tries to persuade her to 'lead the people' in emotion. Difficult, if not impossible when you have been taught all your life never to show your emotions *under any circumstance.* She is asked to fly the standard of the Sovereign at Buckingham Palace at half-mast, and though it is utterly against the protocol, she allows it. She also agrees to talk to the nation on television, which she does well. Mr Frears, whose best known other work is called *Hero* with Dustin Hoffmann, has put in one brilliant little set-piece; the Queen, quite alone in the Highlands with a broken Landrover, sits quietly by a peaty stream, and for the first and only time, allows her natural feelings to take over. She weeps silently, thinking of her dead daughter-in-law and her over-stressed son, the future King. She is disturbed by the silent approach of a magnificent stag, seeming to sympathise with her, but they both hear the sounds of hunting gunfire approaching (it is the Duke of Edinburgh out shooting with William and Harry), and the Queen tells the great stag to 'scram!'. He trots off, we hope (in vain as it turns out) to safety, and she dries her eyes and awaits the help she has called for on a cell-phone. This is perhaps the most powerful scene in the film.

Later we see the famous moment when the Queen stands with her family at the gates of Buckingham Palace, and lowers her head when the funeral cortege passes. The director does not shirk emotional scenes of an apparently angry populace outside St. Paul's. Nor does he ignore strong and distasteful scenes at Balmoral and the Palace between Blair's people and members of the royal family. I believe Miss Mirren won a Best Actress award for her performance at the Oscar ceremony; one is ignorant of what Queen Elizabeth II thought of it.

24TH SEPTEMBER

Preparing for Chirac's *"adieu"*

Angela Merkel is not only Chancellor of Germany; she is also making quite sure everyone knows where she will stand on the question of Europe's future, after the future political demise of M. Chirac. For instance, in a recent meeting held at Compiègne, Merkel and Vladimir Putin (Russia) rejected out of hand some tortuous proposals by M. Chirac which were meant to lead to a re-forming of the ancient 'axis' (dare we use that word?) Paris-Berlin-Moscow. Angela thus clarifies here position *vis-à-vis* President Bush and the USA. While not exactly throwing herself wholeheartedly into Bush's arms as Britain's Prime Minister Tony Blair has always done, Angela manifestly refuses to permit a Europe unified and defiant against America. Neither she nor ex-KGB boss Putin foresee *three* power blocs dominating the world political scene – USA, China/Japan/India, and Europe.

Europe had the chance at the beginning of Mr Bush's war against Iraq, but no-one did more than mutter recriminations and allow demonstrations, except *señor* Zapatero of Spain, with his mysterious programme involving Himself as Man of Peace (he has more Spanish soldiers serving abroad in very dangerous stations than has any other President of the Government since the Transition). With Blair waltzing with Bush, Germany and France had the chance of establishing Fortress Europe then, but bungled the job, with Putin watching idly from the side-lines. This top-secret summit meeting was, observers maintain, orchestrated in Paris with the diplomatic target of presenting a Grand Alternative to America over the ever-present threat of a nuclear-armed Iran. But it turned out to be a series of chats about diplomatic and economic matters, such as Chechenya and the aeronautical industry. This caused Paris newspaper *Le Monde* to print an editorial accusing Putin of 'betraying' Chirac, while, behind his back, negotiating Russian entrance in the European aviation industry. The adroit Russian managed to use the threat of withdrawal of Russian natural gas as a lever. Chirac has been shown up as the only European leader implacably *contra* the 'American Empire', as he likes to call it.

Angela Merkel, on the other hand, has emphasised her friendliness and faith with Poland, other European states, and the United States, much to the *chagrin* of Chirac. It is interesting to note that this Summit was not attended either by T. Blair or by ZP. One supposes they were not invited. Both are, at this moment, in a curious state of limbo: Blair remains defiantly in the house at No. 10 Downing Street, with Cherie and the children, friendless, powerless, still refusing to go, while the Scottish hordes led by Gordon Brown sharpen their wits for the triumphant moment – any minute now! In Spain, Rodríguez Zapatero has pushed yet another stalwart Socialist out of position by persuading Juan Carlos Rodríguez Ibarra to remove himself from a renewed candidacy for the Presidency of Extremadura. This is a startling move on the chess board. Merkel, Putin and others seem to want to keep persons like Blair and Zapatero at arm's length at present. Indeed, they must be wary of making *any* lasting deals with Chirac, as imminent elections will put either Segolène Royal or Nicolas Sarkozy into the Palace; Jacques Chirac may well retire from politics altogether.

At the Summit, Vladimir Putin was received as the 'great friend', at a sumptuous dinner prepared at the medieval castle in Compiègne. This did not prevent his warning that Moscow may decide to change rules of the game with French oil and gas companies, breaking all previously accepted guidelines. It is patently obvious that Putin's intention is to put Russia back among top nations, with a puissant say in world affairs. He is tired of Russia's modern image as a vast country populated by *mafias* and ruled by converted communists. He also wants to enter Europe as a Member, and on his own terms. Observers say he clarified this at Compiègne. A door was provided in the form of Russia's entry in EADS (the formerly mentioned European aerospace industry). Putin had not advised Chirac that this was his intention before the Summit.

20TH OCTOBER

The end of free speech in Russia?

The recent murder of a mother of two, Russian journalist Anna Politkóvskaya has caused much anguish in that huge country – but little surprise. The assassination came at a moment when nationalism surges like a tidal wave, and is made worse by the actual crisis In Georgia, and the continuous crisis in Chechnya. Anna was a fervent defender of Chechen interests, and never stopped accusing Russian troops of atrocities committed in that state. She had no fear of Russian leaders and politicians whose arbitrary methods and xenophobia can only lead to more bloodshed.

The reporter's favourite target was President Vladimir Putin, whom she bit regularly in her columns. Her pen was most acidic when Putin announced more and more repressive moves against Caucasian states that should have been free, but have never been free. Anna's body was found dumped in the lift in a block of flats in Moscow, where she lived. The street is called *Lesnaya* and the number on her door 8. She was found on Saturday 7 October; the Russian press insists that her death should not surprise anyone. Informed people have been saying for years that Anna would be eliminated. They add that certain very well-known persons were not actually present, though they were not far away when the murder was planned. Anna was shot four times by a professional, that is clear; the pistol and some empty shells (no finger prints) were found by the police in the building. She had just arrived from shopping, but did not have time to fetch more bags from her car.

A police inspector says that the hidden TV camera installed above the porter's cubbyhole records a man of medium height, wearing a baseball cap (of course). The recording is very bad indeed, and has been tampered with, as is usual (we are told) in modern crime. Rosinsky an assistant public prosecutor told reporters that a hard disc and several documents have been removed from the woman's computer and flat. He said, "Her latest articles and other material will be of great help to us in the investigation, and will lead us to the instigators of this crime." You'd better believe it.

The police have dismissed the idea that simple robbery was the motive. They say the murder was meticulously planned beforehand. The atmosphere in Moscow is never easy, and it isn't considerably more uneasy now, reminding many of the years before the end of the Soviet when any criticism of the Government or its Leaders, or attempt at the exercise of free speech, was punished by imprisonment in a lunatic asylum, actual incarceration or death.

Anna's articles sought to illuminate, little by little the darker corridors of power in the Kremlin. She had become a thorn in the side, but especially in Mr Putin's side, though he had been elected as President. She had been making grave and apparently substantiated accusations against the methods and ideology of the President, who, one remembers, is an ex-boss of the KGB.

World opinion says that Russia should immediately condemn the assassination, and bring the guilty ones to justice. But silence is maintained in the Kremlin. Since the year 2000 there have been twelve such murders of journalists, with no noticeable reaction from the government. It seems that hundreds of years of Tsarist repression, followed by seventy years of Soviet oppression have been suffered by the Russian people to no purpose. Russia is now, at least nominally a democracy, but a democracy where thinkers who speak their mind clearly run a considerable risk.

6TH NOVEMBER

VW reduces staff in Spain, Portugal and Belgium
The start of another Great Recession?

With the world still a bit punch-drunk after the news that the Ford Motor Co in the USA is 'experiencing difficulties', we will probably need another drink because Germany's own giant, the Volkswagen Group based in Wolfsburg is about to reduce staff in three European Union countries – Spain, Portugal and Belgium. Allow me a quick observation about the Ford fiasco first: they should never have bought Landrover and Jaguar for reasons obvious at the time, and anyway the British government should never have allowed them to. Britain has already lost the greatest symbols of the British automotive industry – Rolls-Royce and Bentley – to German companies BMW and VW. Surely an effort could have been made to save Jaguar and Landrover?

Horst Newmann, personnel director at VW says: "we must confront the spectre of reduction of staff in Western Europe. That is where we experience our worst problems at this time. We shall reduce staff there, as we have reduced staff here in Germany. The car market in Russia, China and India grows apace, but at the same time countries like Spain lose their advantages, because of high costs etc. If it is possible, we will try to avoid actual closure of factories."

Motoring experts think that the possible closure of plants in Spain, Portugal and Belgium is part of a plan greatly to expand the main VW plant in Wolfsburg, but Herr Newmann denies this. We do know that the assembly line in Belgium producing the famous VW Golf is to be transferred to Wolfsburg.

Britain has lost Rover as well; one of the most famous near-luxury marques, Rover vanished because of governmental indifference and inept management of financial and human resources. Only a short time ago one of the Rover range (the75) was declared Best Car in Europe, but now you cannot buy a Rover anywhere. In one week, everything went haywire, and Rover's Solihull works were offered at the bargain price of one sterling pound. Volkswagen will probably recover. They usually do. They own Audi and the originally English Bentley as well, and the company assures us the order books are full.

Banco Espiritu Santo

The Board and its CEO are naturally furious. The Portuguese banking empire named after its founders, the Espiritu Santo family has been told to close its doors in Madrid and Barcelona and freeze the private accounts of its clients. This is a governmental order, made apparently because the famous Anti-Corruption Squad in Spain wants to examine (at their leisure it seems) certain accounts held with this bank.

Far from doing this discreetly, as one might expect, police barriers were erected, police sirens shrieked, newspaper photographers were told in advance, and the whole country watched the exercise on television. It should be noted that the TV cameras were placed in position some time *before* the raid, and one wonders why.

President of the bank Ricardo Salgado said: "the Spanish authorities wanted to examine certain accounts, amounting to some 5.5 million euros, but in order to do so they blocked *all* the accounts. We are indignant, and consider the operation disproportionate and artificial, especially the TV cameras running before the operation took place. It is logical that TV viewers automatically assume the bank itself is the subject of a raid, and not because we hold here certain accounts that we, like any other major bank, happen to hold.

A death sentence for Saddam

In European countries where there is no death sentence the media expressed astonishment and repugnance, after a Baghdad court sentenced ex-dictator Saddam Hussein to hang. The Americans are blamed for permitting the ex-leader to be judged by his own countrymen, who would obviously return only one verdict after years of abuse and repression by Saddam. Newspapers insist that if he had been examined in a Western court, he would certainly have got life imprisonment, a very different thing to a public hanging with the TV cameras whirring and the sound full on.*

The media also thinks execution of Saddam can only exacerbate the awful condition of present-day Iraq, where civil war rages, inept politicians misrule, and the Western greed for Iraq's oil is obvious.

The hanging was carried out by an amateur, and the cameras were indeed whirring, and everybody complained about the flashbulbs explording in their face while they tried to enjoy the macabre scene.

22TH DECEMBER

Europe – breath bated . . .

While all Europe waits with breath duly bated for the results of the French presidential elections – will the new occupant be sarcastic Sarkozy or republican Royal? – the Union seems to prefer the usual wild spending spree during the Christmas period, letting the rest of the world get on with it. The rest of the world is not doing very nicely thank you, what with President Bush wondering how the hell he got in this Iraq mess anyway (ask Colin Powell); Prime Minister Blair fast recovering street cred in Britain, to the bafflement of Mr Gordon Brown, whose divine right to become the next PM is being challenged by Mr John Reid, a fellow canny Scot. In Russia President Putin is quickly organising an almost Soviet-style recovery, determined to put his country right back to where it was – one of the two giant powers. Putin, a clever, ruthless man, (how else did he become No. 1 in the KGB?) does not use the threat of nuclear weapons. He uses an infinitely more subtle blackmail – withdrawal of Russia's enormous natural gas supply to the rest of Europe if he is refused what he wants. And then there is this outbreak of poisoning . . .

In Spain the so-called 'Peace Process' is up a gum tree, because President of the Government Zapatero will not and cannot promise total autonomy and actual independence to the Basque Country, whose illegal representatives in Batasuna also insist on poor Navarra being included in the deal – naturally without asking Navarra if she would like to be torn away from Spain's protective bosom. As I write this one of those rare meetings between Zapatero and the head of the Opposition, Mariano Rajoy is being held at the Moncloa Palace. At the photo calls these two men will shake hands and smile, but the fact is they do not get on together in any area, political or non-political, and that is why Spain is not being governed very well at the moment. It is not just that the Popular Party seems unwilling to assist, or even discuss anything with the PSOE; it is because it becomes increasingly evident that many if not all of Zapatero's ministers of state are inept. How else could the *Ministerio de Fomento* have arbitrarily withdrawn Air Madrid's licence to run an airline (however inefficient it was), leaving something more than 300,000 customers who had paid for their tickets without an airline to fly them out of, or into Spain. At the moment of writing virtually the whole of Barajas Airport is peopled with the late airline's disgruntled customers, many of whom have slept on the hard floor for the last five days, with an Iberia sandwich for comfort. In Central and South America, there are at least 150,000 Spanish residents who had flown to be with the family for the festive season on a return ticket, only to find they must buy a new single in order to get back to Spain. It does not take genius to know that *Fomento* should have given Air Madrid three or four months to settle its affairs and meet its commitments to customers; but no, the company was told its licence would be withdrawn in three days. Understandably, Air Madrid refused to do anything about the chaos – let the Ministry sort it out, said the directors; we've been closed.

23RD DECEMBER

Mr Otegi thinks the worst

Judging by recent events, it is obvious that Arnaldo Otegi, Fernando Barrena, Mikel Zubimendi, Jone Goirizelaia, Rufi Etzeberria and Juan José Petrikorena, and other leaders of the political party made illegal by the Aznar administration are not pleased. In Bilbao, these gentlemen have appeared before the offices of the Socialist Party in the Basque Country to demonstrate their displeasure. They accuse President of the Government José Luis Rodríguez Zapatero of molesting 'the confidence' which must be present in the 'Peace Process'. Zapatero very much wants his initiative to move forward, and so does everyone else in Spain and possibly Europe too, as the ETA organisation has been a fatal thorn in Europe's flesh for far too long. If ZP succeeds in bringing the leaders of ETA to a table with a little humility, and perhaps an attempt at some showing of repentance for the decades of killing and maiming, with the fantastic result of a total ceasefire and the disappearance of ETA – it will be a magnificent victory on ZP's part, and will ensure the PSOE as Spain's elected government for years ahead. But Arnaldo Otegi is not so sure. In fact he is displeased. "This process is quite dead," he said, and added, "it isn't possible . . . it's not even feasible." As spokesman of this illegal organisation, Otegi is of course a radical, and some journalists braver than others whisper that his connections with ETA are perhaps closer than one would expect of someone who wants to see Batasuna legalised, and himself leading it in Congress. This is to be expected, as Batasuna always was the 'political wing' of ETA. The spokesman roundly condemned the present Administration, standing before the cameras and microphones that rather tend to follow him around; he said that it is the Government's fault that the Process is slowing down rather than speeding up. "They shouldn't put the onus on me to make the necessary effort," he said. Zapatero was in

Brussels at the time, and in reply he came up with a classic: "I do wish all those who see so many difficulties and impossibilities would work together with us towards a lasting peace." In other words, only the Popular Party stands in the way of peace in the Basque Country. This is because Rajoy (PP) advises caution, and reminds the Government often that there are many associations of ETA's victims in Spain, who would rather see the terrorists who killed their relatives behind bars than sitting in regional or national parliaments – which is precisely what will happen. It is nine months since the armed band announced their wish to negotiate a permanent ceasefire, but most Spanish journalists agree that neither side have advanced an inch. The Government would find it difficult to do so, because Batasuna on behalf of ETA demands 'respect' for the party, and its immediate legalisation, as well as promises that will not be broken regarding the future status of the Basque Country. That status is perfectly simple to describe; total independence from Spain for the Basque Country plus Navarra and the French Basques. If these demands are not met, Otegi has made quite clear that there is no peace process, and everyone knows this means that the killing will start again, probably early next year. In the meantime, to keep everyone on their toes, there were buses burned by 'street terrorists' in San Sebastian on December 21. The police did nothing while youths turned passengers out of a double bus and set fire to it with Molotov cocktails.

Spain's opinion makers are undecided about Pinochet

Given Spain's liberal bias, there should have been universal toasting with champagne. General Pinochet of Chile had escaped the claws of Spain's judge Garzón, but finally died of old age safely in his own country, not in gaol. He had stuck to the title of Head of the Armed Forces, but had almost disappeared from any political stage. Chile's politics have moved on.

In many ways, Pinochet was Chile's Margaret Thatcher, and her Francisco Franco too. Ask a Chilean about Pinochet and it is like asking a Spaniard about Franco. There will be eager accusers and defenders. The subject is not subjective. It is not easy for Chileans or Spaniards to be objective about these two generals. But it is risky to compare Pinochet with Thatcher. Both names, if introduced, can stop a conversation dead. You know what you think about them, and you are not likely to change your mind. It used to be the same with Winston Churchill. There were always the 'old drunk! Warmonger you know?' lot. Equally, there were the 'fight them on the beaches!' patriots. It is said that in Cataluña for instance, the subject of General Franco is best avoided in conversation. In a bar, it is sure to end in a brawl, though the dictator died thirty-one years ago. Things were the same for at least a hundred years after our own English civil war. Thinkers spoke carefully about Oliver Cromwell.

Historian's judgments have not yet really come to terms yet on the Cromwells, Oliver or for that matter, Thomas; nor on Generals Franco, Pinochet or Margaret Thatcher. They will remain 'controversial' years. Books are written about them, and programmes presented on TV, but this will not settle the case. The facts are there, but the controversy continues. The problem is ourselves; we are each of us individually split into factions. These leaders have become conflicts within us.

It is much easier with really bad men. Idi Amin was an ex-sergeant in the British Army who ate political enemies whose limbs were kept in the 'fridge. Adolf Hitler wanted revenge on the World, for its treatment of Germany at the Treaty of Versailles, but above all he wished to eliminate Stalin's Soviet Russia. He killed six million Jews as an afterthought. Pinochet took power from Salvador Allende, a Marxist who managed single-handed to bankrupt a once prosperous country within two years of being legally elected. At the time of Pinochet's *coup,* Chile's annual inflation stood at nearly 3000%, but Pinochet was, I suspect, like Franco, a mediocre man. Margaret Thatcher was not mediocre, far from it, but her judgement was doubtful, and her philosophies difficult to pin down. Her singular career was terminated by her own party and 'friends'.

Now, Pinochet and his terror camps remains a bitter memory for many but Chile has emerged as the No. 1 economy in South America. No Chilean has ever 'had it so good'. Where is the sense in it? Ask any thinking Chilean if he *seriously* would have liked President Allende to do as he wished, which was to build a Marxist/Socialist state in Chile. He and his wife will cheerfully go into the street with a placard declaring his thankfulness to God for the death of dictator Pinochet, and then go home (I beg your pardon, to one of his two or three homes) in the imported Cadillac. He would not have been the owner of three homes and an imported Cadillac if Allende had not been shot in the presidential palace. He would be a good socialist sharing a cold-water flat in Santiago with four other families, and he would be no stranger to queues.

In just the same way, no modern Spaniard would really have wanted Spain to become yet another atheist satellite of the Soviet Union, which was the declared intention of the leaders of the Second Republic. No Chilean or Spaniard can be confident that such a regime in their country could have been averted by civilised or gentle means. This does not mean that very few (whatever they may *say*), are not bothered by the means chosen.

Augusto Pinochet, a terrible old man, died not long before Christmas, 2006 and I doubt if his soul will rest in peace; I also doubt if the historians will find themselves in mutual agreement over him for many years to come. Meanwhile, Chile races ahead under a firm female hand.

Zapatero & Rajoy – two's a crowd

For the first time in nine months the leaders of PSOE and PP met yesterday, 22 December, and talked together for 90 minutes or so. Results were only too predictable, given that these two powerful men dislike and distrust each other. On those rare occasions when ZP actually takes his seat in Parliament, he and Mariano Rajoy snap at each other like bad-tempered terriers. One supposes that an entirely private meeting between the two at the Moncloa Palace will have at least have produced something. It produced nothing. The President of the Government had made it clear that the meeting was more of an obligation to the Spanish people than an actual attempt to analyse or *perfeccionar* the Peace Process for the Basque Country he is so determined to complete. At no time during the conversation would he deny or accept that senior members of his Cabinet have already had secret meetings with leaders of ETA and the illegal political party Batasuna. The Leader of the Opposition is therefore still in the dark on this fateful question. Whether or not he should be in this political limbo is up to the Reader to decide, according to his/her political creed.

So the Peace Process remains what it was before yesterday's meeting – purely and simply a weakened negotiation with an armed terrorist band, with two distinct possibilities arising from it: (1) Total peace and no more killing in the Basque Country and throughout Spain and parts of France, the dismantling of ETA, weapons and explosives handed over; the award to the Basques of total autonomy and independence from Spain. (2) On the other hand, if the Peace Talks should fail, Spain will face the very real possibility of the end of the temporary ceasefire, and the resuming of terrorism, with all that implies. With an agenda as awe-inspiring as that, no wonder Zapatero and Rajoy got nowhere in their first private meeting for so long. Both their political careers depend on the results of the Peace Process. Meanwhile, the safety and security of the Spanish people also depends on these results. The Spanish Press seems to consider the word 'stalemate' the most appropriate.

CHRISTMAS, 2006

England: the language

In 1906 the Fowler brothers (HW and FW) published *The King's English;* in 1926 HW published *A dictionary of modern English usage.* One hundred years, and eighty years respectively after the first of these 'bibles' of perfect English delighted and astonished English-speakers around the world, one wonders what wry comments the brothers would make if they could materialise in 2006? Both were obsessed with the over-use of faulty or ungrammatical English in their period.

Henry Watson Fowler (1853) was a schoolmaster at Tonbridge and Sedbergh. He was not a muscular Christian, being rather agnostic in his views, and puritan to boot. He went for a bracing morning swim every morning of his life whatever the weather. In *Modern English usage,* Fowler was let off the reins by his brother. He attacked solecism, semi-illiteracy, pretentiousness and especially what was later known as *journalese.* Today, he would be turning in his grave. This is a European column and it is interesting to note that while the Fowlers were at it in England, a German called Karl Krauss was doing the same in Vienna, with German. He wrote in a journal of his own called *Fackel,* of which the funniest item was named 'Desperanto', in which Krauss quoted frightful examples of fatuous and pedantic articles published in the press. Krauss ran a parallel column in which he translated the awful gibberish into decent German. Both Fowlers did the same with the English language in their books and articles. I should very much like to do it in this periodical with a lot of the stuff sent for publishing, because (it must be said) much of it is illiterate. But the odd thing is that the articles need not be illiterate. If their writers only took the trouble to read over carefully what they have produced on the word processor, aloud, they would easily reveal the frightful mistakes in grammar, punctuation, spelling and syntax they have made. But I fear some of our contributors will claim they *do not have the time* for correction at home, before sending their efforts off by electronic mail.

Things have come, as they say, to a pretty pass. For example, I have discovered I am not the only film fan on this island who watches modern British DVD films *in Spanish!* I do this because I simply cannot understand the language spoken presumably in English by actors in the film. I have to turn to my Spanish spouse who will translate for me, because she seems to understand the gobbledegook better. Rather than interrupt her enjoyment of the film, I prefer to watch it in Spanish, where the dubbing actors enunciate with precision, and provide some expression along with an appreciation of the various emotions expressed in the scene.

I believe I have written elsewhere that I sat with my family in a café in the South, with an English family at the very next table. Try as I might, I could not make out what any of them were saying – those who talked, that is. The paterfamilias sat in awful silence, drinking huge quantities of beer and suppressing belches with the back of a cabbage-like hand. The poor waiter couldn't understand either, and appealed to me for translation. The matriarch gave her order to me: "Oilevdesymeasim," she said, pointing to Garganta. I shook my head hopelessly at the waiter. But my wife had understood! *"Ella quire comer el mismo que él"* she explained. Poor HW and FW! All that work in 1906 and 1926 for nothing.

2007

21ST JANUARY

Mr Blair and his Peers

The cheerful smile on Tony Blair's actor's face, which lightened up gloomy Islington drawing-rooms, has worn off a bit. It must be bad enough to be treated like a leper in exclusive Downing Street, tolerate catcalls and polite booing in a Women's Institute, and feel Gordon (Braveheart) Brown's hot breath down the back of your neck; to dream of his reproaching eyes begging you to let him in. And now the British press has upped and discovered one of Blair's tastiest and most profitable little businesses, as well. It is enough to make any decent man throw in the towel: is this the way to treat a Prime Minister who was once head boy at Fettes. It seems he was selling peerages in return for political favours, so much easier now that the head boy has got rid of those damned hereditaries sleeping on the nice benches of the House of Lords.

A case concerning a rather large loan offered to Mr Blair during the election campaign of 2005, in the form of a 'party donation' seems to have caught up with Desperate Dan McBlair after all. And the noose is growing taut, because Ruth Turner, a high-ranking member of Blair's court, a lady responsible among other matters for external relations, was the fourth person arrested by the police in connection with this 'Lordship for Cash' scandal. Turner has spent several uncomfortable hours being interviewed by senior police officers, before being released – on bail.

The sale of peerages is not a modern phenomenon at all. Ramsay Macdonald ran a regular boot sale of attractive baronetcies after the Great War; both Edward Heath and John Major were not averse to healthy party donations in return for a gong. Nor was Harold Wilson, who made his PPS into Lady Falkender, though *Mrs* Wilson's opinion of the former private secretary was not high. Margaret Thatcher is not in the list, as she thought badly of *this kind of thing*, and said so.

The importance of this case is that the Prime Minister himself was interviewed by the police in the last week of 2006. This was the first time in history that a prime minister in office has been questioned by the law in connection with an alleged crime. Turner was known as the doorway by which people could gain access to Mr Blair. We are told that the questioning did not involve any loans, but rather her attempt to 'pervert the course of Justice'.

Scotland Yard believes that documents and other evidence have been 'tampered with' in Downing Street. At stake are loans of more than 20 million euros 'donated' to New Labour to help with the 2005 election costs. The papers also deal with elevation to the peerage of the four mentioned above. Each one has been a donor of funds. The PM is most indignant: "Ruth Turner is a person of great integrity; I have the greatest consideration for her and will always feel confident in her work!" he said. She tells pressmen that she admits to nothing, so there, which is to be expected. The three others are Lord Levy, collector of personal donations made to the PM, and two more donors – Christopher Evans and Des (mond) Smith. They are out on bail.

The police state that they will have finished their investigations by the end of this month (January), and that will have to decide what action is to be taken. The major problem is how to prove that documents have been messed about inside No. 10. They might have to question Mr Blair again.

Another lord, Goldsmith by title has said he will not be involved. He is the chief legal advisor to the Prime Minister, which makes it difficult for the Lord Chancellor, also in Blair's Government. It is said that the Lord Chancellor thinks Goldsmith should indeed involve himself, and the quicker the better.

France: Ségolène's partner doesn't agree with her (at least in political matters)

We know now for certain that the only two candidates for the Presidency of France early next year are the Socialist lady Royal, a smashing looking woman of fifty-three, and, opposite her, heading the UMP party, Nicholas Sarkozy. The polls show *him* with a lead of perhaps ten points over *her*. Meanwhile she has decided to call herself *La Zapatera de France*, and indeed there are gross similarities. Absolutely no-one in France or Spain really knows what Royal thinks, or what she might do if she becomes President, because she never directly answers a question, precisely *señor* Zapatero's method in Spain. where poor old Mariano Rajoy (PP) has been trying to get President Zapatero's actual proposals for dealing with terrorists out of him for the last two years with no success.

The beautiful Ségoléne has no husband, but she *does* have a partner, with whom she has had four children. No ordinary chap this, because he is in fact the Chairman of the Socialist Party of France (PSF). He is called François Hollande. He may prove excellent at pillow talk with his girl, but the couple seem to disagree with each other about practically everything else. He would like Royal to be more open in her campaign, especially on fiscal matters, whereas she keeps her mouth tightly closed. Such is the ambiguity of the situation that her campaign manager, Arnaud Montebourg, recently said, rather exasperated, "there is only one trouble with Ségolèle Royal, and that's her mate!" This was a little too much for a generally irritated Hollande, who promptly fired Montebourg. Some say that *this* was a little too much for Royal, who rather liked the clever work done by her campaign manager, and we must assume that some of the pillow talk has become rather heated lately. Seriously though, the nice lady really will have to make her convictions clear soon. No-one knows if she intends to soak the rich (lots of people are very rich in today's France) as well as the poor (who always get soaked no matter what the name of the party is). Possibly she is afraid of losing the middle and upper class vote if they think she will raise taxes even higher. Sarkozy has defiantly said he will face the challenge of changing the tax system altogether, because it is unfair and top heavy. Ségolène will have to 'get her act together' if she is to beat Nicholas Sarkozy, who is no beauty (these things are important to French people), but has an excellent, speculative and searching brain. He is also quite ruthless, a quality you can never have enough of if you intend to live in the Elysée Palace.

5TH FEBRUARY

"For God's sake, go!"

"I'm afraid you'll have to put up with me a bit longer,' declared a defiant Anthony Blair, still Prime Minister of Great Britain and his own loyal subject. He finds it difficult to believe that so many of his own colleagues, as well as the Leader of the Opposition, long for his resignation. After all, this was the young man with a great future ahead of him who took Britain by storm in 1997, invented New Labour and a lot besides, and persuaded English people to become resigned to the fact that senior politicians told lies constantly, and to good effect. He has also presided over the very worst 'nanny' government Britain has ever suffered.

He is supposed to go before the summer hols, which was his promise to the country and Gordon Brown, but on the other hand, since when has Mr Blair kept a promise? If he does, it will be in June, at the request of his own Chancellor of the Exchequer, the afore-mentioned Brown, a canny Scot like Blair, only a *true* one, unlike Blair, who only has a Scots surname, Scottish antecedents, and went to Fettes, a Scottish school. Luckily no-one dares tell him the damage he is doing to his own party by sticking like glue to the inside of the front door at Number Ten.

There is one matter which may help Blair come unstuck, however; that is the 'funds for peerages' scandal – if it were to become a matter for the Courts. So far it hasn't. Lucky Tony. Did the Prime Minister actually sell peerages to eager (rich) people in return for lovely and lively contributions to New Labour funds? It seems quite likely he did, but how important is that compared with all the other questionable things he and his lieutenants Peter Mandelson, Jonathon Powell and so on (the list of names must be as long as Pinocchio's nose) have done since 1997 – discovered or undiscovered.

Mr Blair has actually been questioned twice by Scotland Yard officers, a rare matter indeed for a British PM, on matters pertinent to this case. Soon enough, I suppose, an Official Report will be passed by the police officers to the Home Office, where yet another ministerial Scot, Mr John Reid, is anxiously awaiting them. Reid is among Blair's most ardent antagonists, and no-one can be sure he won't try to upset Gordon Brown's imperial ambitions. If anyone can do it, Reid can. He is made of the sort of stuff that created and maintained the Empire; guile, ruthlessness, lack of tact, plenty of brains, and the gift of the gab – as long as you speak Scottish and can understand what he is on about.

Whatever Reid does or doesn't do about the reports, the judges will have to reach a conclusion that will satisfy both the British public (generally speaking the British public couldn't give a double damn about *lords* anyway) and the gutter press. As always, there are scapegoats around, unless they vanish in the direction of Estonia with a one-way ticket: Lord Levy for example, whom the papers daily remind us is up to his neck in the scandal; not to mention poor little lady Minister Ruth Turner. The *Sun*, flagship of Murdoch's Byzantine empire, says – *"It's only a matter of time!!"* and, what a surprise, managed to spell 'matter' with two ts.

Nevertheless, even if Blair manages once again to creep out from under, he is treated by everyone as already politically dead. Perhaps he should not have joined Bush so boisterously (and expensively) in the Iraq disaster. Nothing pleased the hypocrites more than the Bush/Blair 'war on terrorism' pantomime. But, it must be said that if the war *had* succeeded, and Iraq was now on the way towards peaceful democracy (instead of twenty years of civil strife) it is on the cards that Blair would be difficult if not impossible to budge before he finished his premiership in the normal way.

2ND MARCH

Tid-bits from Britain

In a sadly disturbed, shaken Britain, the Education Secretary Mr Johnson has helpfully told the Qualifications and Curriculum Authority that schools must emphasise 'global warming, the British slave trade and the anti-slavery campaign (eighteenth century), Britishness (sic), the British Empire (snarl!), racism and ethnicity, immigration, the Commonwealth and cookery'. Surely Mr Johnson missed out a few more juicy items, such as the warming of cocktail sausages in tins. I suppose it is frightfully useful to teach children about these things, and examine them on paper later to see if what is taught has sunk in, but I seem to remember our ancestors preferring, instead of 'Britishness', to teach 'Greek-ness' and Roman-ness, reading and writing-ness, and plenty of maths-ness to boot. One has to ask why Mr Johnson, in his wisdom of course, prefers our children to learn more about baking tarts than the composition of a sentence. He must be right, because he is Education Secretary, but is he qualified to instruct head teachers to emphasise popular moaning's over what was the British Empire?

It seems a pity that governments have decided to make laws over what our children are taught. Surely what should happen is that schools, universities, academies or whatever you like to call them, private or public, should get together at fairly massed meetings (like the Headmasters' Conference), where, armed with their experience and the ability to choose, they may decide on a suitable curriculum? Nanny governments are all very well, but they ought to leave education to the experts. Also in Britain, it appears that detectives investigating the 'loans for peerages' bramble-bush are feeling they are getting no-where. They claim that their questions are answered by half-truths, prepared by lawyers, and that no fresh evidence or new information is being offered. There is light at the end of the tunnel, however, because Mr Anthony Blair's political secretary Mr McTernan has begun to sing a revealing aria about meetings between donors and politicians that lead to knighthoods and ermine. Then there was the arrest of Ms. Turner, head of government relations at No. 10 Downing Street. Then again there was the arrest of Lord Levy, Mr Blair's principal fundraiser. Now it seems at least two prominent people will be charged with 'conspiracy to pervert the course of justice' – that is, if the prosecutors agree with the police. Meanwhile, a stunned Britain has had to face up to the fact that the Prime Minister has been interviewed *twice* during an official police investigation. I believe quite a lot of Britons find this rather shameful.

To make things easier to bear, comical Mr J. Straw has proved what a divided party New Labour is by ignoring Mr G. Brown's proposal to lump together party funding, the honours system and House of Lords reform in the near future when, as he thinks, he becomes a non-elected Prime Minister. Mr Straw imagines that House of Lords reform should be a separate issue. What is more, he appears to think that present reforms to the Upper Chamber (made by this Government) can only lead to scandals like 'loans for peerages'. He suggests the Lords should be half-elected and half-appointed. Oh dear, what a *furore* that would cause! Perhaps Mr Blair and Mr Brown will suddenly realise that Britain's equivalent of the US Senate should only contain hereditary peers who have no need to make loans to party funds because they have been peers since birth, and have no particular axe to grind. It is usual to find that people with no axe to grind make good and honest debaters. Sensible debate is all that is asked of the House of Lords. I heavily suspect that Mr Blair and his cohorts ruined the old-style Lords because they thought (quite mistakenly) that a person who had inherited a title could only be a *toff*. And *toffs*, with New Labour, were *out*; *out* with Gerald, Duke of Westminster, for instance - a clever, subtle and successful businessman who could have made a tremendous contribution to sensible debate - and greatly helped to control the excesses of a power-mad Cabinet. Replace any silly old Earl with a Mr Jones-Smith who knows which way to vote and can be trusted to have not one single idea of his own. It seems that the once laudable fact that the silly Earl's escutcheon was carried into battle in the thirteenth century, and that the carrier's descendants have known something about 'ruling' ever since – usefully provides the very simple reason for Mr Blair kicking him out of the House of Lords. But with what do you replace him? Easy, flatter a chap by dangling a peerage before him, and wait a moment while he gets out his cheque book. But, and what a big but it is, don't get found out, because it doesn't do, even in modern, crazed Britain, to fill the House of Lords with your cronies, *and* charge them a not inconsiderable sum for doing so; this might be pushing the boat out too far.

Britain will have to sit through the 'Princess Diana' case again

Mr Mohammed Al Fayed has won a crucial battle in his personal crusade to further investigate the deaths of his son Dodi, and Princess Diana of Wales, in a Paris tunnel. Mohammed has claimed since the event that it has never been satisfactorily explained, and that 'attempts were made to bring about a cover-up'. A senior Court in London has judged that a trial should be re-opened, and, even more to the satisfaction of Al Fayed, that it will be conducted before a jury. This is what the millionaire owner of Harrods store has always wanted. The decision goes against an order given by the investigating judge, Elizabeth Butler-Sloss, who had reserved for herself the last word. The Court surprised many by declaring that the death of Princess Diana happened under circumstances that 'could be prejudicial to the health of part of the public'. I am not quite certain what this strange phrase means, or how it applies, but the media assault recently on Kate Middleton, Prince William's girlfriend, was most certainly prejudicial to *her* health. She has taken legal action, and has been told the case will be heard before a jury. The Court has clarified in a statement that constituting a jury is appropriate. It will be able to make recommendations about possible future changes, probably radical, in the laws which are supposed to protect the great and good, including members of the royal family, from unwarranted harassment by the media.

Al Fayed is said to have received the news of a further investigation and 'trial' with unreserved good humour. 'This is a great victory, but it is only part of my ten-year battle to see justice done," he commented at a press conference. Even better news for the Egyptian was that the senior Court has admitted the possibility of investigating the allegations made by Fayed against the Prince of Wales and his father the Duke of Edinburgh. Fayed has always claimed these two members of the royal family were 'implicated' in 'a plot'. Few intelligent members of the British press believe that the Prince and the Duke will be called upon to give evidence before a jury, and nor does the presiding judge, the afore-mentioned Elizabeth Butler-Sloss.

Meanwhile, the two princes, William and Harry, have had published a letter in which they hope that the trial, which should happen in May, will prove 'open, just and transparent'. The judicial investigation will examine as principal evidence the dossier prepared during the last three years by Scotland Yard detectives. In that document the police declared (what they must have assumed was the end of the case) that the Princess, Dodo Al Fayed and the French driver died in a fatal car accident. Yesterday's decision by the senior Court does not take this conclusion as final. The British public, Diana's children and ex-husband, the ex-husband's father, and *his* wife (who happens to be the Queen) and a startled world will have to go through all of it again. Mohammed El Fayed, whom I believe has still not achieved his much desired British nationality, must nevertheless be overjoyed.

18TH MARCH

Great Britain prepares – various aspects

I attended a little supper party the other day. The conversation became heated, almost frenzied (for the English, because voices were *raised* beyond the usual hush); the subject dealt with the fading last days of Mr Anthony Blair's premiership. Most guests were of liberal bent, with one or two exceptions; their conservative views were naturally unpopular with the free-thinkers, but the general consensus of opinion was that if Blair had manage to dismantle Old Britain with New Labour's help, his long awaited replacement, Mr Gordon Brown, will finish the process, though without Blair's undoubted charm.

Another, more personal topic was the Mayor of London, devout Marxist and ex-member of the British Communist Party, called 'Red Ken' Livingstone. No-one could suggest Livingstone had mismanaged his opportunities to take political advantage of his becoming mayor of London. He assumed this mantle in 2000, when everybody else thought the position was lowly, with little power, fewer finances and hardly any staff. Only Livingstone realised that the newly created post of mayor of London would offer the largest electoral mandate in Britain. He also knew that if he toed the line, he would be voted more powers, money and staff by the House of Commons. It is possible that Anthony Blair thought the job of mayor of London would prove a sinecure of no significance, as Miss Austen would say. He was wrong. Under Livingstone, a clever fellow, the mayoral budget has tripled, as has the mayor's staff. Ken Livingstone has his own embassies spread across the world, even in China and India. His team's costs have risen dramatically from £12 million in 2000 to £33 million in 2006. Blair made another of his risible mistakes when he told Britain that the office of mayor of London would only cost Londoners three pence per week. In fact it has now added £300 to the average householder's annual council tax. It is widely suspected that Mr Livingstone spends around £100 million a year on 'marketing'.

To be fair, Red Ken has achieved a lot. For example the transformation of Trafalgar Square into an almost continental pedestrian's *plaza* where citizens can sit in terraced outdoor cafés without running the risk of being overly dive-bombed by a passing pigeon. But he has also killed off that most *Londonesque* icon and tradition – the double-decker red bus. His congestion charge has not failed, as many claimed it would. He has bashed the rich with it, as was predicted; if you drive your horrible 4x4 in Kensington, Belgravia or Knightsbridge etc., you'll pay £25 a day for the 'privilege'. *That* was pure Old Livingstone 'get the toffs' stuff all right, and congestion in London streets has not changed a bit.

Livingstone has used his mayor's powers to get around the planet preaching his lifetime Marxism to other countries. He has been overseas twenty times since 2000 – at London's cost naturally. He has tried (and failed) to have meetings with socialist dictators such as Chavez of Venezuela, and of course, Fidel. He really does have 'embassies', as if his mayor's parlour were an independent 'country', in Brussels (natch), Pekin or Beijing (or whatever it is called this week) and Shanghai (shades of the unmentionable British Empire, which used to think of Shanghai rather as if it were St. Albans). He is said to be setting up further embassies in Mumbai*, and New Delhi (or New Delhi).

* *ie. Bombay*

1ST APRIL

Iran bites the lion's tail (or what's left of it)

Just as Tony Blair's last agonizing weeks of premiership come haltingly to an end, a positively Thatcherite opportunity (remember the Falklands?) presented itself. On 23 March, fifteen British soldiers including one woman were arrested and lifted off their dinghy between Iraq (where they were serving) and Iran. The British Government protested. It was claimed the big dinghy was in international waters when the Iranians swooped on it. Iran (at the time of writing) is still holding these British soldiers prisoner, and forcing the woman among them to don a headscarf and appear on videos suggesting it is time for Britain to withdraw the national contingent from Iraq. The result is a diplomatic *impasse* in Europe as Britain and Iran speak measured words to each other. The Iranians have a volatile, not always stable president who keeps talking of wiping Israel off the map, and '*Death to the Infidels*!' etc. Blair is coming to the end of ten years as Prime Minister of a country that, let us remember, not very long ago was super-friendly to Persia (now Iran), and protected Iraq (training her soldiers using British officers and NCOs). At first, Teheran promised to release the female soldier, Faye Turney, but then changed its mind and used her as a puppet, supposedly writing impassioned letters to her family and Blair. In these she 'confesses' Britain's 'guilt' and presence in Iranian waters at the time of their capture. Well of course. Tony Blair spoke in the Commons last Wednesday. Using Westminster as his platform he begged the international community to increase pressure on Iran, and insist on immediate release of the hostages. President Ahmadineyad was contemptuous in his reply, demanding abject apologies personally from Blair and his chiefs of staff. Foreign Minister Margaret Beckett breezily announced the freezing of diplomatic relations with Teheran, except those dealing directly with the captives and their speedy liberation. Blair also appeared on TV (which can be seen perfectly well in Iran) and made it clear he hoped Britain would not have to 'seek other measures' than peaceful and productive negotiation. British military authorities clarified that the nautical arrest took place in Iraqi not Iranian waters. Not caring a bit, Major Afshar from the Irani war office said, "the logical solution in this matter is for British authorities to recognise that they have made a mistake, apologise, and promise they will not again enter Iranian waters." He went on to explain that both the laws of Islam and ordinary humanity had led them to decide to release (as soon as possible) soldier Turney, but in the meantime, soldier Turney has appeared several times on Iranian television begging forgiveness for having 'invaded' Iranian territory. She showed the camera letters she had apparently written 'without pressure' to her father, admitting her platoon's guilt.

Blair now says these televised humiliations are a serious mistake: "It is utterly shameless to use people in this way," he said in a nationwide broadcast. In fact he is refusing to negotiate any more: "The only way out of this crisis is for Iran to release our soldiers as quickly as possible." Back came the major: "This unacceptable performance by the British has forced us to re-think the possible release of the soldier Turney. But the taciturn reaction of the British Government has made this impossible." This is what I suppose is called 'psychological warfare', but knowing this hardly helps the anxious families of the fifteen soldiers held in prison. Nor has an exchange of fire between an Iranian consulate's guards in Basora, Iraq, and a passing patrol of British tommies helped much. The British commander involved said it was a lot of nonsense, that he and his men were on a routine patrol, and that he had no idea an Iranian consulate stood there anyway. No one was hurt, but tempers are fraying.

13ᵀᴴ APRIL

'Great' Britain

Iran returned the fifteen marines it captured in what the British authorities still swear were Iraqi waters. The
fifteen were photographed smiling and healthy, their heads intact on their shoulders despite the declared wish of many Iranians. And off they flew. The general reaction in Britain has been of total indifference. Britons couldn't care less. No demonstrations outside the Iranian embassy in London have been seen. In 1984, a woman police officer called Fletcher was shot dead by terrorist occupiers of the Libyan embassy, and the attention of the entire British population was centred via TV cameras on this part of London for twenty-four hours, until a small detachment of SAS men stormed the house and removed or eliminated the terrorists.

What has happened, ask several eminent English historians, to the spirit of Boadicea (or Buddicca if you insist); of Edward 1, of the Black Prince, of Henry V, of Drake, Raleigh and Frobisher, of Nelson and Wellington, of James Wolfe, of the entire British population, in or out of uniform, during two World Wars? Where are the Churchills and Thatchers. Where for that matter is the shade of Palmerston who sent two British ships of the line to Athens with orders to bombard the Greek capital if apologies were not made to a British citizen who had had his shop raided by malcontents? Where is 'the strong arm of England'? Britain is seen by the civilized world as spineless, sunk in a morass of booze, obesity, prosperity, fast food, football and porn. No Briton is apparently interested in Britain's global role – if she has one. Britain's armed forces (possibly the most efficient in the world) are not connected with the public conscience. Blair's matiness with Bush and a dubious, probably useless invasion of Iraq saw to that. Reports from the UK suggest that the kidnapping of fifteen British soldiers aroused nothing more than a huge 'no comment'. Eyewitnesses state that Iranian troops crossed into Iraqi territorial waters and kidnapped at gunpoint British marines operating at the specific request of that irrelevant and very expensive invention called 'The United Nations', supported by the democratic government at Baghdad. The marines were actually carrying out routine customs and excise operations. No-one fired a shot in protest. The kidnappers took their hostages to Tehran where they were video' d, thankfully not beheaded or stoned, which is what demonstrators in the streets demanded. British consular authorities in Tehran were denied access. The snatching of these marines was a deliberate act of war. When only two Israeli soldiers were kidnapped by Hezbollah last year Israel promptly went to war. The British just sigh and go to the super.

British servicemen and women are being killed in Iraq by troops trained and financed in Iran. A prominent British lieutenant-colonel in Iraq has stated that the vast majority of attacks on British troops in Iraq are funded by Iran. The British people have another cup of tea and switch on the football. I suppose one must reach the unpalatable conclusion that both politicians and public are indifferent to the idea of an enemy nation involved in the murder of British troops. The general idea seems to be that Iran's actions these days are the price Britain pays for involvement in Iraq, but this is surely ironic, since Iran and Iraq were at each other's throats in a bitter war for years, when Iraq was 'governed' by the late terrorist Saddam. According to a recent poll, less than one third of the British public would be unable to trust any British government that suggested military action might be necessary against a direct threat to national security. The more vulgar British newspapers report that most Britons consider American presence in Iraq as a greater threat to world peace than Iran's President Mahmoud Ahmadinejad and his nuclear pretensions. You may ask yourself the question that several senior US Army officers asked: "Why didn't you protect yourselves" The answer must be that the British marines were under orders not to. It would make sense to surmise that the Iranians chose a *British* force to kidnap, not an *American* one. After all, it *is* the British who have announced an imminent withdrawal of forces from Iraq, and the fact that there have been no massed demonstrations in British streets, nor drum rolls, no sharpening of swords . . . prove the Iraqis are right.

What do Blair's crew want? Are they interested in national security? Is Britain relaxed enough to become a neutral country armed to the teeth with nuclear weapons fast rusting in their sheds? Does Blair now claim global impotence, after being brave enough to go in with Bush alone, with no support from that wonderful fraud The European Union? What next? Might not the Iranians grab another handful of British troops and demand in return Iran's ownership of southern Iraq? If the Brits were returned humiliated but unharmed because of some secret bartering – the release of ex-members of Saddam's Revolutionary Guard caught by American soldiers in north Iraq, for example – it will be a pretty kettle of fish. From now on, whenever Iran wants a little more, all they have to do is cop a few more Tommies, wherever and whenever they wish.

I must return to British reactions to this sad episode. Out of the twenty Britons I spoke to specifically on this subject, only one cared enough to wish Britain had more backbone. He said, "these days everyone in politics is a Neville Chamberlain; if there had been the same lazy indifference to real threats in 1939, the world would now be divided into three parts, the United States; Europe ruled by Germany, and the Far East dominated by Japan, with a bit of elbowing occasionally by Russia and China!" He may be right. Many readers will find him wrong. What Britons should be thinking is that no hostile state should even dream of attacking Britain, British interests, and especially British armed forces, without wondering first about the consequences. Is that jingoist, or rational?

13TH MAY

What the papers say . . .

President of the Spanish Government José Luis Rodríguez Zapatero is so engrossed, not to say enveloped, by problems just at the moment, he hardly ever appears to re-assure Spaniards that he is still there. He does however make appearances at meetings of his own party – the PSOE – where he will always be assured of a welcome. He was *not* assured of a welcome at a quick meeting held by Mr Anthony Blair (UK), M. Nicholas Sarkozy (France's future President), and Frau Angela Merkel (German Chancellor), ostensibly to say goodbye. Mr Blair had officially announced his retirement from the premiership of Great Britain and of politics in general. It would have been nice if Blair could have said goodbye to Sr. Zapatero as well, but the latter was rather openly ignored. To be fair even a quick meeting would be difficult for poor ZP – he has looming municipal elections to fight, his own home, the Moncloa Palace, seems to be rent in divisions; one of his senior committees, which deals out advice on economic matters, has been named as 'sinister', and his attempts to bring ETA's violence and mayhem to an end are fading.

The *Tribune de Genéve* limits itself to re-stating that these forthcoming municipal elections are nothing more than a prologue to the general elections which will be held next year. A prologue that will tell Spaniards which way the wind is blowing. The paper confesses bewilderment over the Spanish Government's feeble treatment of ETA terrorists, such as De Juana Chaos, who murdered twelve *Guardia Civiles* (among many other victims) in Madrid's Plaza de la República Dominicana in 1986. This individual was sentenced to hundreds of years imprisonment, but was recently photographed strolling about a Spanish seaside resort with his *novia*.

The American weekly *Time* has a lot to say about Sarkozy and Gordon Brown. This will be a fine political couple, says the *Time* writer, which may well produce far better relations between the United States and Europe, and bring about a new political geography of the world. The weekly predicts a new coalition - Britain/Germany/France (no mention of poor old Spain) and devotes no less than twelve pages to it. Could it be that the United States does not trust Sr. Zapatero? Might his premature withdrawal of Spanish forces from Iraq have a connection with *Time*'s blindness? Might Sr. Zapatero's very public refusal to stand up in Madrid while Old Glory was carried past him have influenced Americans in some negative way? Might Sr. Zapatero and his colleagues' open anti-Americanism have embarrassed Merkel, Sarkozy and Blair?

In Brussels, *The Observer* has been busy analysing the Spanish Government's puzzling foreign policies. Europe has decided on its policy with regard to Cuba, for example, and other dictatorships, such as Venezuela. But Spain's government follows quite a different path. Foreign Minister Moratinos is always popping off to Havana for a puff of a cigar with Raoul Castro or even his recovering elder brother. Sr. Chavez of Venezuela is also accustomed to entertaining Sr. Moratinos if he feels up to it. The paper is not certain 'European values' are being observed by the Spanish Government.

Three mediums, the *International Herald Tribune* in Paris, the BBC in London, and *Forbes* in New York, seem bothered by the new Spanish *Ley del Suelo* (land laws). They are disturbed by possible effects on zooming and booming speculation in this sector – land values in particular. But they too are bewildered. What was the point of pushing this new Law through? Is it an attempt to stop land speculation, which, given the nature of today's capitalist-dominated world, is unstoppable anyway.

In London, the *Financial Times* assures us that all grand European leaders 'are knocking' at Sarkozy's door, certain that the 'New Trio' in European politics will prove the most influential since the conception of Europe as a single entity. Once again there is no mention of Spain as one of the twenty-five. Yet Spain is a member of the 'G8' group of the most powerful and influential countries in the world. What is happening here?

27TH MAY

Ireland

Ireland has been one of the greatest success stories of the European Union. Not only has she prospered, and become a target residence for thousands of expatriates from all over the Twenty-five, but since a comparative peace was established in the British North, even once sad Ulster and Belfast have become attractive too. Certainly the English, who had been flocking towards France and Spain during the Blair years, are now turning eager heads towards the Emerald Isle instead. Dublin herself has become a new centre of culture. Always beautiful, the city is crammed with theatres, art galleries, and colourful life – where everything used to be so grey and dismal. A great deal of the merited praise for the 'Irish Revival' can be heaped at the door of Bertie Ahern and his *Fianna Fail* party, which has just been awarded at the polls a historic third mandate: not only historical, but unique. No Prime Minister or political party has done this before.

At the time of writing, FF has obtained 78 seats out of the 166 in Parliament in the complex and sometimes puzzling electoral system – even more complicated than that of the presidential elections in the USA, in which a chap who has actually won less votes than another chap can still become President, as we saw in the Bush/Gore mishmash in 2000. According to RTE (Irish public television) yesterday, *Fianna Fail* will have won approximately 41.6% of the vote by this morning, rather as the party did five years ago, though hints were made that the final figure might be a little less. FF's partners in governance during the last two legislations, the Progressive Democrats, were projected as having suffered a small loss of seats, perhaps standing at 2.6% of the vote, which would still leave the coalition with the sum of 44.2%, substantially more than the nearest opposition, with only 36.2%. The opposition is also formed by a coalition, led by *Fine Gael (*with 26.3%) and the Irish Labour Party, with 9.9% of the vote.

Many readers, especially Irish partisan readers, will wonder where *Sinn Fein* appears in this imbroglio – the answer being 7.3% of the vote, itself a much lower figure than expected only a few weeks ago. The Green party, also projected enthusiastically, appear to have won only 4.8% of the vote. Irish newspapers attribute the not very astonishing success of *Fianna Fail* exclusively to Bertie Ahern, prime minister since 1997. With ten years under his belt and the prospect of five more ahead, Ahern has left other European leaders such as Tony Blair of Britain and Jacques Chirac trailing behind. These two have now gone anyway, whereas Ahern is he put it recently, 'just settling down in the job'. Ahern's party is of a central disposition, aided by the liberal/right of the Progressive Democrats. Victory was ceded yesterday by the Labour Party, when its leader, the interestingly named Pat Rabbitte recognised that Bertie was *Taoiseach* again. 'We have a long night ahead of us,' said this pessimist, 'but I don't think we shall see many surprises.' The Labour Party is a diminutive partner of *Fine Gael* (Gaelic for Irish Tribes), which stands firmly at centre/right. The Labourites will expect to take part in the governing of this burgeoning and vibrant new Eire. Irish Tribes is the second most important political party in Ireland, but not once has it managed to win the greatest prize, in the 75 years that have passed since an independent nation (Eire) was carved in the largest geographical part of this island, that passed many bloodied centuries as England's near neighbour, never a comfortable one.

24ᵀᴴ JUNE

Sarkozy suggests a job for Blair

I am all of a dither. Just when everyone in Europe was beginning to praise Nicholas Sarkozy to the skies, on account of his winning the second and last stage of his presidential bid with an amazing count of 68% of the vote – *M. Nic* blurts that he will promote the candidature of Mr Tony Blair as first President of the European Council. Or so says *The Financial Times* in a leader. The newspaper informs us that Sarkozy has already told Angela Merkel, of his proposed support for Blair, as well as several other leaders among the twenty-five. European Union leaders are meeting as I write this, and Blair is attending the Conference as one of his last public acts before handing over the premiership of Great Britain to the unelected Gordon Brown on 27 June (in three days' time). It doesn't matter whether or not I consider the proposal insane, however, because the same newspaper reports that official Downing Street sources maintain that Blair will not take up any prominent public position when he leaves Number 10; that he wishes to retire from politics, withdraw to contemplate the wonder of his works, and write his memoirs etc. Still, he has until the year 2009. Furthermore, according to *The Financial Times,* 'theoretical conversations' about his possible future post 'are not a part of the Union's agenda at this time'. Some correspondents don't find this an absolute refusal since Blair has always shown a 'strong interest in the image and persona of the Council's President'.

Germany and Poland

It is not practical, but emotional, to look at the historical uneasiness between Germany and Poland; one must remember that the latter country was invaded and occupied by the Third Reich, and then (after the War) abandoned By Roosevelt and Churchill to the embrace of Soviet Russia. Angela Merkel, the energetic chancellor of present-day Germany, is at present trying (at a distance) to force Poland's prime minister Jaroslav Kaczynski to enter more into the spirit of Europe, by agreeing to the terms under which the Constitution's statutes must be reformed. Merkel is not helped in this Herculean task by further opposition in the rotund form of Poland's President, Jaroslav's twin brother Lech Kaczynksi, with Merkel and other presidents at the Conference. Poland is among the most recent arrivals in the Union, and the country which (at the moment) gets most financial aid from it, while Germany is the founder member of the UE which contributes most to the Union's costs. "We badly need a new contractual base," said Merkel in a speech she made in Meseberg, and went on, rather dramatically, "but we cannot spend so much time and attention on ourselves." I wonder what she means. One thing is certain: Poland is as 'euro-sceptical' as Britain, or even more. At present meetings of the EU Poland is planning to use her veto over a reform of the statutes within the European Constitution, a reform that both France and Holland put paid to in referendums not long ago. So the nightmare (for Merkel anyway) proposition is that Poland and Great Britain should refuse to join in the fun; GB is represented by a Prime Minister (Blair) who is due to leave Downing Street on 27 June, and Poland by the less obstinate twin. It is Jaroslav who holds the real power, and he stays put in Warsaw.

Not since the era of Margaret Thatcher (a stern and unyielding anti-Marketer) has there been such a hullabaloo in Brussels. Angela Merkel, faced with the obstinacy of the Polish twins, has even threatened to go ahead with plans to change the statutes without the agreement or support of Poland (or Britain for that matter, though Blair has said he will provide no opposition). Angela hopes that given time the Poles will change their mind. It seems likely therefore that following Germany's lead, the Inter-Governmental Conference will start examining the statutes with a view to reforming them.

17TH JULY

Berlin: Tom Cruise and a hornet's nest in the wolf's lair

Just as I write this, a huge Hollywood movie is being made in Germany. The star is the diminutive but acrobatic actor Tom Cruise, and the backing company is United Artists (which maintains its famous name but is probably owned by a North Korean laundry chain). The film has stirred up a storm in Germany, for a number of digestible reasons: first, Mr Cruise is about a foot and half too short to play the German hero – Colonel Count Klaus Schenk von Stauffenberg; second, Cruise is a leader in the Scientology movement worldwide – and much of Germany believes this particular religion to be worse than Nazism; third, many Germans and Austrians are wondering why an American actor has to play the part of a widely admired German aristocrat, whose resistance group tried to bring the Second World War to a halt at the 'Wolf's Lair' (Rastenberg, East Prussia) on July 20, 1944. They ask why couldn't a German actor play Stauffenberg?

At the time of the Conspiracy the Count had only one eye and one arm, and had lost most of his lungs on the Russian front. He had won the Knight's Cross twice, and had laurels added to his three Iron Crosses for valour. He was loved by the Army and the people, and therefore loathed by Hitler's toadies. The Fuhrer himself said on many occasions that he could not trust any '*von*' an inch. The firing squad that shot him had to be secretly infiltrated by three 'trusties' because the officer in charge believed ordinary German soldiers would not shoot their hero. The name of the film due on our cinema screens in mid-2008 is *Valkyrie,* and the director is Bryan Singer. The movie's German co-producers with Cruise and his partner Linda Wagner claim that they were permitted to film at the former

German general staff headquarters in Berlin, where Stauffenberg worked – and was shot in a courtyard after his bomb plot failed. Shot, strangled, hanged etc. at the same time were about half the leading German and Austrian military aristocracy, plus many civilian mayors, town clerks, chiefs of police and so on - anyone whom Judge Julius Streicher chose to accuse of complicity.

The problem lies in the present German government as well as the Stauffenberg family, of whom more later: the government believes Scientology to be a purely commercial enterprise that takes advantage of vulnerable people (this is of course debatable), and that one of its best known adherents should not be playing one of the few heroes from the Nazi era in Germany's history. Social Democrat Klaus Uwe Benneter said, "Stauffenberg is being played by an actor whose sect, through dubious methods, attempts to lure people and make them pliable. This is a slap on the face to all upstanding democrats, all resistance fighters during the Third Reich, and all victims of the Scientology sect." A firm reply came speedily from Carl Woebken, head of the German studio co-producing with Cruise/Wagner: "basically, some politicians are using the popularity of Tom Cruise to become popular themselves," he announced, and went on, "this is not a Scientology film, it is a Bryan Singer film, and Brian Singer is Jewish. We want to show that during the Nazi regime there was heroic resistance. The personal beliefs of Tom Cruise must be separated from his skills as an actor. He is one of the best actors in the world in heroic roles, and that is why Bryan Singer approached him."

One of Klaus's sons is Count Berthold Schenk von Stauffenberg, himself a retired German general. He has spoken out against Cruise: "he should keep his fingers off my father!" In case this was not strong enough, he predicted the film would be 'terrible kitsch anyway'. Not so a younger son, Franz Ludwig von Stauffenberg, who said, "We each have our own opinions; a family is not a corporate entity." Franz Ludwig is a former member of the European Parliament. He added, "I am amazed that in discussing the most important case of German resistance against the Nazis, we should be arguing about the suitability of an American actor to play a role." Not to be outdone, *his* son Caspar told the German newspaper *Bild am Sonntag,* that he 'doesn't have any fundamental problem with the film," and, "I am not going to change my mind."

28TH JULY

'Don't turn again, Livingstone!';
the fight to become Mayor of London begins

In July, after several weeks of procrastination, Boris Johnson threw his hat in the ring. To be mayor of London (note: *not* Lord Mayor of London, which is quite a different thing) means to manage the most vibrant city-state in the world, a centre for finance and commerce, with an enormous and always growing population, four international airports, a hugely famous fast-flowing river and a million tourist visitors per month. The first Mayor of London was, and still is, a hard-shelled communist called Ken Livingstone, who introduced congestion charges to reduce the heavy traffic (failed), compared a Jewish journalist to a concentration camp guard (sniffed at), and praised a radical Islam religionist called Al-Quaradawi (caused intake of breath). Livingstone has also made pals with the Venezuelan dictator, Hugo Chávez (no comment). He has also, as had been pointed out in these pages, turned Trafalgar Square into a pleasant meeting place as agreeable as the Piazza de San Marco.

Boris Johnson is a journalist and editor and Conservative MP for Henley. He rides a bicycle, has a great mop of genuine ash-blond hair, went to Eton and sounds like it - David Cameron went to Eton and makes every effort *not* to sound like it. Boris's father is also a writer and MP called Stanley. Boris was an extremely successful editor of *The Spectator* for five years, and probably would be still, were it not for his political ambitions. The Election does not take place until 1 May, 2008, May. Londoners will be examining the two most important contestants (out of forty!) for the next nine months. One who has already published a vitriolic assault on Johnson is the hornet Polly Toynbee. In *The Guardian* (of course) she called him, between other one-liners, 'a right-winger, Europhobic, a jester, a toff, a self-absorbed sociopath (sic) and a serial liar'. That's enough to be going on with, but I don't think this kind of frivolity will affect Mr Johnson too badly. Toynbee was, if my memory serves, the editor of a paper which announced it would *publish* the full names of anyone *accused* in a court of molesting children. She did not clarify what she would publish if the accused were found innocent.

Boris has been accused of 'non-seriousness' before. Mr Livingstone, not to be left out under any circumstances, has also said of his forthcoming rival that 'he would be seriously damaging for the capital.' And 'did you know he didn't even bother to turn out to vote for free travel for old age pensioners in London?' There was more to come: 'he doesn't pay sufficient attention to the debate about Crossrail!' And still more: 'it would be beyond a joke to put someone in charge of London who has no experience of managing anything at all'. Some observers of the beginning of this scuffle have noted that Mr Livingstone has never achieved anything outside politics in his life. Mr Johnson managed to run Britain's most prestigious and financially successful political weekly for five years. I see something like hysteria in Toynbee's and Livingstone's attacks.

Andrew Gimson has written about Johnson: 'People love him because he makes them laugh, but also because they glimpse the hurt young kid behind the laughter. Boris's vulnerability is akin to someone like Marilyn Monroe's; it is part of his attraction, and like her, he can use it to seduce audiences pretty much at will'. Stanley Johnson has written: 'over the years I have learned not to be surprised by Boris. As a parent, I remember attending a performance in the Cloisters at Eton where Boris was playing the title role in *Richard II*. It was fairly obvious that he hadn't learnt the part, but he winged it splendidly, inventing on the hoof a sequence of nearly perfect Shakespearian pentameters'. Andrew Gilligan has written: 'I think it is better to have a serious man being a buffoon (Boris Johnson) than a buffoon pretending to be a serious man (Ken Livingstone)'.

Nicholas Boles, who was one of the Conservative contenders, but who backed down in favour of Johnson, has said: 'Ken Livingston's reputation as an unbeatable incumbent shouldn't be taken at face value. He has sort of written himself into the script – he's part of the furniture of everybody's life in London- so people can't really imagine life without him. But he has never got more than 36% of the first preference votes. I think I stood a chance, but I think that Boris has a much, much better chance'.

One thing is obvious in London. Boris Johnson's campaign to win the mayor's job is but a few weeks old but already it has put a smile on the face of politics. Now some may find this a loosening of the seriousness of the electoral process, and some have gone into print by calling it 'an indictment of the state of political culture.' Does this mean, oh liberals and freethinkers, that politics can't and mustn't be entertaining? Perhaps it is the very artificial seriousness of modern politics (when we all know how *sincere* many modern politicians are) that makes it so dull and deathly boring? In the case of Boris Johnson, humour reflects his tremendous capacity as a communicator. He is one of those people who stretch out a hand, saying 'what can I do to help?' He cannot just be dismissed by the Left as 'a toff' as if that is the end of that. Does candour and good humour make one 'a toff'? Surely this is better than trying to be 'the man in the street', and 'the modern man', claiming friendship with the best pop groups and dropping his aitches on purpose? Why are '*toff*' and '*posh*' terms of opprobrium? What can the latter word mean? Have you seen and heard '*Posh* Spice'?

Johnson has said: 'when I look at the streets of London I see a future for this planet, a model of co-operation and harmony between races and religions, in which barriers are broken down by tolerance and humour and respect – without giving way to bigotry, or the petty balkanisation of the Race Relations Industry'. If Mr Livingstone is going to beat Mr Johnson in May next year, he must conquer his need to see the capital of Britain as nothing more than a playground for his communist collectivism and as an available stage for his private brand of leftism. (*Note: Boris Johnson won the election and is now Mayor of London*)

13TH AUGUST

Nicholas Sarkozy eats hotdog with the Bush family (and tries to solve the kidnapping of Ingrid Betancourt)

The new President of France has been privileged by an invitation to eat hamburgers, hotdogs and other healthy picnic items with the President of the United States and most of his family. Unfortunately Sarkozy had to tell his host on arrival at the Bush country retreat at Walkers Point, Maine, that his wife Cecilia and two daughters were unable to accompany him at the picnic because of illness. George Bush told him "donworryboutit". Then the Frenchman decided to tuck in after all.

What better way to gain confidence between the two presidents? Admittedly Sarkozy had been rather rough with Mr Bush and his ideologies during the French presidential campaign: which would you choose? Hot dogs and hamburgers and the marvellous view from the grounds of this private estate of the Bush family, or than the stuffiness of Washington D.C., or the false modesty of Camp David. Mr Bush holds M. Sarkozy in high esteem, as he is one of the only two foreign leaders ever to have been invited to join the Bush family at Walkers Point. Mr Bush usually invites other world leaders to his ranch at Crawfurd in Texas (the state Mr Bush claims to hail from). The other big chief who got to Walkers Point was Vladimir Putin of Russia who got to spend a day or two fishing with Bush last July. But no picnic, no hotdogs or hamburgers, just talk, talk, talk and some crabs from the rocks. Nicholas Sarkozy got US fast food delights *and* Barbara Bush and Bush daddy, Laura Bush, twin sisters Jenna and Barbara, brother Jed from Florida and another sister. No doubt Sarkozy was able to smooth things a bit with his colleague. His predecessor, Jacques Chirac, had been scathing about Mr Bush, and refused, along with Germany, to join him on his perilous adventure in Iraq. Reporters claim that the two presidents spent around twenty minutes of the visit talking privately about climate change, the Lebanon, the Sudan and Iran. If they had a map between them M. Sarkozy was probably able to point out to the most powerful man in the world where these places are. One remembers that Sarkozy was much criticised during his electoral campaign for his apparent interest in regaining the friendship of the United States. He was especially attacked for his attitude by Ségolène Royal. If that lady had won, I doubt she would have been invited to munch hotdogs with the US president. She would have been lucky to have got served in a Howard Johnson in Newark, even if she had passed successfully through Immigration Control.

Sarkozy *did* once say that if he became President of France he would not allow his country to become a 'vassal' of America, but that was all right because Mr Bush thought a 'vassal' was a kind of ship. Having demolished the hotdogs, the two new friends established their next meeting point – this autumn – when Sarkozy arrives in New York to address the General Assembly of the United Nations.

While the United States and France hold remarkably similar views on subjects like Iran and the Lebanon, there is a bit of a problem over climate change and what allegedly causes it. One of Sarkozy's principal arguments in his campaign was that the American giant was not pulling its weight in the planet-wide battle against air pollution. Disagreement also exists over commerce and business agreements. But it is possible that Bush and Sarkozy may find another twenty minutes, in the autumn, in order to make their points and re-arrange things. *Donworryboutit.*

7TH SEPTEMBER

The French resurrection

I return to France in this sideways glance at Europe. France is an active founder member of the Union, and what happens there eventually affects us all. Sarkozy's conservative winds of change are blowing away the cobwebs of Gaullism, though many Frenchmen are still convinced that M. Sarkozy is a (much smaller) reincarnation of the General. M. Sarkozy won the Presidential elections in May partly because he attracted a goodly section of right-wing extremists to the voting booths. Because of this, the National Front lost perhaps 15% of its regular supporters, who now stand firmly with the Monsieur. He based much of his campaign on the twin subjects of French national identity, and immigration. For the socialists, this indicated a future president to be avoided at all costs, because he was too right-wing. But events in France of late led to most Frenchmen wishing perhaps in desperation for a conservative government similar to that of Mr George Bush Jr. If so, they were mistaken, because nothing will convert the new President of France into a neocon; as his foreign policies demonstrate. He has formed a government in the sure knowledge that long-held traditions in French foreign and home policies dictate that the country seeks practical agreement, or consensus of opinion, not only with other great nations, but also with the other great parliamentary Party. He gave the Exterior folio to a socialist, Bernard Kouchner, he who had been formerly Minister for Humanitarian Affairs. Another socialist, Jean-Pierre Jouyet, is looking after European Affairs. A socialist ex-mayor, Jean-Marie Bockel is Minister for Cooperation and Relations with the rest of the French-speaking world. Socialist Fedela Amara is Director of the NGO set up to defend the interests of women, a job she now combines with heading the Ministry of Housing Development.

The next important initiative has been to polish up the whole European project and image. Since the failure in 2005 of proposals for a European Constitution, nothing has been more foggy than deciding what could be the best way to improve the mechanisms by which Europe is governed, and by whom. Sarkozy however appears to see no hurry, and certainly will not his rock the boat by awaking the sleeping dog (the European Constitution) because he knows he will be bitten.

He has however managed to persuade other leaders to adopt a positive view about what he calls 'a simplified treaty'. None of this is written down, but appears to interest most of the representatives of the Twenty-Seven. If it works, it will be Sarkozy's doing. Again, if it works, it might do something to assuage the euro-scepticism of countries like the UK and Poland. Sarkozy has not broken his campaign promises, in which he was optimistic for a 'political' Europe, not just a commercially free federation. The readiness of the new French Government to take the initiative in all international conversations concerning climate change seems to be another signal that Sarkozy is determined to reinstate France as a world leader among nations. He is also strengthening French cooperation connected with development, security and confidence among the Mediterranean nations. He has made presidential official visits to Algeria and Tripoli. He has also visited the almost permanently troubled zone of Beirut. He has said that he accepts this is a great challenge, and that it may prove a long and arduous task. If he should serve two terms in office, which would prove nothing out of the ordinary, he may have enough time (he certainly the guts) to achieve something in this thorny element.

Sarkozy has also shown where his sympathies lie by backing all efforts to free the Bulgarian nurses imprisoned in Libya. These women have been (falsely) accused of deliberately injecting children with the AIDS virus. Before and after his election as President, he has been engaged in intense negotiations with Libya, very much in the name of Europe. Colonel Gaddafi was a reluctant host to these discussions, until Sarkozy was wise enough to send his own wife to do the negotiating. Now, apparently, there is more hope. I *am* bothered, however, by Sarkozy's avowed intent to force through legislation which will enable France to castrate persistent paedophiles and rapists. Not that I do not agree that something should be done, but it is what can evolve from such a drastic reaction that upsets me. It is a small step from cutting off testicles to cutting off heads, and this has, I believe, happened before in France.

2007

10TH SEPTEMBER

Spain: a third Party at last

It was bound to happen. Our Leader will shortly have to carry on his own peculiar style of politics with not only the ten million Popular Party voters opposed to it, but a brand new political party, positioned between the Centre and the Left. It was Rosa Diez, the socialist dissident from the South who, perhaps inevitably, founded the party, backed by intellectual writer Fernando Savater and philosopher Carlos Martínez Gorriarán. Mikel Buesa, leader of the anti-Zapatero Basque movement *Foro Ermua*, which has been prominent in its savage opposition to the President of the Government's attempts to bring peace to the Basques *apparently at any cost* – is not very far away either. Mikel Buesa promises not to leave the *Foro*, but intends to combine his work with the movement with active and fruitful membership of the new party. It must be said that the Popular Party has not swallowed this at all. Several PP spokesmen have declared they are sure Buesa will leave *Foro Ermua* just as soon as the new party begins to take decisive shape.

Rosa Diez is spokesman for the party, at present called UPD (standing for Unity, Progress and Democracy). It seems that the new party has already gained 10,000 members, many of whom are dissatisfied ex-members of the two principal political parties PSOE and PP. The problem, as one of these put it (anonymously) to the press, is that Mr Rodríguez Zapatero has been President for three years, but has only made one positive action. He withdrew Spanish forces, doctors, nurses and policemen from Iraq at precisely the moment when they were most needed. Not even his most ardent fan can deny he did this for any other than purely political reasons –

certainly not pacifist ones; he moved Spain's forces almost directly to Afghanistan, where they kill and are killed regularly. Perhaps we could add another positive move; he sacked his first choice as Minister of Culture and replaced her with a good, hard-working fellow who knows his job and its importance. At a first meeting held in San Sebastian, Rosa Diez said that 'our greatest task right now is to present our message to the people.' The party would seek adherence from 'people with experience and prestige; people with plenty of patriotic sentiment, a sense of State, a need to defend ourselves against the divisive motions at present rocking the boat. These people may well have differing viewpoints and arguments: some will favour ecology above all else, while others consider the economy more important: for example, seeking to obtain at last a zero deficit.'

In Madrid on September 29 a first grand event will be celebrated, at the *Casa del Campo*. We may expect many speeches, and a good turn-out. The Spanish people have been bewildered, confused, and finally angered by the actions since 14M 2004 of *both* senior political parties. Mr Zapatero has set himself up in the Moncloa as a sort of unapproachable Cardinal Richelieu, leaving his lieutenants of both sexes as spokesmen. His sole (and rather disappointing) political policy seems to be limited to a continuous attack on the other main party, with an emphasis on blame. Blame for everything from climate change to Iraq. Meanwhile, Mariano Rajoy and *his* lieutenants have replied in kind, instead of ignoring the vulgarity and getting on with providing a coherent opposition. Now, with the arrival of Rosa Diez, Savater, Martínez Gorriarán and the popular Mikel Buesa, Spain will be in a better position to make progress within the European Union, and perhaps restore her prestige internationally. We doubt the probability of Diez insulting the American flag, as ZP did. How he must regret it. Relations between the USA and Spain have hardly ever been lower than at this moment. For example, the American Embassy has quietly fired all its Spanish employees.

5TH OCTOBER

Ségolène: the price she must pay;
French socialist barons get their revenge

Since her humiliating defeat in the French presidential elections, Mme. Royal has had to face at least two books published by outstanding leftie intellectuals, and a whole library of newspaper articles written attacking her with no quarter. The French Socialist Party now resembles those famous cartoon scenes of a terrible soccer match between wild animals in the Disney film *Bedknobs and Broomsticks*. In this case the ball is Ségolène Royal, while crocodiles, panthers, vultures, hyenas, gorillas and other charmers do battle without much protection for the poor ball from the referee David Tomlinson. In fact there *is* no referee.

Two recently published books will do as an example of the mayhem within the Party: one is written by no less than Lional Jospin, and the other by Claude *Allègre* – and there is nothing *happy* about either, if you will forgive the pun. Ex-Prime Minister Jospin is probably the most prominent socialist since Mitterand, or was until the sudden eruption on the political scene of the glamorous Royal. In his book he blames the woman for losing the election to Nicholas Sarkozy, calling her an 'unfortunate mistake', claiming that she has 'drained the Party of all credence', and accusing her of trying to have the same appeal to the French people as the worst of the radical right-wingers. Allégre, an ex-Minister of Education, comes from the rarefied world of the French universities, and the inner circle of socialist scientists. Both he and Jospin share the same conclusion: the rapid ascent of Royal, her confident defeat of all other aspirants to the candidacy, her failed electoral campaign, her own incalculable ambition have combined to throw the Party into the worst disarray the labour party has known for decades – in fact since the re-founding of the Party itself in 1971, at the Epinay Congress. The reasoning of both Jospin and Allégre has caused both left and right of the Party to clamour for yet another re-founding of themselves as a party – starting probably with its name.

Both gentlemen coincide again in their criticism of the apparent total absence of any human feeling in the beautiful lady. One goes as far as saying that she has 'turned the Party into a 'nest of rats seeking to devour each other'. Jospin writes in his *L'Impasse* (One-Way Street) – 'she hasn't got those human or political qualities necessary to get the Party going again, not even before the next presidential election.' Allégre adds his own bit of venom – '*la défaite, chantante* (she goes singing to her defeat). He also compares her to Eva Perón, the wife of a particularly disastrous president of Argentina, 'a cabaret dancer who grabbed power capable of eliminating without scruple any competitor'. I say, chaps, this is no way to treat a lady, even in France. But there is more; after describing Ségolène as a 'dancing girl with the human qualities of a cheap cabaret artiste' Allégre claims she is worse, for she has robbed the Party of its ideals, its ideas, and political identity. He moans that she has converted the Party into a 'ship without a course, divided in fragments or worse'.

Well I suppose Lional Jospin should know; he has been a participant and chief actor in all the great ideological adventures of the Left during the last thirty years. He wanted to eliminate capitalism, to apply socialist ideals with rigour, support state interventionism, and stand up against any liberalising pressures from the European Union. He was Premier from 1997 to 2002. With this kind of experience behind him Jospin accuses Ségolène of 'leaving the rails, blinded by her own adventure'. Once again he compares her with the Extreme Right as she constantly attacked 'political elites' (which really means the most important political parties). This is an extraordinary thing to say, especially about a left-winger with a popularist façade and the rhetoric to go with it.

19TH OCTOBER

Getting into Europe: not as easy as it was

Not very long ago, finding another suitable and attractive country to live and work in, when you were not actually a native was comparatively easy; no longer. The countries of the European Community (27) are definitely showing much more attention to who is let in and who is not. Examinations for wannabees are becoming more rigorous. Some states are pretty tough with their own nature, too, in case it should not coincide with a prospective immigrant's own views. Denmark, for example, has a brochure prepared which says, quite bluntly: "whether you like it or not, sexuality and nudity are openly expressed and exhibited in public places. Newspapers and magazines publish plenty of articles about sex and sexual relations, and all carry advertisements of a sexual nature, with ample illustration. This is the result of evolution in a society which enjoys a liberal attitude towards sexuality as a whole." Thus Denmark bares itself to 'New Citizens' on the website of the Ministry for Foreign Affairs. In effect, it is saying 'you have been warned! If you don't like it, don't come.' This programme was installed as long ago as 1999.

At the end of 2005, the conservative government of premier Anders Fogh Rasmussen started forcing potential immigrants to attend special examinations, in the language, and both the culture and history of Denmark. The Ministry of Integration explains: 'the objective of these tests is to ensure that foreigners who wish to become Danish have good general knowledge about Danish ways of life, Danish history, and understand the Danish democratic system, so that they may more easily integrate with the population.' In simpler terms, 'forget about bringing your four wives in burkas, and as for stoning citizens publicly, don't even go there': expressed decently of course, in Danish. Ah! You don't speak Danish, then learn it, and fast if you wish to become a Dane. The Danish example, similar to that of the United States, reveals a growing tendency, found admirable by many, towards insistence that potential citizens strive to become as 'Danish' or 'American' as everyone else, and leave whatever remains of their country of birth, in the matter of traditions, dress, manners, customs etc. behind. Exams must be passed, to show that governments are perfectly serious. To this end, at least nine EU countries now employ this type of examination, after courses of integration and tests for loyalty etc. Oddly enough, it was Holland – formerly notorious for a customary laxity in these matters, which introduced much tougher tests for immigrants, in the middle Nineties. Right now, in addition to Holland, Denmark, the United Kingdom, France, Austria and Germany have established examinations for prospective immigrants who crave a new nationality.

In the UK, the test is called "To live in the United Kingdom" and consists of a 45-minute exam containing 24 questions about the British way of life. One of the questions, for instance, asks the entrant *where* he or she will find Geordie, Cockney or Scouse accents. In France, the test is called "Contract of Acceptance and Integration" and includes a hard test of the French language, and can only be taken after attending a course in 'civic formation'. The candidate must be able to ask for an interview in French, tell the time in French, or describe a medical problem they might have – in French. In Holland, the test is named "Basic Test of Civic Integration". It consists of an hour's exam embracing questions on Dutch history, geography, and the language itself. One example:- "Who was William of Orange?" In Germany there exists a special test for persons of the Muslim faith, a test exclusively designed for would-be immigrants from 57 different Muslim states. One of the pertinent questions in this test is phrased as follows:- "what is your position regarding an affirmation that a wife belongs to her husband and that the husband may hit his wife if she should prove disobedient?"

21ST OCTOBER

Cherchez la femme

France, it appears, is having 'a bit of woman trouble' these days. Mme Sarkozy finally decided she did not wish to be Mme. Sarkozy any longer, nor did the magnificence of French presidential living appeal to her. "I don't like the public life at all," she announced, and continued, "I prefer to live in the shadows." The divorce has unleashed a storm of comments in the European media, where everybody claims to know confidential things about the sexual life enjoyed (or perhaps not enjoyed) by everybody else. In Lisbon, Sarkozy himself was embittered: "Forty-eight hours ago, the media was shouting about a possible general strike in France, and its effect on everyday life. Now however (at the European Council meeting) no reporter has asked me about this threat made by the chief unions. All they want to know is about my divorce and my family life."

Cecilia Sarkozy has been rather nice about her (now) ex-husband. Only hours before Sarkozy announced the astonishing news to the European Council (and you cannot get much more public that that) Cecilia said: "Nicholas is a virtuoso of politics. Now he is installed in the Elysée and will do a great deal for France and the French people. It is as if a great but impecunious violinist were suddenly presented with a Stradivarius." Mme. also confessed that she had first run off with an intimate of her husband's to New York in 2005; not only an intimate friend, but one of Sarkozy's closest advisers. She says she was 'profoundly in love with him'. Asked why she had then decided to return to France and take a reasonable part in the electoral campaign that ended with Sarkozy safely installed in the Presidency of France, Cecilia said: "I returned because I believed both of us could build something together again, but it proved impossible." Having said that, several French newspapers claim that Cecilia took part in the campaign without notable enthusiasm; it is certainly not easy to forget (or perhaps forgive) her decision not to vote in the second and decisive election. "I wasn't feeling well," she said, "I am not designed for public life: what I want is to live in peace, in the shadows, in tranquillity." Still, Cecilia admits that she enjoyed a good deal of the twenty years she spent with Nicholas, two decades spent mostly in vigorous and numerous political battles, with the eventual target of entering the Elysée Palace by the front door.

New French finance minister

One of Sarkozy's first appointments when he became President of France was Christine Lagarde as Finance Minister. Following a fairly spectacular career in international law, this Frenchwoman became something like a star in the United States. The magazine *Forbes* didn't hesitate to name her the fifth best female executive from Europe. Sarkozy insists that he is changing France. He might well shout, "This is not the old, Gauloise-smoking, endless lunch, anti-globalisation France. This the France of Change, not Decay. Here to prove it is the first woman finance minister in a Group of Seven economy, and a woman who made it very big in the United States!" Christine herself admits she likes challenge. She was working (for the law firm Baker & McKenzie) in the US and becoming more and more irritated by the American idea that France was in decline. Which is why when she was invited (actually by the Prime Minister) to join the Sarkozy team in such an important rôle, she accepted. Lagarde is married and has two sons. She is thin and tall and has grey hair, which will probably become greyer in due time. She got a degree at Le Havre, later studied law in Paris. After this she took a Master's course in political science. Once qualified to do so, she took an offered job with Baker & McKenzie, always specialising in labour and anti-trust laws. She became chairman of the corporation's international committee in 1999.

In June 2005 Domenique Villepin, then Prime Minister, got her to join the government as minister for foreign trade. After Sarkozy's triumph, she briefly became minister for agriculture and fisheries, but was rapidly asked by the new PM, François Fillon, to become finance and economy minister.

5ᵀᴴ NOVEMBER

Italy and Germany

Newspaper reports across Europe resound with news from Italy. They report that the Italian police are processing expulsion orders for 'European Citizens'. In itself this sounds odd, but the reason given for the actual draconic process is the 'danger' these citizens of the European Union apparently represent. At the end of October the government began preparing expulsion orders especially for Rumanians. A spokesman in Rome for the appropriate government department, Carlos Mosca, admitted that 'there exist expulsion orders for certain foreign residents, which are being processed by the police'. To accentuate his point, Mr Mosca went on: 'taking a hard line is necessary, because faced with these beasts one must act with the utmost severity'. Not content with that, *signore* Mosca added: 'the equation 'respectable citizens/disreputable citizens is not equal'. In stepped Minister of the Interior, Giulano Amato, who said recently that the decree 'does not mean a witch hunt for Rumanians, only delinquent Rumanians'. This event is on a national scale, and is therefore significant at EU level. The movement has been proposed for a long time, but things came to a head when an Italian woman was brutally assaulted by a man allegedly from the afore-mentioned middle-European country.

Italian newspapers, never backward in coming forward, burst the news with popular headlines such as: 'Rumanians! Green light for expulsion!' *(La Republica)* and 'Woman attacked in Rome dies!' As it happens, the poor woman involved in the murderous assault was one Giovanna Regianni (47), the wife of a captain in the Navy. She was attacked, robbed and dragged to a sparsely populated area in the outskirts of the city. The police immediately arrested a suspect, a Romanian living in a shack nearby. He was found to own clothes covered in blood, after being accused by a woman of the same nationality who denounced him for the crime. The man has confessed to robbery, but denies homicide. The police, meanwhile, perhaps animated by the Navy, whose admirals are angry, cleared all the Rumanians out of the shacks and exported the whole lot of them. Then the shacks were pulled down. Newspaper reports indicate that at least five thousand Rumanians have been, or about to be, deported. Naturally, this action has woken up the liberals; Salvatore Cannavo, leader of a party called 'The Critical Left', has denounced the police action as 'plainly racist'. Not to be outdone in a moment of crisis, the leader of the political Right, Gianfranco Fini, has mourned that such an action has come 'too late'.

Berlin

While New York is busy building commemorative skyscrapers over the Black Hole left by the collapse of the twin towers, Berlin, a city not without bad memories too, is beginning its own clean-up of infamous places – more famous now as 'places of interest for tourists'. One of these used to be a big complex in what was once called the Prinz Albrecht Strasse. This was the general headquarters of the Gestapo. The street has been re-named Niederkirchnerstrasse, and forms a large city block bordered by the Anhalter Strasse and a building designed by Gropius. During the War and before it, these headquarters were used by Hitler's Gestapo mostly for imprisonment, and scientific 'experiments' which do not bear looking into or describing. The huge empty space will now become a 'Documentary Centre' which will bear the name 'Topography of Terror'. Mayor of Berlin Klaus Wowereit says the new building will become one of the focal points of the city, and adds that 'no other place better represents terror and genocide'. Half a million visitors are expected to visit the new Centre each year, in the future. The construction will be in the form of an open-air park beneath which lie the dreaded basements used by the Geheime Staatspolizei for unmentionable purposes. Visitors who are brave enough will be able to visit what is left of these basements too. Here millions of Jews, homosexuals, gypsies, priests and socialists were used, abused, and left to die after transportation to the concentration camps.

19TH NOVEMBER

Two dear old aunts who don't like each other very much

France and Britain have always pretended to get on, as near neighbours at least. When De Gaulle was forced by circumstances to come to Britain and 'run the War in France from British shores by brooking no interference from the British' he did his worst to grin and bear it. Historians now say that after 1940, not only was half France a zone unoccupied by Nazi Germany /under Marshal Petain) but that *resistance*, in terms of real, determined, violent and organised resistance to a foreigner occupying your country's soil by force of arms – was not as high as some claimed it was. Be that as it may – historians from both nations are still squabbling over the point – Britain's new unelected Prime Minister Mr Gordon Brown from Scotland has just squashed his own Foreign Affairs Minister David Milliband by forcing him to change the great speech he was about to make at a European level meeting held in Bruges.

Murdoch's London *Times* calls it a 'humiliation'. Milliband was going to launch a thoroughly pro-Europe message, totally in line with what he assumed was 'the Sarkozy Line', and which poor David also assumed would be Brown's line, after his ten years of experience as Chancellor of the Exchequer. With those years under his belt, surely Mr Brown would know enough about France and her part in the Union, under the direction of several different Presidents and Premiers. Brown must have known that Sarkozy greatly desires much bigger military cooperation between the twenty-seven nations that comprise the European Union. But no: Brown changed the speech, a little late because most of it had already been filtered through to the press. Milliband had to say: "We have no intention of doubling the work already done by NATO or others by introducing a new

European military institution. We'll carry on how we are right now, using the institutions we already have." Before, Milliband had intended to speak of Europe as 'a model power for the rest of the world', but Brown changed this to representing Europe as merely 'a regional power'.

This strange event took place a few days after the world saw the new great mateyness between the two presidents Sarkozy and George Bush. Perhaps the Scot sees the renewed friendship as a potential threat to 'the Special Relationship' that has always been supposed to have existed between the USA and Britain. There have been plenty of critics only too ready to rubbish this notion, usually by claiming that if by 'special relationship' you mean Britain doing what she is told by any American president, then a special relationship (of a kind) does exist. But Gordon Brown is not the kind of man Mr Blair was. The son of the manse is not going to be put on a lead by Mr Bush.

There is also the question of jealousy. Sarkozy has started well. Brown has not. He is much criticised in the press and media for his apparent hesitation and lack of will. Commentators say he was waiting too long for supreme power in the UK, and that now he has it, he doesn't really know what to do with it. Oh dear, if this is true it is but a repetition of what happened in Spain. Since he became president of the government in that country, Mr Rodríguez Zapatero has shown remarkable reluctance to do anything except smile, while his foreign policy seems to depend on personal relationships with Latin American dictators of the Chavez/Castro kind. Meanwhile, Sarkozy announced this week to the European Parliament that he will use the French presidency of the Union next year to reach new frontiers in the powers achieved by Europe for her own defence. According to *The Times,* Milliband had intended to use his speech at Bruges to contradict everything said by Margaret Thatcher, when she spoke in this city in 1988. The Iron Lady had opposed the construction of a federalised super-European state. This speech was and is the basis of all 'euro-scepticism', and though this comes as a surprise, it would appear Mr Brown is as 'euro sceptical' as Margaret Thatcher was.

14TH DECEMBER

British Army affairs

The British Army might be one of the smallest, in terms of manpower, but it is also accredited by most military authorities as being one of the most efficient and best equipped. The Wilson government started a trend, however, which attacks the very soul of this great armed institution: the idea, image and essential history of *The Regiment*. Most of these are hundreds of years old, and the list of their battle honours is impressive, if not a little awesome. The honour of the regiment was no little thing. The name, also, of the regiment, was no little thing, but recent governments seem to have been determined to belittle these names along with their traditions. By chance I came across a Note from the British Embassy in Madrid. It mentioned a young bugler playing something plaintive at the Cenotaph. Apparently he is a British soldier, belonging to something called 'The Rifles'; just that: 'The Rifles'. I suppose this unimaginative title was the idea of some 'expert' at the War House. What could it mean? Was the article correct? Yes it was. The Internet tells our researchers that 'The Rifles' is the term used to describe a new regiment formed by amalgamating several very well-known regiments into one, and 'thinking' up a collective name. This was the practice started in the late Fifties. For instance, I joined The Royal Norfolk Regiment, 9th of Foot on September 4, 1958, but by the time I was demobbed this once noble name had become 'The Royal Anglians' by a merger of the Norfolks, the Suffolks, the Essex, the Beds and Herts and I think the Cambridgeshire regiments. A lot of military history wiped out by some civil servant. 'No longer civil and no longer a servant' aptly said W. Churchill.

Well, 'The Rifles' turns out to be a light infantry group formed by making a coalition of the Devonshire and Dorset Light Infantry, the Royal

Gloucestershire, Berkshire and Wiltshire Light Infantry, the Light Infantry itself and the Royal Green Jackets. The first two were amalgams even before the amalgamation! The light infantry you will remember are famous for marching at high speed when on parade or on route marches – 160 paces per minute. The Spanish Foreign Legion, similar in many ways, does the same thing. You had to be remarkably fit to be a member of these light infantry units. But why did the Ministry of War have to call the new group 'The Rifles'? The name is ridiculous. You might just as well call the Royal Marines 'The SMG' because they are issued with sub-machine guns.

The concept of British light infantry was the brain child of General Sir John Moore, who died during the battle of 'Corunna' (*La Coruña*) in 1809. He had established the original regiments at Shorncliffe in the early nineteenth century. If the eggheads in Whitehall had to find a name for their tasteless commingling of these illustrious and resounding military groups, why didn't they go the whole hog and dub them all by the name of one - *The Light Infantry*?

Scotland

This astonishingly beautiful country with its sparse population has many deep rivers sparkling with salmon, and one Salmond glittering in his elegant old office in *London*, where he is, oddly enough, the *First Minister for Scotland*. He has recently claimed rather proudly that the Union with England will end by the year 2017. If not before. Alex Salmond much prefers his seat of power in London to what he calls 'the sanitised Continental-style layout of the Scottish Parliament'. Last May he led the Scottish National Party to victory, which brought an end to a half century of Socialist domination of Scottish politics. He added that some new studies just released suggest that Scotland is not the poor man of Europe – as many people, including many Scots – think. In fact, he says Scotland is the sixth richest country in the world. "It would be absurd to argue that such a prosperous country would be anything other than a country of great economic potential. There is no question but that Scotland is in a relative surplus, none whatsoever".

We will see in the eventual and inevitable Referendum what the Scottish people really think.

2008

4TH JANUARY

Kiev (Ukraine): modernity and greed upset an outpost of the Empire

The USSR used to rule fourteen republics, divided into many non-Russian speaking peoples, always indignant that Mother Russia should turn out to be a brute with a huge moustache and a liking for killing – mass killing wherever feasible. Of these non-Russian nations, the biggest and most nationally conscious was the Ukraine. In 1982 her population was already 70 million. Under both the tsars, and later the Politburo, the Ukraine drew special attention, usually of the grisliest kind. Even under modern conditions, with Tsars long assassinated and Stalin and Lenin in their mausoleums, the Ukraine is virtually divided into west and east. The West stretches from Kiev westwards towards the Polish border. It used to form part of the old Austro-Hungarian Empire, and was more 'Europeanised' Ukrainians in the West read and write in Roman letters, not Cyrillic script. Most are Catholic. In the East, where the countrymen have lived for centuries under the thumbs of Russian tsars, and if they are religious at all, it is Orthodox.

Since the fall of the Berlin Wall and the 'end' of communist rule (most of today's politicians were members of the Party once) the Ukraine has become free to hold democratic elections and become as rich as everybody else – not necessarily through honest toil. Westerners have come from the USA, and from the rest of Europe, not to mention Japan and China and India, to join in the bean feast, and in many cases honest toil has not been *their* guiding inspiration either. Make a very quick million bucks and get out is more like it. In the Ukraine, you could be a tall, spotty youth with a backpack and a Wisconsin accent who showed up in Kiev and lived under a bridge for a short while. Then you cornered a positive source of income in an otherwise unused hole in the markets, and within ten years you find yourself spotless, dressed by Savile Row, with three or *dachas* and this year's Bentley Continental. Your huge fortune might come from a media empire publishing neo-liberal economic news and forecasts. Your magazines and cheap pamphlets get their facts from *The Economist* and *the Wall Street Journal.* You could have been Robert Fletcher, an American who became a 'millionaire's mentor', instructing Ukrainians how to get rich quick for huge fees. *He* published a magazine too, called, with unpromising grammar – *The Rich's Club.* He went too far, tried to get out of the country on a false passport and got banged up.

In Kiev, the Catholic religion has been mostly replaced by 'markets-and-mass-consumption'. As a result, what appeared to be growth and development has been enormous – and a catastrophe. Unlike the West, Ukraine has not enough watchdog financial journalists publishing advice in a daily column; there is hardly enough watchdog media; where are the American or British armies of eagle-eyed lawyers expert in dragging potential marketers from court to court wrapped in a mile of red tape? The Ukraine's elite are mostly coarse ex-peasants who were there first, with their armament factories, and their franchise to sell Kalashnikovs.

Kiev, that is ancient Kiev, is fast vanishing beneath a grotesque building boom, turning what Russians used to refer to as their 'most pleasant big city' into a brick and cement jungle of ill-designed skyscrapers and collapsible blocks of flats. As the court system doesn't work – never has – any young tycoon with good connections in the town hall can find himself a nice, large, unused carpark and convert it into a low neighbourhood of little charm, with a, unattractive but money-spinning skyscraper of a mere 26 storey in the middle.

As the chief status symbol of the newly rich is a motorcar, hundreds of thousands of German, Japanese, Scandinavian and home grown cars now litter the streets and create traffic havoc. The less intelligent, Slivovitz-fuelled citizens tend to drive down the crowded pavement in a SUV. Most citizens of Kiev carry a handy handkerchief fixed to their nose in downtown Kiev, where air pollution nearly rivals Pekin's.

7TH JANUARY

A change of mind after the presidential elections in the 'other' Georgia

With a population estimated at just over four and half millions, Georgia is not quite in Europe, but has great strategic importance for Europe. Through Georgia flows a crude oil pipeline towards the nations of the European Union. The country is also near, perhaps dangerously near – both Iran and Iraq. In this double report we are not discussing the American deep-southern state which carries the same name. In Tbilisi (formerly Tiflis), capital of Georgia, locals found it difficult to remember such a shower of predictions made by inquiry polls, before the presidential elections held last November. However, when the shouting had died down, and the votes had been counted, it appeared that President Mijail Saakashvili had lost his job, and the victor was the leader of the opposition, Levan Gachechiladze, with thirty-one percent of the votes. Mr. Saakashvili seemed to have only twenty-four per cent of voters' confidence. Such was the howl of protest from the former President's party, with cries of 'Fraud!' prominent, that the opponents had to go on to a second bout, which takes place tomorrow, 8th January.

Among the most vehement protesters is the national TV channel 'Rustavi-2', which, accompanied by a chorus of denials by three other local channels, is certain that Mr. Saakashvili actually obtained fifty-two percent of the vote. Electoral fraud seems to have been proved, but whatever happens, if this was the true figure, it makes a second round look silly and unnecessary. The same inquiry reports Mr. Gachediladze as winning support from twenty-eight percent of the electorate. Someone is getting the figures wrong, especially as another poll reveals a third candidate, business impresario Badri Patarkatsishvili (the names!) as having won nearly twenty-one percent. Perhaps the oddest thing of all is that the first round only attracted a total participation of forty-six point four% of those with a vote

The supposed winner, Gachedchiladze, has threatened to bring his supporters out into the streets (in Georgia this is ominous indeed) if the original results are 'manipulated', as he claims they might be. Whatever the results of the imminent second round, electoral fraud should be counted out, as the sheer quantity of foreign observers crowding the streets of used to be Tiflis should prevent any cheating. There are over eight hundred observers eagerly awaiting the great day, over half of whom have been sent by a typical European Commission body called the Organisation for European Security and Cooperation. Watch this space.

Spain: the State versus the Church; things get worse

The Pope himself has entered the fray. In a speech made before 180 accredited ambassadors to the Vatican, Benedict XVI condemned on 7 January 'the worrying attacks on the integrity of the family unit, founded since time immemorial by marriage between men and women'. The Pope at no time mentioned names, but this was unnecessary, since all those ambassadors knew that the Pope referred to Spain, where the President of her Government recently launched a tremendous attack on the Church after it had organised a massive demonstration on behalf of 'the family unit' in Madrid. Not only the Italian press, but papers around the world have not ceased commenting on this direct confrontation between an openly atheist government and the Catholic Church. Shades of the 2nd Republic are closing in.

Mr Zapatero's government has never been easy in its relations with the Church, but senior vice-president María Teresa Fernández de la Vega tried hard to establish a direct link between the Spanish administration and the Vatican. She was rejected by cardinals who told her relations must be cordially established between themselves and the Spanish Conference of Bishops (a sort of clerical trade union made up of the bosses). Zapatero replied by sending as ambassador to the Vatican the popular Francisco Vázquez, and things got a little better. The senior vice-president was well received in Rome when she attended the investiture of three new Spanish cardinals. Then foreign minister Moratinos received special attention when he went to watch the beatification of 498 Spanish martyrs.

Now, it seems that Mr Zapatero, always eager to represent discord, or at least to sow it, has decided to return to the practice of confrontation. The

Church is a solid wall between agreement and disagreement, since its dogma cannot accept the idea of (1) rapid divorce; (2) marriage between persons of the same sex; (3) abortion, or (4) decisions which prevent parents from being able to choose an education for their children which includes religion. No Spanish bishop can change his own or his church's views on these subjects, and others, without a series of church reforms. These can only be expedited after a lengthy conference between all the world's cardinals – in the Vatican. Meanwhile, the world's onlookers see nothing but strife between Mr Zapatero's government and a leading Spanish institution. Things can only get worse.

21ST JANUARY

Of a Union, a Council, NATO and Vlad's Russia

Just next door to the grandiloquent European Parliament building in Strasbourg, where delegates from twenty-seven states send their chosen representatives to debate for the good of the European Union, stands a more modest palace. No Russian sits in the European Parliament, but the smaller building houses the Council of Europe, which has forty-six member states, including Russia. The Council became a fact following Churchill's 1946 speech in Zurich calling for 'a United States of Europe'. Perhaps Winston's American mother had influenced the old man's tongue, because the French and the Russians showed themselves none too fond of this allusion to North America. Nevertheless and notwithstanding, the Council was set up under that title, and early representatives of the United Kingdom were Harold Macmillan and Duncan Sandys, the latter Churchill's son-in-law. No-one from the British Labour Party sat in the council, because the late Forties and early Fifties the Reader will remember was a period when Labour refused to have anything to do with anything 'European' under the sun. It is as well also to remember that neither the Council of Europe nor the European Convention on Human Rights, nor even the European Court of Human Rights have anything but a cloudy relation with the European Union. The Council remains an essentially British concept, as indeed is the Court.

The Council's 46 members include Switzerland, Norway, Turkey, Armenia, Georgia, some non-EU Balcan states – and Russia. The parliamentary assembly meets in vigorous debate four times a year, and tends to get things done, unlike its grander sister next door. In the Council, custom demands that deputies call a spade a spade – if they have indeed 'seen a spade', to quote Mr Wilde. Recently, female deputies from

Scandinavia and German lady Social Democrats quarrelled violently over what to do about prostitution.

Several European newspapers have pointed out that Russia, under Mr. Putin who seems at present to be moving gently from the presidency into premiership, despite her poor record on human rights, has the support of British conservatives in the Council. In fact it would appear that Mr Putin and his loyalists are working hand-in-glove with Tory MPs to promote the Russian line: this includes an attempt to put in place Putin's choice, as head of promoting democracy and human rights on the continent. Please do not chortle, as Frankie Howard used to mutter. We are told that whoever is president of the Council of Europe is always given the green light by Governments eager to avoid the European Parliament's criticism of their own versions of democracy and records on human rights. But we are also told that there is an exception – Russia. Far from trying to make Russian laws and practices conform to Council of Europe terms, Moscow is spending huge sums seeking to influence the Council, and arrest any criticism of the Kremlin's home and abroad policies. Were the reader to investigate the Council, using the ubiquitous Net, she will find that the Russian delegation to the Council is not only one of the biggest, but includes key politicians who lead the most important Russian committees. Each of these potentates is backed by a team of multi-lingual experts who can get over the Russian point-of-view in any language.

The Kremlin is intent on wrecking any plans to monitor elections in Russia or her satellites. Mr. Putin has cleverly reverted to the old Kremlin custom of insisting on criticism of the West's own record on democracy and human rights, while at the same time treating any attempt to do the same thing with Russia as external interference. Meanwhile, when NATO assembles, Russian members openly insult other delegates, despite the fact that Russia was originally made welcome in the euphoria excited by the end of Communism. A veteran British labour MP (a Mr. George) was only last year called 'insane' by a Russian MP. He has long been chairman of the House of Commons defence select committee.

When a woman minister from Georgia (an ex-satellite that causes the Russians a lot of pain) finished her speech recently, the leader of the Kremlin's deputation said, "In Russia we know there are two things it is pointless to debate with, a radio and a woman."

Great Britain: what can they do with Prince William?

What indeed? If one were the Queen and the Duke of Edinburgh, grandparents, or the Prince of Wales and the Duchess of Cornwall, father and stepmother respectively, it would be difficult to imagine a more eccentric career move for the future King of England than a job in journalism. Nevertheless, we are informed by very correct sources that when Prince William has finished his military career (this year), he will start doing his 'work exercises' with a newspaper. Perhaps it has been thought (by the Royal Family) that a short period of reporting and writing for the press might be an excellent 'first job' for the heir to the throne. Come to think of it, following the rather unsettling experience Britain had after revelations of Princess Diana's close relation with the British press, it is not such a strange idea after all. William might well have learned a great deal about manipulation of the press from his mother, and spending some time with a national newspaper may even the intellectual balance, so to speak. It is possible too that employing William in a newspaper might put a brake on the nefarious activities of most of the vulgar press who cannot resist intrusions in the private life of persons like Kate Middleton; I doubt it. The *paparrazi* find royal romances, on or off, a temptation too tempting to avoid. We learn that Clarence House has dictated that the very last subject they want reported by Prince William is anything to do with the Court – such as it is. Reports also indicate that a very senior member of That Family has said, 'I think the idea is excellent. The Prince should learn how the media works. I should like to learn that myself".

Prince William, in accordance with family rules, has already served his time in the Army. He is now in the RAF, learning to be a pilot and obtaining his flying licence, just as his father and two of his uncles before him. His brother Harry has stayed in the Army as a career move, and is apparently showing promise as a professional in that branch of the Armed Forces. Towards the end of this year William will, again according to family custom, enter the Senior Service and become a sailor for a while. Meanwhile, his father has just broken the record in all British history for A Prince of Wales and Heir to the Throne…waiting to ascend to it. This may come as a surprise to those who thought that Edward VII held that record. Given the longevity Elizabeth II has inherited from her Scottish mother, and given the Prince of Wales' actual age now, who knows? Poor Charles may never occupy the throne, but his oldest son will*, and that is why a period of time spent as a journalist is so interesting to the rest of Britain. Afterwards, William may well go to the Foreign Office to learn diplomacy, or the Home Office to learn how to use double-speak to confound his enemies. Who knows?

* Unless he goes to the Middle East, where foreign journalists are generally beheaded by 'the Muslim State'.

Homosexual couples aren't less stable: official

The European Court of Human Rights, in Strasbourg, has just condemned France for disallowing the adoption of a child by a Lesbian couple. We are informed that this sentence is without precedent in European jurisprudence, as it tacitly implies that the 'mother' (one of the two women involved) was treated with discrimination. What is more, the magazine *Development Psychology* has just published an article which supports the idea that relations between a couple formed by the same sex are just as stable as those to be found in any heterosexual one. The article emphasises that homosexual couples are equally compromised in romantic terms as their heterosexual equals. Investigators from universities in Washington and Illinois (USA) assure us that gay unions are no less healthy from the psychological point of view.

Research shows that out of all the couples studied, of both opposite sexes and the same, interactions and adult development are the same. No great divergences have been observed; in fact a recent study declares that 'generally speaking, both male and female homosexual couples are no different in their responsibilities to each other, or social inter-action, as any heterosexual couple, though we should point out that there is a noted tendency among the females to resolve problems that may arise more efficiently'.

18TH FEBRUARY

Kosovo's independence may set a dangerous precedent

Fully backed and supported by the European Union, encouraged by the United States in the form of each one of the candidates put forward by both the Democrats and the Republicans, praised by Great Britain, and dreaded by Spain, the Government of Kosovo has unilaterally declared its independence from Serbia. Naturally, Russia has objected. Just in case, the European Union has sent more than two thousand special police, judges, lawyers, and Union functionaries to the region to show solidarity with the Kosovans, and generally keep a wary eye on things. In Pristina, Kosovo's capital, it was and is well known that the Serbian Government had plans to make Kosovo a kind of 'Cyprus' – a permanent state of disarray in which two different nationalities strive (in most cases) to live together in an uneasy peace. In Cyprus, this means Turkey and Greece. In Kosovo, it means Albanians and Serbians. Boris Tadic is President of Serbia, and he repeated that threat during his recent inaugural speech. Even while he was making it, the Kosovan Parliament was approving a series of measures (actually suggested by an ex-President of Finland) designed to make the process leading to independence from Serbia smooth – or at least not as rough (or violent) as much of the European press has insinuated.

During the week before yesterday's historic Sunday announcement, the Albanian Kosovans for their part spent every day exploding fireworks, dancing in the streets, flag-waving, and listening to rather inflammatory speeches made by some of their leaders. The Serbian section of the population remained sullen. The Kosovan prime minister proclaimed the formation of a new branch of the Government, loaded with a million or so euros, which would help deal with 'daily problems' of all the minority groups in the tiny new State – especially the Serbs, while at the same time 'guaranteeing the equality of everyone in Kosovo'. "The door to my office will always remain open, so that I may listen to the needs or worries of each and every Serbian citizen in Kosovo," assured Mr. Hashim Thaci, an ex-guerilla leader who had much to do with the Balkan troubles in the 90s of the twentieth century, and who was known to have caused many casualties, especially among Serbian farmers. It may be that the gesture was designed to be recorded by the multitudes of foreign reporters at present swarming about the capital.

From the European legal point of view, the United Nations Organisation has laid down rules about the maintenance of a truly multi-ethnic population. Historians know that this existed well enough *before* the dreadful Balkan wars that scarred everything in Middle Europe, and were such an embarrassment and disgrace for the European Union. Since the wars 'ended' the ideology of everybody living together in harmony has virtually vanished, and many international observers feel that things are not going to be easy.

In Serbo-Kosovan territory, such as the town of Mitrovica, thousands of Serbs demonstrated in the streets and squares against the secession. Their ring-leader claimed that he would never permit the 'monstrous declaration of independence to hold any sway in 'Serbian territory'. It was not long before home-made bombs were being thrown at Serbian shops and businesses across Kosovo.

In Moscow, the Kremlin watched grimly, perhaps a little reluctantly, given the fact that the destiny of Kosovan Serbs has not perturbed the Russian Government unduly up until now. Radio Serbia reports a *comunicado* from the Kremlin, actually the Foreign Ministry, saying that the independence of Kosovo will force the Russians to 're-value' and 're-assess' the situation in respect of the laws of international Rights, a veiled reference to Russia's own problems with Osetia and Abjasia, also threatening unilateral independence. Russia has, however, recognised the independence of Georgia, though unwillingly. Serbian Prime Minister Vojislav Kostunica prefers to take the victim's role in his speeches, as if Serbia has been hard done by History. This admirer of Russia claims that the European Union wishes to reduce Kosovan Serbs to 'the position of slaves'. President Tadic says he will withdraw his embassies from Pristina.

17TH MARCH

The indiscreet charm of M. Sarkozy

I write again about France and her almost new President. Nicholas Sarkozy is a baffling mixture of two distinct characteristics: he has the political skills of Metternich and a startling propensity to act like a clown. The French Presidency lasts for five years, and it seems that many French people (now sorry) voted for the new folk hero; the honeymoon is over and only 37% of those who wanted Sarkozy want him now, according to a recent poll. What happened? Could it be the sudden divorce from a popular wife? The immediate wedding with a new glamorous model? But we are talking about France, a country where people are not shy about marital matters. A nation where most men are considered effeminate if they do not have the statutory wife and brood, plus a couple of pliant mistresses, should surely not censure their President for being so French? This acceptance of love, marriage and adultery is as much a part of France as the *Marseillaise.* Nancy Mitford, a Francophile and besotted mistress of General de Gaulle's chief advisor, used to repeat that French men did their most serious thinking in bed.

The Financial Times: "The popularity of the French President has declined precipitously during the last few months, with public opinion apparently little impressed by his presumptuous style, the exhibitionism shown in his private life, and his incapacity to maintain his promise to raise the standard of living." Strong words. A member of the *Academie Francaise* has written in *Newsweek* about the marked differences is style shown by Sarkozy and his predecessors at the Elysée Palace. "He (Sarkozy) is always the one to take and make decisions; always. With previous Presidents, this has not always been the case. Sarkozy is always at the centre of things, especially when they are newsworthy. Presidents have always *wished* to be at the centre of things, but *this* President is permanently in the front-line of news." French newspapers accuse

Sarkozy of wanting to be "the bride at the wedding, the baby at the christening, the corpse at the funeral – but in every case to leave his mark:" more strong stuff. In another piece in Newsweek, the journalist compares Sarkozy favourably with Tintin. William Pfaff, a resident of Paris almost all his life, continued; "this is not serious. If anything characterises France, it is being serious": fair comment, in a country where children use the formal *vous* when addressing parents or relatives, and even lovers do the same. Sarkozy fans (there still *are* plenty of Sarkozy fans, myself included) console themselves with the fact that the opposition has found no way of using Sarkozy's eccentric style (half stand-up comic, half senior statesman) against him, even given his apparent fall into disgrace. His socialist rivals continue fatally divided. This began when they realised that the glamorous Ségolène Real was a dangerous no-no, seriously damaging the unity of the French Socialist Party. In one of his brilliant Metternich-like moods, Sarkozy sent his most powerful rival, ex-Minister of the Economy Dominique Strauss-Khan off to Washington, to substitute Spain's Rodrigo Rato as chief of the International Monetary Fund. I say, 'Metternich-like' because this apparent promotion may also be Strauss-Khan's swansong, as the world's economy is beginning to stagger, with worldwide recession hovering around the corner. It will be convenient for the French to put the blame on Strauss-Khan, or discredit him in some way. An American political assessor has said: "If Sarkozy had not sent Strauss-Khan to Washington, the latter would now be the overall boss of the reformed and strengthened French socialists, and that would never do".   The French President is fascinating to watch precisely because of this extraordinary mix of political astuteness, and the impression he gives at times of being a wounded spirit with the world against him personally, capable of dismissing French problems with a merry quip and a smile even more false than the rictus that crosses the face of the Spanish President of the Government.

1ST APRIL

Ireland

The emerald isle has always been a problem to the Irish, who in history could not wait to leave their beautiful, sad home to populate new cities in the United States, or serve as mercenary generals from Latin America to the Philippines. Ireland was always a problem for the English too. They thought of Ireland as their property, because it was so near, and sent kings, princes and Lord Protectors to burn the towns, bothies and churches, and starve the few Irishmen left. Irish satirical wit Jonathan Swift wrote a famously tongue-in-cheek article in the English press suggesting a 'solution' to the Irish problem which (as always) was famine because the potato crop had failed. His 'solution', mass cannibalism, caused a rumpus.

In the 1990s, however, a miracle occurred. Ireland quite suddenly became the most dynamic economy in Europe, accompanied by growth rates that far outrun any rival. The republic, with a population of not much more than four million citizens, had suddenly turned itself into one of the richest nations in the West. A new generation of Irishmen appeared –not the gaiter'd road worker or hod-carrier in unwelcoming English cities of the nineteenth century, but gentlemen clad in Savile Row suiting and Lobb shoes, doing international business with style and a good bit of Irish blarney. The Celtic tiger had arrived.

The Irish economic miracle has become one of the most exhilarating and happy success stories of the last thousand years. But (there is always a 'but' you may have noticed) in a few short months this has turned round, and amid collapsing property values and a frightening forecast of imminent financial meltdown, the Celtic tigers have changed their roars to a mild, plaintive mew. An economist in Dublin says, ruefully, "Growth is going to slow down dramatically this year. We are facing a real contraction in the housing market." Does this mean that the transformation of Ireland was a mere bubble forced by the airs of property speculation and cheap money? Or was it built on something harder which will outlast present troubles? 20 years ago, Ireland decided on a two-decade experiment with supply-side economics that startled the world, and made Thatcher and Reagan's policies look like Marxism in comparison. Above all, taxes were slashed, always a good move if you are prepared for high risk. The Irish opened their economy to the world. Competition was encouraged. World companies began establishing factories and offices in Irish villages, towns and cities.

The astonishing result was a continuous period of sustained and sustainable growth, leaving the rest of us looking silly. In 2005, the Paris-based OECD decided to update its list of the five richest nations in the world, something measured by per capita GDP. Ireland was on the list, joining the United States, Norway, Switzerland and Luxembourg. The pundits said "this is a remarkable achievement". A Dublin economist went further. Jubilantly, he announced that Ireland was already richer than the UK! According to an organ called 'The CIA World Fact book', the estimated Irish GDP for 2007 was $45,600 (compared to $35,300 for the United Kingdom). What was it about Ireland that produced this wealth so quickly? Norway has tons of oil and a tiny population and burgeoning tourism. Switzerland and Luxembourg are stuffed with money in secret accounts, and besides, they have hoarded cash for centuries and always been neutral in wars. Ireland seems to be a long way from anywhere, and has suffered from centuries of unrest, murderous religious wars, and huge emigration. It even got itself stuck with the euro.

Perhaps it has all been too dynamic: very low taxation, mass immigration for a nice change, plus the euro which has meant permanently low interest rates. It has all made a heady cocktail. House prices have quadrupled in ten years. But now it seems the hangover is going to be on a Bertie Wooster scale. In 2007, Ireland had the worst housing market in Europe. Prices were falling by 7%. Only Germany came close, with 6%. According to a gloomy forecast by the Allied Irish Banks, the decline will continue this year. As prices drop, the Irish are not building new houses. House completion fell by 12% in 2007 and could halve again in 2008, says the Construction Industry Federation. Someone else with lowered eyebrows has said the number of new houses built will drop to 40,000 by 2009. This is serious, and it is happening in Spain too, a nation where socialism is preferred, but prosperity only comes when socialists are not elected.

14TH APRIL

A gossip column

And now for something completely different: gossip magazines are all the rage in Europe these days. A new one, called *OK* has just published its second edition, containing spectacular photographs of the people famous that week. These magazines sell well. The photo/stories always include European royalty, especially the younger set; also featured are the older, much older celebs whose members have had so many facelifts they must now have their bodies lowered; then there are the *'actress/models'*, and their boyfriends. The latter must have gymnasium bodies and be unshaven (at least on their cheeks) to complement the beauty of their *actress/model* of the month, or, in some rare cases, the year. Just for once let us forget about terrible old politics, and transform European Focus into a (temporary) gossip column.

I remember from the memoirs of David Niven, a notorious womaniser, his account of a film actress called Mary Astor, rightly famous in the Thirties and Forties. She was an astoundingly pretty woman who could have been 'the girl next door' or play sweetly innocent younger sisters. Mr Niven tells us a different story, and he was in a position to know. It seems Mary Astor was a very busy girl indeed in Hollywood. While everybody thought she was just the nicest thing around since sliced bread, it seems Mary was occupied in getting to know every male in California between the ages of eighteen and eighty. Not only that, but she was a clever sweetie who kept a diary. Scandal rocked America when the diary was at last revealed: its pages contained entries describing bedroom performance, those gentlemen who wore toupets, those gentlemen whose breath stank, those gentlemen who would perhaps have preferred their own sex to Mary Astor's. She never left anything out in her gleeful reminiscences. Niven writes enchantingly about Miss Astor, in his own book of memoirs called *The Moon's a Balloon.*

I have been reading about a twenty-first century actress/model in various gossip mags myself. She is apparently thirty-four years old, which seems just about perfect for an actress/model. Also, appropriately enough, she is beautiful, with the sort of figure most chaps would die for. It appears that Miss Inés Sastre the actress/model has also been a very busy girl: she is married, but separated from, an Italian businessman called Alex Corrías, and has an eighteen month old son called Diego. The estranged couple married in London in April, 2006, and went to live in Rome. In 2007 they separated. Inés settled down with her baby son in Paris, where she had once studied Sociology and the French language at the Sorbonne. This is no dumb catwalk skeleton.

Though she has only been married once, Inés has never been bereft of male friends; in fact the list is remarkable: One wonders how she found the time needed to be an actress/model. In 1991 (when she was seventeen) she enjoyed friendship with a Spanish aristocrat called Juan Ignacio Sáinz de Vicuña Primo de Rivera. But in just about the time necessary to speak his name, she had left his circle to join one José Joaquin Güell. This young man was rapidly fired (though he had another fling with the actress/model in 1996). In 1994 our heroine started a relationship with one Jean-Marie Something, but before the gossip columnists could establish what his surname was, Ines was off with Luis Carvajal Hoyos, son of the *Marqueses de Isasi.* The Isasis are an old established aristocratic Andalusian family with *cortijos* and horses and that sort of thing.

As lovers go, Luis went, and Inés became friendly with an Anglo-Saxon for a change, Tim Jeffries, ex-husband of actress/model Koo Stark, herself daughter to film tycoon Ray Stark, and one of the quasi-fiancées of Prince Charles. Staying with the English-speakers for a bit, Inés became associated with a Scottish lord called Simon Fraser, before being rushed off her pretty feet by an Italian aristo called Alessandro del Drago. Italians were not the flavour of the day, apparently, because in a flash Inés was been squired about by an Argentine filmmaker called Javier Torres. It was also around this time that the name of Inés Sastre even became associated with the then unmarried Prince Felipe of Asturias. This was in 2000, but Sastre herself hotly denies the association.

Even busier than Mary Astor, Inés continued her exciting life with Nicolás Vallejo-Nájera, (now married to singer Paulina Rubio) before becoming bored with yet another upper-class man and rushing off with lawyer Max Bianchi. Torts and judges did not fascinate however, and when Belgian billionaire Michel de Maleingreau beckoned, *she very* nearly married him. In fact, the year 2002 saw the announcement of their engagement. Eleven months later all was over: Irishman Nick Taylor, plus golfers Colin Montgomerie Juan Andrés Vizcaya joined the lengthy list of our girl's conquests .

Then came marriage - with Alex Corrías. If there is a common denominator, it is that Inés' ideal must be tall, sporting, and from high society. The matrimony with Corrías over, Inés is now to be seen with a young Frenchman with all the right attributes, called Gregory Reznik.

29TH APRIL

Much ado about nothing at all

Writer's block is a well-known syndrome, affecting and irritating at one time or other a goodly proportion of all those men and women who (usually vainly) try to make a living with the keyboard. The block is not helped by a heat wave hitting first (as always) the Peninsula, later the Canaries. In Tenerife we have suffered temperatures of nearly 40° C over the last five days. No-one sleeps. Clothes are wringing wet half an hour after putting them on. And, worst of all, nothing is happening. Nothing supports writer's block better than a state of inanition.

Oh yes, a tuna fishing boat ran over its national limits near Somalia, as Spanish fishermen do right round the world, but was caught by *pirates*, not by local authorities. Negotiations were set up to seek freedom for the crew – and they succeeded. No-one wants to talk about the freeing of the hostages too much, but the Spanish and world press assume that the Spanish Government opened a fire hose of money and directed its jet at the happy corsairs. Piracy on the high seas, by the way, is fashionable these days. Everyone goes to the cinema, and to the greater glory of Disney, three episodes of *Pirates of the Caribbean* have probably cajoled many an innocent sailor into assuming that there is money in them seas – flying the skull and crossbones as if he were Captain Morgan.

Rosa has some embarrassing questions for Carme Chacón

The magnificent and courageous Rosa Diez, as a Deputy at Congress for her own party, *UPyD* (known already by political columnists simply as '*Y*', or 'Oopiday'), has registered a whole range of official questions at the *Congreso de los Diputados*. These official questions have to be answered during open debate in Congress, and by the appropriate Minister or Secretary of State, however unwilling she may be (I shall always use the feminine personal pronoun now as there are more females in the Cabinet than males, and the males are a pretty indifferent lot, compared for example with Carme Chacón, our charmingly pregnant Minister of Defence, or our dragon-like Senior Vice-President, or *La Álvarez,* who plainly couldn't give a damn).

Rosa Diez wants to know if it is true that Spanish troops in Afghanistan have been exercising troop movements in transport labelled with a Red Cross. Diez demands answers, following a fairly sensational report by the daily *El Mundo;* investigating reporters had revealed that armed soldiers have been employing helicopters belonging to the Spanish Red Cross to get from one war zone to another. All is fair in love and war, I suppose, and it is less likely that the Taliban will aim their rocket launchers at the Red Cross. Nevertheless, Rosa Diez reminds the Administration that the Geneva Convention states that the sign of the Cross and the red Half Moon cannot be used under any circumstances than those connected with health installations. She adds that 'their use, if it is meant to deceive the enemy, constitutes an act of perfidy and may be seen as a grave infraction of the Rules' So Rosa Diez tables the question: 'Have the Spanish armed forces illegally used the symbol of the Red Cross for their own purposes?' If some wretch from the Ministry of Defence has to admit to this in Parliament, Rosa has another tabled question: 'On how many occasions has this device been used?' And another: 'Has the Ministry of Defence begun the appropriate investigations concerning the irregular use of the Red Cross symbol?' And yet another: 'Has the Ministry of Defence made a suitable apology to the international Red Cross, should the answer to these questions be 'yes'?'

All in all, Rosa Diez' party *Upyd* has tabled thirty questions of this calibre. These must be answered by someone in the Administration with supreme authority. It would be best if that person were the Minister herself, but it seems on the cards that her advanced state of gestation will prevent her from rising from her seat in *Las Cortes* to judge Rosa's impertinence.

Spain bats for Cuba

The Madrid Government will spend much of June urging the lifting of sanctions against Cuba before fellow members of the European Union. What is more, Spain demands complete removal of the sanctions. They were imposed in 2003 after a Cuban putsch against seventy-five 'dissidents' (Cubans who do not support the Castro regime) who were imprisoned. The sanctions, which included a reduction in official European visits to Havana, were in fact suspended in 2005, again following demands from Spain. This time, however, Spain, represented by Foreign Minister Moratinos, wants the sanctions banned. Cuba has been one of the Ibero-American states most wooed by Zapatero's Government since the PSOE won the elections in 2004. Miguel Angel Moratinos has been Foreign Minister since then and has followed his leader's policy of a strong union between Cuba, Venezuela, Bolivia and other anti-US nations, in the face of criticism from the Opposition in Parliament, and frequent protests from the American Embassy. Not only protests; at one stage a new US Ambassador arrived in Madrid and promptly fired every Spanish member of staff without a word of explanation.

Relations with Cuba will be at their best during the coming week, when the famous EU/Latin America Summit is held in Lima, capital of Perú. Readers will remember an incident at last year's event when the King of Spain told bully Chavez of Venezuela to shut up and listen while Mr Zapatero was speaking. Now that dictator Fidel is ill and out of action, replaced by his brother Raoúl, Moratinos will be hand-in-hand with the new Cuban chancellor, Felipe Pérez Roque. Fidel might be 'out', but he is still very much an *eminence grise* in the running of the Cuban state. Last year during the 'Council on General Matters' in June, Spain tried without success to get rid of the 'measures' agreed upon by all other members of the Union. But Spain did manage to achieve something: In the accord signed by all European Ministers of Foreign Affairs there would be no mention of adverse attitudes towards Castro's Cuba adopted since 1996, presumably because of Cuba's well-known stance on civil rights, or rather *lack* of them. Europe has sent a strong request to Cuba to start the democratic process in the island, a transition not foreseen or accepted by Fidel. Europe also demanded more pluralistic government, and immediate respect for human rights, freedom of the press, and 'recuperation of sustainable economic growth'. Europe also called for 'dialogue' (oh dear), between all social levels in the island. Commentators suggest that this is Europe's signal that the Twenty-five wish to have freer dialogue with Cuba, in Brussels. However, despite Spain's dream of opening European doors to Cuba (and vice-versa), the Spanish Government gave Cuba a year to 'sort itself out'; this means no more dictatorship, the beginning of democracy, votes for all, the release of political prisoners, and a benign Raúl Castro. Spain put the bite on, by threatening to recommend the resumption of measures and sanctions if the Cuban situation had not radically changed within twelve months.

Now, it seems, the Ministry in Madrid considers the required changes have taken place. It is believed that measures adopted by Raúl Castro in these last few months are positive and permit, in theory at least access by Cubans to various goods and services which were previously banned, such as computers, mobile telephones (poor Cuba!), hotel beds etc. (did you know that under Fidel no Cuban, unless he was in the government, could stay in a Cuban hotel?). Madrid also believes that there have been good results in mechanisms of dialogue concerning human and civil rights. After all, Cuba has signed plenty of international agreements over civil rights, and *four* dissident prisoners with health problems have been released from jail (actually these four were expelled to Spain).

It is recognised in Madrid that the various changes we have seen in Cuba are not spectacular and that much remains to be done before the island nation can be seen as a fully-paid-up member of the democratic world. There are still plenty of conscientious objectors to Fidel's regime lying in Prison, and Spain will awaits the return of their stolen Cultural Centre, nicked by Fidel's men in September, 2003. The reader can find many more details of the situation viz. EU/Cuba at www.europa.eu.

Things get worse for G. Brown

All things go in cycles, so they say, and British politics is no exception. There is a strong swing towards the Tories showing, especially in by-elections. In the popularity stakes, it would seem that though David Cameron is a toff and an Etonian too, he stands well above Mr Brown with the British people who have been accustomed to various forms of near democracy for a thousand years; having an unelected Prime Minister is *not* popular. Labour did not do well in the municipal elections of May 1st, though it was Labour Day, and following the crushing defeat at Crewe & Nantwich, things are looking very serious. Labour had held that seat for nearly 30 years. The Conservatives took it away from them, the first time this has happened in a by-election for 26 years. If my memory serves, it happened when Margaret Thatcher was beginning to make her presence dominant. The Crewe & Nantwich result shows a 17.6% swing towards the Conservatives (they lost in 2005 by some 7000 votes, and have just reversed this, winning by 7,800 votes). For the first time in many years, it really seems as if the swing towards the Tories is happening, and there is serious doubt over whether Labour can win yet another mandate in the next General Election. In the municipals held in parts of England and Wales on May Day, the Labourites achieved their worse results in 40 years (24% of the vote as opposed to 44% for the Tories). This must have caused some heart-searching for Mr Brown and his few friends. Even the BBC, through its Political Director Nick Robinson, admitted that if Mr Cameron becomes the next PM, the process really started at Crewe & Nantwich; it will be remembered as such. A joyous David Cameron declared (without his usual caution) that the end of Tony Blair's New Labour was at hand. Mr Brown chose to blame the end of the economic boom in the UK (something the experts have been predicting for years). He had already promised to 'take all the measures necessary' after the disastrous results of the May Day municipals. Nothing has been done, and the newspapers believe that Mr Brown has not proved to be the PM they were expecting, after some successful years as Chancellor of the Exchequer. Perhaps the endless wait for the key to No. 10 has exhausted Brown's invention and Scots canniness? He likes to remind the British that he alone is the best figure to lead Britain through the marshes and bogs of recession and depression in the years to come, given his supposedly brilliant record as Chancellor. Mr. Robinson at the BBC, remembering Brown's "It's the Economy, stupid!" speech, was just as phlegmatic when he changed this slightly to "it's the Leadership, stupid!" And while we are on the subject, several high rankers in the Labour Party are showing their dissatisfaction with Gordon Brown. Graham Stringer, for instance, has called for 'some heavyweight' in the party to substitute for Brown in the next Election – "so as to avoid disaster!' It is significant that Brown himself went nowhere near Crewe & Nantwich during the campaign leading to the by-election 'for fear of producing negative results'. First to take advantage of this extraordinary decision was of course David Cameron, who practically set up camp there during the campaign. Newspaper articles claim that the electorate at Crewe etc. punished Labour for having been negative enough during the campaign to centre it not on promises of positive results, but with vile attacks on the personality of the Tory candidate, Edward Timpson. In other words, it was the same old Labour garbage involving the 'Class War', which most Britons thought as dead as the dodo. With the resounding success of another Etonian, Boris Johnson, in the election for the mayoralty of London, plus the pathetic failure of Blair's hunting ban, the class nonsense was generally seen as awarded *null points* by the British people.

It is even suggested in certain periodicals that Mr Brown has actually fallen into a state of depression – something I should have thought practically unheard of in Downing Street – purely because of his exceedingly bad press. No other PM has, at least in public. When Harold Macmillan became the target of satirists and rough comment in the press, he scotched it by going to Peter Cook's Establishment Club and showing every sign of enjoying himself. When Douglas-Home came under heavy fire because he was 'The Fourteenth Earl of Home', he responded by talking of 'The Fourteenth Mr Wilson'. Castlereagh admittedly shot himself, but not because of his popularity ratings. Mr. Brown has several months to recover his poise and possibly his popularity before the Labour Conference.

Spain: a smack on the wrist for M. Trichet

Just when Mr Zapatero of Spain had everyone hypnotised into believing that the economy in that country was zooming upwards, and that a smile on your face is worth more than a boot up the bottom from your bank manager, along comes M. Claude Trichet (President of the Central European Bank BCE) to announce that interest rates of all kinds are may (or may not) rise noticeably following the next conference on 3 July. What a blow for ZP! So much so that the President of the Government chose a brief visit his home town of León to administer a sharp rebuke to the French accountant (Zapatero was in León to give an award to a nun, Obdulina Fernández, now named *Leonesa del Año)*. The President rapped M. Trichet over the knuckles for provoking, he said, an immediate increase in European inflation. He asked for 'responsibility' and 'prudence'; but who is more responsible, or perhaps irresponsible? A President who announces that his Government will take immediate action to avert more crisis than already exists, measures to prevent more increases in the cost of diesel fuel (so that national transport workers will come back to work and stop striking) – or a President who denies the existence of any kind of crisis, and wants us to believe in his own make-believe world? On 4 October, 2007, Zapatero told us that the *Euribor (*acceptable inflation in Europe*)* had reached the ceiling and would rise no further. It then stood at 4.64. It now stands at 5.5. On 29 April, 2008, Zapatero told us "inflation will now start its descent". Inflation in Spain was then 4.2. Now it is 4.7. On the same day, 29 April, ZP informed Spain that the ongoing increase in unemployment was 'a small setback'. By the end of May, however, unemployment beat all previous records. One month later, on 29 May, the President announced that Spain's growth was at a level higher than the average in Europe. Spain's growth in the first three months stood at 0.3%, while the European average growth stood at 0.7.

In León, Mr Zapatero said this: "I would recommend more prudence in what he says to Mr Trichet. We all respect the independence of BCE, but we also expect responsibility from it. Yesterday (Friday), the Euribor rose higher, and so did the price of crude, to an exaggerated extent, and these things occurred after an announcement made by the President of BCE." Government sources consulted by the media admit it is unusual to see such a friction between the BCE and the Premier of a member of the European

Union, but they added that hearing such an announcement from the President of BCE is also unusual. "*Señor* Zapatero has said in public what all his colleagues really think, but do not speak of, or if they do, they do so in private". In fact, not one European leader has criticised Trichet's words, even the normally outspoken Nicholas Sarkozy of France.

In answer to Mariano Rajoy's complaint that he cannot find any tangible measures being taken by this Administration to counter rising inflation and frightening unemployment statistics, Mr Zapatero said (in León) that the Cabinet had decided on 20 measures to re-activate the economy. Among these will be found the famous 400 euros devolution this year to taxpayers on their *declaración de la renta;* the devolution of IVA paid by companies month by month, the amplification of the availability of official credits, the 'speeding-up' of the process by which public building becomes licit, the plan to aid construction workers left out of work by the slump (is there a slump?) by using the sum of 200 million euros, and a new plan to stimulate the fading automotive market. Car buyers must be persuaded that fuel prices have reached *their* ceiling as well. On that point, Minister of the Economy Pedro Solbes has expressed doubt. He is after all a vice-president of the Government, and people tend to listen attentively to him. Perhaps he will be accused of irresponsibility and lack of prudence by The President of the Government.

In the meeting at León, the President of the Government admitted 'some difficulty in the short run', and asked the Spaniards for 'patience', because measures taken by the Government to counter an economic crisis cannot take effect in a day. He repeated what his lady senior Vice-President has been repeatedly saying: "The Government is studying the problem and is preparing itself, as the situation evolves, to present new measures should they be necessary". It must have been gloomy, when you and your Cabinet are so publicly atheist, for Mr Zapatero to present an award for good works to a *nun*.

Housing needs in Britain

When I was a boy growing up in rural England, a village consisted of a large house or castle in ruins, a church with a roof problem, a village green where cricket is played and Guy Fawkes is burnt on November 5, several dozen farm-workers cottages, a village school doubling as a Friends' Meeting House, the village bobby's house doubling as a police station, a large, attractive house *not* in ruins (with a Daimler in the drive), and the village pub. Most of all, the village meant peace, silence you could actually hear at night, the melancholy of church bells summoning on Sunday. Town and city life was not much different, but unrest and violence sometimes broke the silence of the night. The latest in vandalism, called the 'Eco-Town', directed by the Government, will soon change all that rustic stuff. Now, restful urban or rural silence has been replaced by a new kind of Goth – the liberal young English hating silence because it might make them attend to their own, often terrifying thoughts. The quiet village street is now scarred by screams. Down the pavements gleaming with vomit pools stagger drunken, shaking sluts of either sex, pudgy navel protruding, garish tattoos on fat shoulder; women hardly bothering to cover the breast, men showing the top two inches of the cleft in the buttocks. You must pretend not to see them, or look at them, for if you do, a glass half-full of beer will be broken by contact with your face.

The 'Eco-Town' is the very latest weapon in the British Government's determined campaign to empty over-crowded towns and fill the green countryside, making it brown, or 'progressive'. The Eco-Town means the planned destruction of the green belt by suburbs as a measure for the protection of the environment. There is of course a Minister responsible for this lunacy. Her name is Heather Blears. She must have studied George Orwell at school, for her speeches are full of typical Orwellian euphemisms, contradictions, distortions, and 'officialise' disguised as earnest advice. Thus, Blears says the public is to have a 'larger say on local planning issues', but prevents it happening by making the system 'streamlined' and 'efficient', and removing 'bureaucratic hurdles' – Orwellian for overcoming local objections to development schemes. Blears and Brown Ltd. are setting up something called 'The Independent Planning Commission' (unelected) which will greatly assist one of Blears's favourite terms – 'Community Empowerment'; this calls for local councils to re-present themselves as community empowerment champions, set on 'reviving local democracy'. Actually, though Ms. Blears probably does not know, what she is after is Stalinist control. In the development battle, 'democracy' comes out a poor loser faced with a pact between politicians (greed), Whitehall bureaucrats (cunning), property firms (greed again) and retail monsters (you name them).

I shall give an example: take your average village or hamlet, much changed by Progress from the description in the first paragraph, but still an English village. The large house and extensive gardens lie in a conservation area in this village, and the owner of the attractive house wishes to demolish it and his gardens, in order to build two blocks of modern flats. This would seem to be vandalism to neighbours and the local district council, who throw out an application made by the owner. The council has therefore done its job, which is to protect local heritage and uphold the wishes of neighbours and public alike. The owner's bid to destroy a protected house and garden for reasons of commercial greed would appear to have been thwarted by the body placed there by government. But, thanks to Ms. Blears, it is not so. 'Community empowerment' has made its move. The house-owner applies again to the Government's invented Planning Inspectorate, which has the power to override any decision made by a local council. The Inspectorate gives permission to the owner to bulldozer his own home and garden and build two apartment blocks. This is why the description 'Stalinist' is cruelly appropriate. The point of even *having* a planning department in the local council is lost. At least fifteen Eco-Towns are to be built across England's once green and pleasant land. Each will provide between 5000 and 20,000 homes. This is happening because the Government tells the British that there is an urgent 'housing need', a 'chronic housing shortage'. There is allegedly a 'disastrous shortfall' in the number of new homes being built every year. Again this is Orwellian in concept, because the Government itself has told us that there are at least 800,000 empty properties in Britain.

Italy: Berlusconi on the (tapped) line

She is not a Christine Keeler; nor a Mandy Rice-Davies, especially not a Monica Lewinsky. She is Mara Carfagna, named Minister of Equal Opportunities by Silvio Berlusconi in May this year. Beautiful, dark-eyed and articulate, Mara was a part-time TV presenter and full-time socialite until she caught the sight of Berlusconi, who is fancied by the Italian public as a ladies' man. Someone in the Government of that excitable country got hold of some recordings of hottest telephone conversations, apparently held between Mara and Silvio before he elevated the ex-*vedette* to ministerial rank. Naturally, the taps have been passed to the press, and an almighty row has broken out in Rome and elsewhere as a result. The row is not just over some injudicious cooing on the telephone. It has become a first-class political storm which might even topple Berlusconi's never entirely stable hold on government. *Il Cavaglieri* himself is furious, but accustomed to the frantic efforts of the Italian Left to unseat him.

Friends in the Centre-Right administration claim that what was said over the telephone was part of a private conversation between two citizens. It should have no political relevance. The Opposition however see the matter under a different light – as one would expect: certain important enemies of Silvio's claim that the tapped dialogue tells us all we need to know about the relationship between Berlusconi and Carfagna, that led to her abrupt elevation to a Minister's office. After all, everybody knows that Mara Carfagna was an ex-finalist in a Miss Italy gala competition. It is also common knowledge that her political experience is nil. One of the Opposition is Massimo Donadi, leader of the IdV party, always eager to take a swipe at Berlusconi. He crudely asks: "What, I wonder, would have happened in the USA if Bill Clinton had made Monica Lewinsky a Senator?" And adds: "In the case of a Head of Government, the limits between what is private and what is public are very fine, and I think the public's right to information must come first". The Opposition also questions Berlusconi's right to insist on a new Law, passed by Decree without debate or consultation, which will permit judges to put newspaper proprietors and their journalists in jail for five years for publishing telephone conversations. Walther Veltroni, leader of the Left, suggests: "if this Government needs to pass Decrees, it should concentrate on salaries, pensions or prices, for these are more pressing problems than telephone tapping".

That Italy is in the middle of a political tempest has been made obvious by Berlusconi's cancellation of all his recent appointments, including his customary appearance on his own show, *Matrix,* broadcast by one of his own TV companies, *Canal 5.* The *Cavaglieri* explained that he would not appear because he did not want 'the many reforms and improvements made by the government to be over-shadowed by insignificant little tarantellas and public gossip which might poison the political debate, and take the public's attention away from things that matter'. The lady in the case, Mara herself, has also declined to speak on the matter. In a cold ministerial statement, Carfagna said: "I have no comment to make on these intercepted private conversations, nor on any other stupid manipulations. They do not form part of my work in this Ministry". However, as so many of Silvio's most loyal colleagues are spending so much time on the air-waves vigorously defending their boss, it becomes clear that they *are* bothered by the implications of illegal interception on an ordinary telephone line, because if the Head of Government's line can be tapped by someone (*someone in a position to do so*), listening-in could become a regular practice – if it is not already. Gianfranco Rotondi, Minister in Berlusconi's Cabinet, said: "All Italy speaks on the telephone like Berlusconi; joking, making allusions, using a dirty word occasionally: that is what we Italians are like". Before leaving this Italian storm-in-a-glass-of-*grappa*, perhaps one should go back a little in time; Berlusconi and Carfagna were the protagonists in a similar incident around a year ago. They were both present at a large public *gala* attended also by Mrs. Berlusconi, no slouch in the beauty stakes either. Silvio made some very flattering remarks . . . about Mara Carfagna . . . and Veronica Lario didn't like it. She didn't like it at all, and complained about the cooing of her dove in an open letter addressed to *La Repubblica.* In the letter Berlusconi's wife demanded he should make a public apology. Her husband rejected the idea at first, but, as every *cavaglieri* should, he finally recognised that women are usually right; he apologised.

A stormy 90th Anniversary in Russia

During the night of 16/17 July, 1918, the Tsar of All The Russias and his Empress, their five children, two employees of the royal family and their doctor were shot to death in a cellar at Ekaterinburg. After the murder, a mystery remained for many years concerning the whereabouts of the dead bodies. Witnesses said the inadequately burnt remains were thrown down wells or buried deep in the forests. Some skeletons were found, but scientists could not find those of the teenaged Tsarevitch or his sister the grand duchess Maria – until July of last year – when cadavers recently discovered were, through the DNA process, proved to be the two unfortunate children. Russian historian Eduard Radzinski has also turned up some diaries belonging to Yurovski, who headed the execution squad in Ekaterinburg. What is written in the diary proves beyond doubt that the assassination took place in the manner history has always claimed it did; but the doubt remained about who ordered the killing. Historians have never doubted the motive. The royal family had been moved from one place to another the last year of the Great War, trying to keep ahead of White Russian forces. The latter were doing well against the Bolshevik armies marshalled by Lenin, and no communist wanted a Tsar and his family alive and in 'White' hands, where they could be used for propaganda purposes. The Soviets might have imagined that the family was safely incarcerated in the vastness's of Siberia, but they were wrong, and a White Russian army was known rapidly to be approaching the town of Ekaterinburg.

Historian Radzinski claims there should have been a huge public apology for the mass murder this year, but cynically reflects that the Euro Cup football series rather turned the attention of newly democratic Russia away from the point at the appropriate time. "Russian people *must* accept this terrible moment in their history, and show their repentance. It was a monstrous crime" he writes. What should have happened, and hasn't, was a great ceremony of political and public sorrow to be held in St. Petersburg. The Pantheon of St. Peter and St. Paul contains now all that remains of the calcified bodies of the family and their servants (and a pet dog, whose guilt has not yet been ascertained), as well as those royal predecessors who died under less grisly circumstances. It was hoped that a ceremony would take place there attended by the President of Russia and his prime minister, Vladimir Putin. There is always a problem, and it is grave. The Orthodox

Church of Russia still refuses to accept the facts. This means that the head of the Church, Alexis II, cannot be present at the ceremony – and of course he *should* be. In 1998, when at last the bodies were found, Alexis II did not attend their internment in the Pantheon. The Government, perhaps following the example of Alexis II, seems loth to make a concrete apology, though the country is now 'democratic', and the seventy years of Soviet rule that followed the assassination are just History.

Chief of the remaining Romanovs grand duchess Maria Vladimirovna Romanov has spent years trying to achieve public recognition by the Palace of Justice of the magnicide. She is determined that the government should stand up and admit that the murder of an entire family including four young girls, and a boy suffering from a grave disease of the blood was the work of Lenin and the Bolsheviks. Evidence has been received from a one-time partner of Lenin, one Nadezhda Krupskaya, that she had seen a written order addressed to the Red Army of the Urals, sent from HQ in Moscow, dated 14 July, 1918: this was the order specifically requiring immediate execution of the captive Romanovs. While Yeltsin was President, he ordered (for reasons best known to himself) the demolishment of the house in Ekaterinburg. Until then, the house had been a place for curious tourists to visit. Now it has vanished entirely.

Hopes remain in Russia that a ceremony will at last take place in ten years' time, as a proper hundredth year Anniversary of the murder that startled (and changed) the world, and founded so many years of communism. In a recent inquiry, Russian TV station RTR asked the Russians to identify the person they felt best represented them as a society or nation. The winner was Nicholas II with 275,000 votes: Joseph Stalin and Vladimir Lenin came second and third.

6TH AUGUST

Europe and the USA: how did we survive?

Dear friends Johnny and Marti found a friendly message on the Internet which intrigued them, and promptly sent me a copy. The missive is directed to those of still alive and kicking, who were born in the Twenties, Thirties, Forties, Fifties, Sixties and even Seventies of the last century. To judge by the erratic punctuation and occasionally eccentric language, I think the provenance is American. The point is . . . it is all true! Here beginneth the Lesson:

'First, we survived being born to mothers who smoked and/or drank while they carried us and lived in houses made of asbestos.' Perhaps not all the house was asbestos, but a good deal of it was, and most of our mums 'died for' a Pimms No. 1 or a glass of sherry, to accompany their Craven A with no filter. Amazingly, we entered the ring weighing eight pounds or more, kicking lustily.

'They took aspirin, ate blue cheese, tuna from a can, and didn't get tested for diabetes or cervical cancer.' If your generation was the Forties, both mothers and children would have been lucky, or part of a black market ring, to eat 'blue cheese'. In Britain, everything was rationed, but people with a bit of garden kept chickens fed from kitchen scraps such as potato peelings, and hens rewarded us with nice fresh eggs. I should add that our firesides were kept comfy and moderately warm by burning grimy coal delivered by grinning hulks with black-stained faces and every chimney belched poison gases into the wartime air, but we are still here.

' Our baby cribs were covered with bright-coloured lead-based paints.' And our nappies were fashioned from scissored old shirts and nighties, washed in carbolic soap so often they ended looking like a lot of holes held

together by thread. The point of the *'lead-based paints'* is they were deadly poison, but we didn't know it.

'We had no childproof lids on medicine bottles, doors or cabinets and when we rode our bikes, we had no helmets or shoes, not to mention the risks some of us took hitchhiking.'
Children today are saved from meddling with medicines by tricks that (some) adults understand. A group of fourteen-year old males, including me, took off for Scotland from Hertfordshire on our *derailleur*-geared bicycles with super-dangerous drop handlebars. We kept off the main arterial roads, and covered nearly a thousand miles, staying at youth hostels kept by ruffians; our diet seemed to be Kellogg's Corn Flakes with stolen milk. Not one of us was abused, but around this time (the Fifties) no.one locked their front doors except at night and the family car stood in the open drive with the keys in the ignition.

'As children, we rode in cars with no seat belts or airbags or in-board computers to go wrong and drain the battery.' My father drove puffing his pipe filled with St. Bruno Flake. It always went out, so he lit it again steering with an elbow at 50 mph. The car was permanently filled to choking point with tobacco smoke. Uncle Allan owned a large smallholding and a 1929 Rolls-Royce which he used once a year to go to the races. The old dear (the car, not Uncle Allan) always started immediately on the same battery it had when it was new.

'We drank water from the garden hose and NOT from a bottle. Take-away food was limited to fish and chips or something pink and fluffy at fairs. No pizza shops, McDonalds or Burger Kings.' Our Saturday treat was a visit in the oxygen-free Vauxhall to nearby St. Albans, where a restaurant stood called *The Pilgrims' Rest* with the apostrophe correctly placed. Brown Windsor soup, mashed potatoes and whale meat steaks, followed by real Scottish scones with artificial strawberry jam. No-one, but absolutely no-one, in Europe or the United States was obese. Look at your group photos from the Thirties, Forties and Fifties. Bodies like greyhounds. Today we never eat those terrible starches and calories and poisons, and everybody looks like Humpty Dumpty. Why were we not overweight? 'Because we were always playing outside. We would leave home in the morning and play all day, as long as were back when the streetlights came on. No-one was able to reach us all day: and we were OK. We built go-carts from scraps and rode down the hill with squeals of delights, until we discovered we had forgotten the brakes. We built tree houses and hide-outs in thick gorse. We played with (lethal) stones on river beds. We had no Play-Stations, Nintendo's, X-Boxes, video-games, no videos, no DVDs, no Surround Sound, no mobile telephones, no computers, no Internet, no texting, no chat rooms. We had friends instead. We went outside the house and found them.' I should add that compulsory sports were played at school

every afternoon. But we did have air-guns, given us by unimaginative, uncaring parents. We used to fire at each other from behind trees. Today's public meddlers would faint. *'We fell out of trees, got cut, broke bones and teeth, and there were no lawsuits from these accidents.'* Five years ago some city council decreed that chestnut trees in a public park must be cut down in case a conker fell on the head of a passing pensioner.

'Only girls had pierced ears.' Now both girls and boys have ironmongery dangling right round and down their body, between the tattoos. *'We drank milk laced with Strontium 90 from cows that ate grass covered in nuclear fallout from atomic testing at Maralinga in 1956.'* No comment required. *'Mum didn't have to go to work to help Dad make ends meet. Not everybody made the best football team, or passed their exams, and those who didn't had to learn to deal with disappointment. Our teachers used to belt us with sticks and straps and bullies* always *ruled the playground. The idea of a parent bailing us out if we broke the law at school was unheard of. Their judgement sided with the school. Our parents got married* before *they had children and failed to invent stupid names for their kids like "Kiora" and "Blade".*

Perhaps the most amazing thing about these generations is that they produced stunningly brave risk-takers in wartime, problem solvers of all kinds, and above all inventors without whom 'modern life' would not be quite the same. In fact *'the past 70 years have been an explosion of talent and new ideas. We had real, not politicised freedom, failure, success and responsibility, and we learned the hard way how to deal with it all.'*
What happened?

17TH AUGUST

England needs another Hogarth

England needs not only another William Hogarth, but a Thomas Rowlandson, a George Cruikshank and a James Gillray too. About once every century the English nation for one good reason or other becomes a nightmare. The people develop ugly bodies and minds. The country is prosperous and so are the people, despite government taxation abuses. The powerful liberal lobby overpowers sense and sensibility. The way English people behave badly abroad sets a prototype for foreigners that will linger for decades. In the eighteenth century younger sons of the wealthy did the Grand Tour, which included sinks of vice and depravity. The boys returned with a sparse knowledge of distant lands, a serious drink problem and syphilis. The girls (very few of them since the Tour was deemed a masculine activity) returned healthily and wrote rewarding books about their travels (see Mary Wortley-Montague).

Hogarth (1697 – 1764) sketched and painted the English in England, horrifying foreigners and frightening the horses. Rowlandson (1756 – 1857), Cruikshank /1792 – 1878) and Gillray (1757 – 1815) etched, sketched and painted the English at home and abroad, and their choice of subject became a popular scandal. In *this* awful period of the 21st century English youth go to pieces because of a repetition of weak, immoral governments led by prime ministers who are no better than they should be; because National Service is too expensive to maintain, and because discipline of any kind no longer exists in the schools. The people take no exercise, become obese, bad mannered, bad-tempered and frequently dangerous. Some relatives of mine recently attended a *'posh'* Anglo/Spanish society wedding in Andalucía at which *all* the English invitees spent the day drunk and incapable. Their behaviour during the wedding ceremony itself, and the wedding breakfast afterwards will be remembered with shame by the locals for the rest of their life. The former impression of the English as a nation of gentle, nice, just and beautifully-mannered people was smashed by drunken carousing, and free-range vomiting. Only a Gillray or a Hogarth could possibly re-create the scene.

Some friends have just returned from Crete, a small, intensely old-fashioned island where many British soldiers left their thin, dead bodies in the Second World War. My friends told me they spent just one night in the biggest seaside resort on the island . . . and decided the following day to hire a ramshackle car and head for the mountains. The resort was brim-full of fat Brits with the full complement of tattoos and piercings, drunk as a skunk from breakfast to bedtime, regardless of gender. Cruikshank would have filled his sketchbook with ease.

I am constantly told this is only how English people behave *on holiday.* If so, why? Does the image of your typical Brit have to be so bloody? The Canary people are philosophical about this. Anyone who has visited Playa de las Américas (Las Verónicas especially) at any time of day or night will know what British visitors are like. It is difficult to remember the Dunkirk spirit, and the courage and fortitude of city people during the Manchester Riots, the English Civil War, the Trenches of 1914-1918 and the Blitz when you have to step carefully between pools of vomit and often, blood.

What England needs is a new Hogarth or Cruikshank. Actually, cartoonists almost as accurate and frightening abound in Britain *now;* Martyn Turner, Dredge, Kipper Williams, Bill Proud and Castro to name but five. They should be sent with a commission to depict *the English abroad* for newspapers that sell three million copies or more. The behaviour of our people on holiday should be studied by experts, and the results taught as a special course at university. Something must be done, before the image of an Englishman or Englishwoman abroad becomes indelibly stained.

England: how can immigrants learn the language?

In the last twenty years the UK population has been greatly magnified by immigration. People from the ex-Empire should not have problems with English – in some formerly colonial sub-continents and islands the population has been speaking English for two and a half centuries – and in many cases speaks and writes the language infinitely better than the presently illiterate English themselves, who are not embarrassed by total ignorance of spelling or punctuation. The apostrophe, for example, is thought by most modern English people to be an upside-down peg for hanging up the raincoat; but most immigrants come from Eastern and Central Europe, not the ex-colonies. In thóse countless 'istans', and 'Mittel-Europe', for example, they still see the English as hard-faced toffs trotting in hansom cabs from one atrocity to another in the fog, to paraphrase Anthony Powell. The highest barrier is pronunciation, especially as the original and traditional aids to foreigners' speech – the BBC, language teachers using R.P. etc. - have been damaged beyond repair.

How can a Montenegran, for instance, deal with a language where nothing is pronounced as it is spelled? Hugh Seymour, Marquess of Hertford becomes *"Hue Seemer, Markwis of Harf'd":* Cholmondley becomes *"Chumley":* Leveson-Gower becomes *"Looson-Gore".* Featherstonehaugh becomes *"Fanshaw".* Pennistone becomes (perhaps fortunately) *"Penstun".* If you are Scottish and spell your name 'Ruthven' you will pronounce it '*Rivven*'. I have heard natives of a north London reservation calling their Cockfosters home *"Co-fosters".* The pleasant game of golf becomes *"goff".* No wonder our immigrants are bewildered. Falcon becomes *"fawcon",* according to the 1928 *Times,* but the *Oxford BBC Guide to Pronunciation* (2006) claims *"fawl-khun".* More confusing: should plebiscite be *"plebissit"* or *"plebissyte"* (last syllable rhyming with *night)*? How do you pronounce aspirant (should you want to)? Today it is *"as-pyre-n't":* and centrifugal, *"centRIfugal"* (emphasis on the second syllable). This is the influence of America, where a lot more people speak English than in England. Do you say *"FORMidable"* or *"ForMIDable"*? *The Times* encouraged us to pronounce combat *"cumbat"* and combattant (2006) should be *COMbattant* though I can't think why; there is even a strong suggestion, taken up by newsreaders, that it should be pronounced *"kum-buh-tuhnt.* How do you differentiate immanent from imminent? Eccentrically enough, 1928 suggested stressing the second syllable – *"imMANent".* With imminent, you need to reduce that second 'i' so much the word becomes *"immnent".*

For recently arrived immigrants with the courage (and the cash) to get about a bit, the confusion in place names becomes horrifying (emphasis on first syllable). Alnwick and Alnmouth in Northumberland must be *"Annick"* and *"Aymuth.* Burpham (Sussex) – *"burfam":* Colne (Essex or Lancashire) – *"cone".* What do we do with Hurstpierpoint, a mixture of Danish, Saxon and medieval French? And what about Worcester, Gloucester, Bicester, Alcester, Leicester, Uttoxeter and Cirencester? Imagine having to learn *Wooster, Gloster, Bister, Alster, Lester, Uxter* and *Sister*! And saying *"Kuventry"* when it's spelled Coventry.

More: Debach in Suffolk – *"Debbidge"* or *"Debbich".* Etchingham in Sussex – *Etching'em* with emphasis on the *'em,* or *"ham"* if you are not vegetarian: Frant (in Sussex again) – *"Fraant".* Greenwich (south London) – *"Grinidge", "Grinnitch"* or *"Grennich",* which brings me to 'Estuary' or Essexman's English: I sat perplexed at a table in a well-known resort on this island (pronounced *"ayeln'd)*. The next table was occupied loudly by a family speaking Estuary English. It was impossible for me to understand a word they shouted. I am English.

More trouble with place names: Hoxne in Suffolk – *"Hoxen"*; Ide (Devon) – *"Eed"*; Kirkby (Lonsdale, Malzeard, Moorside or Stephen (Yorkshire or forgotten Westmoreland) – *"Kurby"*; Lowestoft – *"Lowstoft"* or *"Low-stoff"*; Mildenhall however stays as *"Mildenhall"* though some locals prefer *"Mine-all"*; and here's a stunner or stumer = Oughtibridge (Yorkshire) becomes *"Ootibridge, Outibridge* or even *Oatibridge.*

Incidentally, the members of the 1926-28 BBC pronunciation committee included the opinionated playwright G.B Shaw, who tried to divert English spelling in the direction of American English. On the same committee was the phonetician Daniel Jones, who later became the model for Professor Henry Higgins, so *some* good came of the committee.

15TH SEPTEMBER

The Pope in Paris

Pope Benedict XVI came on a visit to France, and got on rather well with the country's President, Nicholas Sarkozy. Religion is probably the least pressing subject in Sarkozy's mind at the moment, with Europe officially sinking fast into depression, a gun-totin' prospective US Vice-President, and smaller congregations in church getting progressively smaller. Still, Sarkozy's idea of 'a positive secularity', presented again to the Pope, went down well. There has always been a large gap between Church and Government in France, just as there is right now in Spain. The bitter legacy of hundreds of years of aggressively strong clerical authority in both these officially Roman Catholic states is still there to see in the reactionary agnosticism of modern governors, and the obstinacy and pride of the prelates. Journalists could see how things were going to be during the Pope's visit to France when Nicholas Sarkozy flouted French norms by going directly to Orly Airport to welcome the Supreme Head of the Catholic religion. Usually the President of the Republic awaits his fellow statesmen in the Elysée Palace. Madame Sarkozy, first lady of France, former singer and present beauty Carla Bruni was at her husband's side at the airport. This was a repetition of what happened recently in the United States, when George and Laura Bush went to Washington Airport to greet the octogenarian Pontiff.

The extraordinary and diplomatic treatment of this wise old man in the great countries of the world is perhaps only natural, as Benedict only has to open his mouth to show the true meaning of Christian teaching, no matter the religious ideals of the audience. Pope Benedict made an encouraging and uplifting speech to the French nation, in which he said among other things that 'the Church in France enjoys a splendidly free regime,' and that 'lack of confidence shown in the past has given way to serene and positive dialogue'. He also said that there existed a climate of 'reciprocal goodwill'. The Pope insists that it is 'fundamental to take note of the fact that a distinction exists between political ambience and religion, as much to enhance our religious liberties as to accept the responsibility of the State towards them'. Benedict is worried by the growing gap in the richer countries between the wealthy and the poor. 'The Church must intervene, as do so many other associations, to offer immediate solutions: how can the poor and the abandoned get help? Let us accept that in these matters it is the State which must enact legislation to assist the poor and deprived and wipe out injustice'.

When it came to the President of France's turn to speak, the Pope listened intently as Sarkozy said 'it is to be assumed correctly that we are Christians. It would be madness to deprive ourselves of the wisdom offered by all denominations. Indeed it would be a crime committed against culture and thought. This is why I stress the importance of what we call "positive secularity". This thrusting philosophy was applauded and praised by the Pope. Possibly because Nicholas Sarkozy is a hardly practising Christian, his speech of welcome to the Pope aggravated his traditional enemies, who found him hypocritical, and said so in the newspaper columns. In fact the French President had first launched the idea last December during a state visit to Rome. Sarkozy had mentioned a 1905 Law which limited (in France) church activities, which he considered antique and out-of-date. "Positive secularity", he insists, should be the guide to making and keeping the peace between Church and State. "Politicians should not preach sermons, and priests should not attempt legislation!" was one reporter's sniffy comment.

One Spanish commentator's gruff response in his column to another religious future was to suggest that the Cardinal-Archbishop of Madrid should not have permitted entry to the herd of Spanish Ministers, appearing recently at the memorial service for the victims of the Spanair air crash of last month. The journalist pointed out that these were the very same Ministers who are trying to rescind the law which permits taxpayers to tick a box on their tax return form allowing a set amount for the Church. What were these enemies of the Church doing in a church, he wanted to know? On another subject, Pope Benedict said he is worried by indications of a new 'Cold War' between Russia and the nations of the West. In his wisdom he knows that Russia has been for countless centuries a permanent worry for the nations of Europe and the West, as well as the great Asiatic nations such as Japan and China. Russia, as does the leopard, finds it difficult to change its spots.

1ST OCTOBER

European Airlines: surprises all round

Amidst the stunning fall of the smaller, cheaper airlines such as Futura, and astonishing mergers such as KLM/Air France and Iberia/British Airways, news now comes about yet another state-owned giant in trouble – though at the moment of writing it would seem the problems with Alitalia are being solved. When the Italian press pronounced that agreement had at last been reached on privatization of the corporation, the public didn't react with much enthusiasm – almost as if they were tired of the subject (wilder and wilder surmises for months) and didn't want to believe what the press said anyway.

Now, it appears that after weeks of declarations from politicians (traditionally taken with a large pinch of salt in Italy), ultimatums delivered, negotiations with trade unions, agreements and disagreements, something is (probably) going to be done about Italy's pride – Alitalia.

Unions representing the Italian pilots and technicians have signed a plan put forward by a group of businessmen, with the intention of absorbing the state-owned company. This is a pleasant change, since this particular union had been in the vanguard of those objecting to the offer made by the *CAI (Compagnia Aerea Italia)*. This is a corporation floated by sixteen leading impresarios. The gentlemen needed a final twelve-hour meeting with the unions before an agreement was reached.

One of the most debated sections of the newly signed agreements dealt with giving the head of land-based technicians a director's rank and authority. Another clarified the position of company employees with regard to guarantees in personal work contracts.

Another sharply discussed point was the union's demand that the new Alitalia should employ 1,550 pilots on full-time contract. A further 139 will be on part-time contracts, giving the corporation a total of 1,689 pilots, a number which should significantly reduce the over-work experienced at the pilots' cost (and the airline's) by employing a smaller team in the past.

These modifications are now added to those already discussed, which contemplate no change in the lower-salaried groups. There are also modifications to the timetable, allowing more opportunity to work over-time under controlled rates.

It has been mentioned in the Italian press that the unions' sudden positive changes of mind might have come about after it was revealed that other European airlines have sought and obtained a piece of the cake by investing alongside the impresarios. They include German Lufthansa, and Franco-Dutch Air France/KLM.

The French know a great deal about Alitalia, having being the brink of buying a controlling share last April. They were thwarted by both the Italian Government and the unions however; they preferred the Germans, who offered many different destinations, whereas the French seemed only interested in connections with Paris.

Meanwhile, Irishman Michael O'Leary, president of Ryanair, said that he found the fusion of Iberia with British Airways 'great!' It was also great news for all the 'cheapie' airlines (those which still survive) because, predicts O'Leary, these mergers of giants always mean an eventual reduction of the twin airlines' capacity, and an overall increase in seat prices. He claims that this precisely what happened after the merger of Air France and KLM.

Mr O'Leary has a reputation for eccentricity, though no-one doubts his business abilities. Some journalists have wondered why the Irishman should imagine that the top men at Air France and KLM had not taken this into account when agreeing to the merger. O'Leary replies to this 'bewilderment' by predicting that the near future 'will be a lot of fun'. What, he asks, will happen to Alitalia (see above), Austrian Airlines, Air Berlin, Sky Europe and Spanair? He is certain the next few months will be hot with mergers, bankruptcies, takeovers and surprises, as the recession cuts into all airline business possibilities, the cost of fuel soars to unsustainable heights, and trade unions (never forget the trade unions) play for heavier stakes.

13TH OCTOBER

France, Sarkozy and the 'neglected' one

Quite recently the big guns in the European economy, France, Germany, Britain, Italy etc., held a summit meeting to discuss what the administrations of each could do to simmer down emotions over the imminent 'catastrophe' of a Grand Recession (awaited not exactly with bated breath, but a certain weary acceptance) by financial experts for at least a decade.

The only problem, if it was a problem, was that Spain, in the person of her President of the Government *was not invited.* The world's press was aghast. Everyone knows that relations between the USA, President Bush, and the present incumbent of the Moncloa are shaky, sometimes rather rude, but Spain is an integral and important part of *Europe,* and there was no seat for Mr Rodríguez Zapatero.

Some columnists asked why. One of the answers came from a senior member of the European Parliament, who suggested that there was no point in inviting Zapatero to a high-level conference about an impending *crisis,* when Zapatero refuses even to use the word. The world must assume therefore that as there is no crisis, Mr Zapatero would not be required to put his position. This may be cynical, but up until now no senior person in the Spanish administration has been heard to mention the c-word.

But one can safely assume that ZP was miffed, to say the least. Suddenly, diplomatically, he was invited to the palace of French President Sarkozy for a face-to-face chat and lots of photo calls, with the Arch-Conservative embracing the Arch Socialist as the solemn guards in their splendid Napoleonic uniforms pretended not to look.

From the moment of their meeting, neither man moved at anything less than breakneck pace. Chancellors, Prime Ministers, Ministers of the Economy, all were summoned (again) to a summit. This time Spain was not forgotten, which is in fact a Good Thing, because Spain is one of the very few countries in Europe where the economy is still on a sound footing, with the major banks declaring their usual obscene profits (if you are interested, take a look at the profits of the Grupo Santander); the petrol companies not lowering their price-of-a-litre by a *céntimo* while the oil producing states have reduced their per-barrel cost from over 100 bucks to an average of 73 etc. As it turns out, ZP was to a certain extent right in not mentioning the word 'crisis', as life trundles on throughout Spain, upset yes by the dreadful weather, with towns flooded, but (as yet) no suited gentlemen (or ladies) hurling themselves in despair from the eighth storey.

A pleased Nicholas Sarkozy emerged from meetings to remark, "I believe I can say that the watches of Spain and France show the same time," in reference to agreements between the two powerful old women over the economy. Some cynics might say (and are saying) that Sarkozy has forgotten something: something relevant. The fact is that the two watches are on two different wrists, and some people are not sure if ZP can bear the weight of his. The same measly cynics say *this* is the reason why ZP was not invited to the previous summit.

Whatever, Zapatero asked Sarkozy if, in his position as temporary President of the UE, he would call another summit, and Nicholas came up trumps and organised it for the following day! Thus Mr Zapatero could assume once again his coveted position as one of the central pillars of Europe. Incidentally, the second summit took place two days after Black Friday (10th October) for the European Exchanges, where closing figures of -8.5% were shockingly normal.

During the second summit Silvio Berlusconi of Italy suggested that the only way out of the crisis was to suspect all activities in the Exchanges. When he was quizzed on this later at press conferences, Berlusconi pretended he knew nothing about this impious idea, though he knew that 'some people' has suggested it as one of the panaceas designed to lead us out of recession. "One hears this sort of thing all the time," he admitted. Italian banks responded by persuading the Italian population that they were perfectly solvent thank you, and that there was no need for worry (or foresee millions of bank clients in long queues trying to withdraw their savings).

29ᵀᴴ OCTOBER

Spain: expensive wheels hit the headlines

The President of the Catalan Parliament is an independist, communist republican (ERC) called Ernest Benach. The Spanish, Catalan and European papers have been having a field day with Mr Benach, who seems unmoved by the fuss. Every official in political office throughout the EU has a car at his disposal, usually with chauffeur thrown in for good measure. Using a motor you do not have to drive (or park) and this is one of the perks. Mr Benach is probably guilty of one major fault; bad timing. In the throes of the beginning of a deep and lasting recession, in Cataluña and all other regions of Spain (and Europe), the President of the Catalan Parliament had had some 'tuning' done on his official motor car that has caused a serious breach between ERC and ICV, two of the fiercely independist political parties in Cataluña.

The Councillor for Institutional and Interior Relations (how do they invent these wonderful working titles?), Joan Saura, has demanded an immediate investigation into the bit of tuning ordered by Benach on his Audi A8 Limousine. The tuning seems to have consisted in new extras placed in the car at a cost of 9,276 euros. These extras include a wood-panelled desk with a relaxing footrest beneath, a television set and connections for both MP3 and Bluetooth. The Audi itself is on the market at the tidy sum of 130,000 euros, but in all fairness to Mr Benach, he got it cheap at 83,386 euros using the 'renting' system (you rent the car over a long period and can exercise the right to purchase when that period is over). During interviews with the international and national press, the Councillor said: "it has escaped nobody's notice that expenses of this kind, incurred while the country suffers a financial crisis, are in any way justifiable. In fact, such *gastos* are offensive". Saura added that though it would be most unusual to open an investigation into the actions of such a senior Member of Parliament, it will be up to Mr. Benach to explain his actions.

The Catalan Opposition, led by CiU, PP and Ciutadans, joined in the chorus of disapproval. They emphasise that this has occurred just as the proposed *Ley de Dependencia* has had to be postponed for lack of funds. They add that the Councillor for Health has just suggested making ordinary people (those without an A8 Limousine) pay for their National Health visits to the doctor.

Leader of UDC Josep Duran y Lleida calls the 'tuning' unnecessary, and the President of the Popular Party in Cataluña, Alicia Sánchez-Camacho is another leader who calls for an 'immediate' and 'intense' investigation. She insists that at times of grave financial crisis, both political parties and their members should be the first to present an image of austerity, especially now, when many if not most Catalan families are experiencing serious difficulties in staying solvent towards the end of each month. Mr. Benach normally uses his chauffeured motor to drive daily from his home town of Reus (Tarragona) to Barcelona where he presides over Parliament. Other senior politicians use Volkswagen Passats, and there is one more Audi, an A6, bought new. Joan Puigcercós, actual leader of Mr. Benach's party, ERC, says he uses a Renault Laguna, though he has the right to use the Audi A6 if he wishes. In fact, Puigercós says he prefers the Renault.

The seriousness with which Puigcercós approaches present pecuniary difficulties certainly contributes towards reducing costs in the everyday running of government, most appropriate at a time when the Antifraud Squad in Barcelona is working on a proposal made by the republican party ERC, in which cases of political corruption will be fully investigated.

The question that nags me is why Benach should want a wooden desk and a footrest in his official limousine? Surely he works long enough hours controlling sometimes fractious and contentious MPs, without labouring on and on during his long drive home. And a TV set? Well, the latter would be nice for those moments of calm in which Mr.Benach could watch Barcelona F.C. beating up some hapless opponents on the soccer field.

In case you think I have forgotten something, I haven't. You are quite right of course. Neither Mr.Benach nor any other politican actually pays for such trifles as these, *himself*. These costs are met, like everything else, by the taxpayer; which is presumably why the European press is making such a fuss.

24TH NOVEMBER

A bitter divorce in French politics

If there are two ladies in international politics who never give up, have the cheek of the devil and the skin of a rhinoceros, they are called Hillary Rodham Clinton and Ségolène Royal. Mrs Clinton survived the Presidency of her charming husband – and his public infidelities – and became the opponent of Barack Abama in the Democratic candidates race to become President herself. Obama won in the end, but it was a near draw, and Hillary will probably become Secretary of State if she plays her cards right, which she will. La Royal pushed herself to the top of French socialism in a failed attempt to beat little M. Sarkozy to the Elysée Palace. Again, as the Iron Duke observed after Waterloo, it was a damned close-run thing.

Far from accepting defeat and retiring to some obscure mayor's parlour, Ségolène prepared her attractive self gamely, marshalled her regiments of supporters, and has just contested the election of a new leader for the Labour party of France. Her opponent was Martine Aubrey. The campaign has split the Socialists into two bitterly opposed factions, as unmixable as oil and water. The result was an even closer-run thing; 50.02% of party members' votes went to Martine Aubrey. 49.98% were for Royal. As Aubrey claims to be an orthodox Gallic social-democrat, and Royal has always been a hard-liner, an admirer of cloth-capped, down-with-the-bosses-and- off-with-their-heads-as-well Socialist with definitely Marxist ideals, there seems to be an irreconcilable divorce in the French socialist party. This gives a decided advantage to M. Sarkozy, whose politics and followers are markedly Conservative.

What kind of union can possibly emerge between the followers of each woman when such personal hatreds are being aired? The campaign showed a bottomless ravine between the two factions. No-one can cross it, because it is too wide, and no-one can throw a bridge across it, in the foreseeable future at least.

Martine Aubrey is best known as the architect of the 35-hour working week. She is as hard as Royal and has no intention of budging an inch for electoral purposes. But she only won by a difference of 42 votes, and that tiny sum will prove no help in the internecine battles to come. As was expected, when the *Royalistes* learned that the difference in the vote was 42, they immediately announced that there must have been 'irregularities'. They will take the other faction to Court, and demand a re-election.

One of the most vocal supporters of Ségolène, M. Manuel Valls, accused the Aubrey faction of organising an anti-democratic *coup*. The actual leader of the Socialist Party, François Hollande, has had no alternative but to ask the Socialist National Council to investigate the claims made by the Royal group, and decide whether to declare the results null and void and call another election, or ratify the result as a victory for Aubrey, albeit a Pyrrhic victory. Readers will remember that Hollande was 'emotionally connected' with Royal for ten years. The couple separated after the 2007 presidential elections which Royal lost to Nicholas Sarkozy.

The bitter fact is that since socialist Lionel Jospin was thrashed in the 2002 elections by the extreme right-winger Le Pen, the French Socialist Party has had difficulty raising its head. Being French, they naturally would not have looked at Tony Blair's stratagem, which was to invent a *'third way'*, or *New* Labour, besides which, French socialists are true socialists, whereas Mr Blair is about as socialist as Charley's Aunt. In fact Mr Blair was probably the most conservative Prime Minister Britain has had since Churchill. But this is *France*. Ségolène Royal has lost no time since early Saturday morning (the vote took place on Friday) before denouncing the election as a 'democratic farce'. She and Manuel Valls sustain the notion that 'irregularities' sabotaged the voting, especially in those zones heavily influenced by Martine Aubrey, such as Nord Pas de Calais, and those dominated by ex-Premier Laurent Fabius in Seine Maritime. Fabius is one of Aubrey's closest followers and supporters.

Finally, for those who do not fully understand French politics, it should be noted that Martine Aubrey is the daughter of Jacques Delors, is 58 years old, has been Minister of Labour (under Jospin), is solidly Europist, anti-liberal, a feminist, divorced with one daughter, and Mayor of Lille.

8ᵀᴴ DECEMBER

Great Britain: a crisis in conversation and confidence

Over the last five or six years I find (looking through my diary) a repeated theme: I have made dozens of entries about one subject – the only too obvious fact that British people hardly talk to each other. They do not 'converse'. I note the same numbing scene in cafés and by beaches and in other places where people meet. If it is a British couple, I should imagine they exchange not more than five words with each other during the meal. Sometimes, the male spends more time chatting with the waiter – more if it should be an (attractive) waitress. The female smokes rather a lot and couldn't give a hoot. The children clutch their cell phone.

I do not expect Oscar Wilde quips or G.K. Chesterton wit. Wilde did not indulge in conversation. His 'repartee' consisted of comic or dramatic epigrams to which there was little or no answer. This is not conversation. Chesterton, like so many other people who live by the pen, longed to speak uninterrupted. He would bash you around the head with numbing anecdotes usually connected with religion. His acolytes drank in every word with their Lafitte Rothschild. In Spain conversation consists of a number of normally intelligent and polite people taking a breath when they can and shouting loudly at each other and never heeding (or hearing) one word said by anyone else. This is sad, because the Spanish are a well-educated and erudite race whose opinions are always worth hearing. But how to do it if everybody talks at once?

I have heard of 'social hostesses' in London who, tired of paralysing silences throughout their carefully chosen dinner, have even gone to the length of placing a 'conversation menu' on each plate, so that when you sit down there is a printed list of suitable subjects to stimulate a good argument. Thus: with the soup, *Iraq and Afghanistan*; *where do you stand*?

With the pudding, *wasn't Churchill just a drunk blessed with the gift of rhetoric?* And so on.

And yet, and yet…place two total strangers (if they are British) next to each other in what airline companies choose to call 'seats', and you can bet they will spend the flight telling each other the innermost secrets of their family, wife, husband, lover etc. They will also invent episodes in their own life that would make even a sailor blush. And they will listen to each other with every sign of interest and attention, even after the fifth Scotch. They have never met before in their life, and will not want ever to meet again.

Confidence: there now, that's a different thing. We have lost all confidence. We do not trust each other. We especially do not trust career politicians or television performers. If World War III were about to be declared, would we heed a word on the telly if it came from the likes of Jack Straw or Geoff Hoon? Or David Milliband? Why did the older ones among us gather nightly throughout the second of those world conflicts to listen to radio broadcasts throughout the horrors of the Blitz by such a man as Churchill. Did we believe *then* that he was just a cigar-waving toff with a quickly emptying brandy glass? Many believe, despite the current demonisation that Churchill did indeed mobilize the English language, one of the subtlest, richest instruments ever known to Man, and use it to do battle in his own special way. Britons have never cared much about politics, it is all one to them, but they recognised the voice of honesty during the War.

Have you noticed that those historians and journalists who now pick holes in W.S. Churchill would not actually be here if he had not lived. So where are the people who gave us confidence? Where is 'The Radio Doctor' whom we heard on a crackling wireless, and took his medical advice about our 'plates of meat' and our headaches*. Why did we take this advice? Because we had confidence in him. If China were about to invade the sceptered isle would we care what Gordon Brown said, even if we could understand it? I am not sure about David Cameron either, but I do think Boris Johnson shows an encouraging amount of the Churchill touch. Churchill was also a political toff from childhood, not above crossing the floor (twice) in Parliament if denied anything, but he (like Boris now) was well aware of the intoxicating success of good publicity. I have recently hit the allegedly easily obtainable three score years and ten, and I do not really want to enter 'the Autumn of my years' as a cynical and disillusioned old bastard, but I do know that the Britain and the British of my youth have vanished into twilight, and I do not find this a happy thought. But…*what to do,* as the poet said.

* Dr Hill, I believe.

22ND DECEMBER

SPAIN: sporting success for the Government

In case you were under the impression that Spain's tremendous winnings in sport during 2008 were to be laid at the door of Iker Casillas and his Merry Men, or Rafa Nadal's magic left hand, or the strong legs of the cyclists, the pluck and strength of the basketball and hockey players etc., the Spanish Government has *news* for you. Inspired by the eminence of the party's political success last year, the *Ministerio de la Presidencia* has published an elegant booklet entitled: *2008: Principal Actions of the Government.* The well-produced booklet lists all the positive results of the PSOE's governance. Among these, in a section headlined Achievements of the Ministry of Education, Social Politics and Sport, you will find an interesting chapter called *The Golden Year for Spanish Sport.* Eat your heart out Iker, and Rafa, cyclists Sastre and Contador, and those other Spaniards who won gold, silver or bronze medallions at the Chinese Olympics. According to the little book 'the year 2008 has been, beyond doubt, the year of Spanish sport. The ADO Programme, plus the Programme for the Paralympics, and the constant support of this Government concentrated in the Centres *de Alto Rendimiento Deportivo* have shown their efficiency in the Olympic Games at Beijing'.

Here is the backroom boys' explanation, kindly clarified by the Ministry, for the Spanish basketball team's winning of the Silver, as well as the seventeen other medals won by Spain in China. But the dance of self-glorification doesn't stop there: the booklet also claims that it was by the action of government that so much athletic success was inspired and achieved. In case some of the athletes who actually won their medals, or competed anyway in difficult or dangerous sports, might be mildly offended by the general tenor of the booklet, a small paragraph has been inserted: 'it must be admitted as well that the effort and dedication of the Spanish sportsmen and women has glowed in its own light during these international competitions'. Oh well, that's all right then.

Later the pamphlet announces that a Spanish football team won the Euro Cup, just after reminding the reader that the Government spent 130 million euros last year on sporting activities in centres of education. One is invited to connect one with the other. In June, after an extraordinary exciting final in Vienna, the President of the Government, who had been there, took quick advantage: 'it was a privilege for me to be there. I am the first president in our democracy to be present at such a final. I shall never forget it'. In case anyone else does, this anecdote is in the booklet. Mr Zapatero went on: 'my generation had the right to see such a triumph. This is only the beginning. The best is to come'. I seem to remember the PSOE's skill in adopting the praise for success in sporting events, as the years pass. Do I not recall television reports of Butragueño's winning goal in the World Cup in Mexico in 1986? Did not RTVE/PSOE manage to superimpose the PSOE's logo at the bottom of the picture?

The Ministry's booklet lists among the Government's 2008 achievements, triumphs in tennis (Nadal and brilliant company), cycling, basketball and hockey. 'Spain is the country with the greatest numbers of tennis tournaments won, and also has more Spanish names among the top 100 than any other country,' crows the booklet. And indeed, the Spanish team (without Nadal) has just won the Davis Cup. Cyclists Alberto Contador and Carlos Sastre get a bear hug from the Minister herself – Mercedes Cabrera: 'Spanish cyclists also showed their superiority in the Olympics, as well as the three greatest tests, the Tour, the *Giro* and the *Vuelta*'. Basketball is singled out too; 'the female team won a historic Silver in the European Cup', the booklet reminds us, in one of the lists of Government achievement.

Government propaganda bears no limits. The Moncloa has managed to include Spanish athletes' personal achievements last year as part of the positive achievements of the Government. It is as though Zapatero himself, accompanied by José Blanco (there to foul the opposition) scored goals in the Euro Cup, climbed all those high mountains, made smashes at the Wimbledon net, or nearly passed out with the excruciating agony of cyclists' cramp. At least there is still not a Ministry of Sport (with that name) in Spain, or we would have to see photographs in the press of the Minister of the Day dribbling a football about or sharpening her hockey stick.

2009

11ᵀᴴ JANUARY

The importance of having gas

President Sarkozy of France, using up his turn as temporary president of the European Union, has been rushing about in his usual frenetic manner. He rushed to Israel and Jordan, as well as Egypt, to try to mend holes broken in an already fragile world peace by Israel's belated but nonetheless violent reaction to constant rocketing from Gaza. The world's press stood by horrified while Israel's air force bombed their former colony. The world's press was shocked by the death of Palestinians, and many front pages were disfigured by dreadful photographs of dead and maimed Palestinian children. The Israelis were once again compared to 'Nazis who ran extermination camps'. Hamas (a Palestinian terrorist group financed and armed by Arab states) has been rocketing Israel for the past ten months, and Israel decided that enough was enough. Unfortunately, as always happens in all wars, it was (and is) the civilian population that bears the brunt.

Sarkozy tried to dissuade Hamas from aiming explosive rockets over Israel, and at the same time urged Israel's government and military not to carry out a full military invasion of the Gaza Strip. The Frenchman got refusals from both sides, as the newspapers knew he would. By the time you read this, Israel may have carried out a full-scale land invasion of Gaza, with the concomitant horrors such an exercise will bring.

M. Sarkozy did much better in his talks with Russia and Georgia. Not singlehandedly, but certainly well in the lead in the talks, he made suggestions that ended in a kind of uneasy peace between the giant and her neighbour, now independent, but for many decades only a prickly segment of the Soviet Empire. This is not to say that Russia will keep Putin or Medvedev's word. After all, Russia had promised to keep most of Europe supplied with gas (of which she has a hugely inflated amount) but is now setting about turning off the taps because of an argument over prices.

M. Sarkozy visited the tiny Czech Republic too. Plenty of political observers scoffed, saying that this small nation state bears too little importance in European and world affairs. Chancellor Schwarzenberg gave his opinion swiftly, however, to Sarkozy. Talking about Gaza, he declared that Hamas actually increased the number of rockets fired at Israel *after* a 'cease-fire' had been signed. Like most cease-fires, this one turned out to be an illusion, and deluded no-one, especially the Israelis. Hamas, true to style, caused the latest conflict by launching rockets deliberately from the most over-populated and unmilitarised zones in Gaza, knowing that the Israelis would be loath to counter-attack directly because of the awesome count in civilian deaths that would inevitably result. But enough was enough, and the Constitution of Israel, a small independent state invented in the post-War period in the middle of the ethnically unfriendly desert, does not cater for mercy if attacked. At least Scharzenberg said what every other leader in Europe was thinking, but didn't dare express. Today, one must be politically correct: Israel is evil, and Palestine is as innocent as a baby in a cradle; which is why so many photographs of slaughtered Palestinian babies have been front-paged.

The Czech Republic should be lauded, not disparaged by politicians and the press. Prime Minister Mirek Topolanek told Sarkozy, on another subject of note, that the European Commission's official line on the ongoing battle between Gazprom and the Ukrainian company Naftogaz is clumsy and mistaken. The EC claims it is merely a 'bilateral commercial dispute'. It is, says the Czech premier, nothing of the kind: Given that both these giants are in fact state-owned, the conflict is purely political, and concerns differences currently held by Russia and the Ukraine itself. While the gas producers (and exporters) argue about prices, Russia has cut off supplies of gas in the middle of a terrible wave of freezing weather right across the continent of Europe. Enter Mirek Topolanek again, in discussions with Vladimir Putin which ended with handshakes, and a promise from Russia to 'create a protocol' whereby gas would continue to flow into Europe via the Ukraine. Actually, the extremely tall Mr Topolanek said he would stay in Kiev until the previsions of the protocol are signed by Russia and the Ukraine.

The European Parliament might not greatly benefit with Ramon Tremosa as a Communist candidate for Spain

The European Union (UE) comes in many forms. It is made up of hundreds of committees. Members of these committees, many of which happily sustain an image conjured up by a well-known saying about committees*, are men and women sent to Brussels or Strasbourg by their countries to represent them. Some, not all of these European deputies or MEPs are to be found in well-paid jobs within the UE because their countries' governments either could not think what to do with them otherwise, or because the political parties they represent wish they didn't. For instance, it cannot be coincidence that Spain and Britain's representatives in Europe are (often but not always) considered difficult, contentious, or an embarrassment by their own parties. In Spain, it has been noticed that members of both the Popular Party and the Spanish Workers' Socialist Party (PSOE) who generally clash with either Rajoy or, perhaps especially Zapatero, are simply sent to Brussels (or Strasbourg), where they can live like kings and do little harm. This last coincides with the fact that no-one within the European Union really know what it is there for. Is it there to provide defence? No. It could do nothing when the population of certain Balkan countries began ethnically cleansing the population of other Balkan countries. If the UE cannot discipline countries within its own borders, how can it provide an adequate defence?

Is it there to rule benevolently over us? It strongly suggested to Britain, for example, that she should stop foxhunting in England. But the UE has *not* yet suggested to Spain that the national sport of torturing live bulls in an arena and killing them in a dance of death – might be stopped. At least the UE managed to impress upon Spain that the common village practice of dropping live animals such as goats from the top of tall buildings such as churches, in order to entertain the populace during *fiestas* might be stopped. Fireworks that set fire to homes and permanently injure passing folk must now suffice for some villages in the Peninsula.

The Catalan political party CiU, has chosen Ramon Tremosa, economist by profession, to stand for them at the June elections for MEPs. Leader of CiU Artur Mas has not noticed what a hornet he is introducing into the peaceful honeycomb in Strasbourg, where nobody in their right senses wishes to do anything else but sleep in committee. Mr. Tremosa started his campaign by stating that in his opinion the European Parliament is 'not important'. This forthright statement proves that Mr Tremosa is not an experienced politician. Many politicians might *think* that the European Parliament hasn't much importance, but they don't say so, especially before elections in June. Might it be that Mr. Artur Mas is, like Homer, nodding? After all, the past and present Eurodeputy for CiU is Ignasi Guardans, who was expecting to repeat his past excellence as Deputy. When asked what he thought about being replaced by Mr. Tremosa, his answer was truly political, in that it was not an answer at all: "Lots of people still do not understand that the European Parliament does not agree with the idea of an independent Cataluña'. Ah, but there *is* some sense in Guardans' remark, as Mr. Tremosa has distinguished himself as an ardent independent, even organising campaigns against the famous *Estatut* before the referendum. In order to show his patriotism, Mr Tremosa also helped to found a political platform called *Economistas por el no*. This organisation is highly vocal in its denouncement of Spain's 'fiscal banditry towards the Catalans'.

Tremosa has had a few words to say about his CiU boss Artur Mas too. Talking about financial agreements made between Mas and Zapatero in the financing of the region. Tremosa commented, 'Mas made a mistake rushing off to the Moncloa by himself and representing the *Estatut* by himself. He might govern, now, a little less as a result, but he will achieve more credits, and make himself heard better.' Asked about these words, spoken in 2007, Mr. Tremosa stands by them. It remains to be seen if, after June this year, he becomes CiU's official representative in the European Parliament, he will follow the party line, or be a pain in the Mas for Artur.

* A camel is a horse designed by a committee

9TH FEBRUARY

Munich this year

The new Vice-President of the United States flew over the pond to Munich in Bavaria to attend the 45th International Security Conference. Representing Spain was our Foreign Minister, in charge of *cooperation* with other nations. Miguel Angel Moratinos said on the day before the conference, 6th February, that as far as he knew he wouldn't be *cooperating* directly with Joe Biden in the form of a meeting. Nor would he be *cooperating* with any other member of the US delegation.

Moratinos remarked that he supposed he would have a chance to say hullo to Mr Biden during one of the official receptions offered in Munich. Or so he hoped, for this affair is 'an informal assembly at which matters affecting security will be discussed, debated and reflected upon'. Though not, it seems, by Moratinos and Biden.

It is reported that the President of the Government of Spain, Rodríguez Zapatero, has not yet spoken on the telephone to the newly elected President of the United States, Mr. Barack Obama. Our newspapers appear uncertain if this means a continuation of the coldness between Spain and America scrupulously maintained by Zapatero since he was elected by the people to represent the Spanish as their leader, and observed with a certain malicious good humour by ex-President George W. Bush.

At the Security Conference, the Vice-President expressly avoided any mention of a request for more European troops to be sent to Afghanistan. He was almost certainly advised to ignore this thorny subject to avoid any bickering from France and Germany. Both these powerful European states are very much against sending soldiers to a strife-torn country where they consider internal conflicts are the Afghans' problem, not theirs.

Mr. Biden did however ask his European allies for 'ideas and suggestions' that might vitally help the new structure in Afghanistan. He was reminded that the latter has been a bitterly sharp dart in European flesh for two centuries or more. Most Afghans would agree with Mr. Biden that their country deserved a rest from continuous violence and discord. It is to be hoped that the rapidly failing powers of the Talebans will contribute towards an eventual peace. Meanwhile, Mr. Biden said that Obama has thought seriously of doubling American forces in the zone, bringing the number up to approximately 60,000 men and women.

One delegate at the Security Conference was more outspoken: Secretary-General of the Atlantic Alliance Jaap de Hoop Scheffer said he fervently hoped the European nations capable of doing so would send many more troops to Afghanistan, and quickly.

Joe Biden reminded the conference that the USA wanted to use a 'European shield' in cooperatio with Russia, against the growing threat of nuclear threats coming from Iran. Biden emphasised that the 'shield' was not in any way meant to menace Russia herself, and hoped that that vast country would cooperate with NATO by join with the European states in presenting a firm front against Iran's pretension to push the rest of the world into Islam, if necessary using nuclear force. Biden said: "We are most anxious to talk with Iran's leaders and offer a clear choice; they can continue their potential aggression, causing more international pressure to be brought down upon them, and become even more isolated in world terms – or they can abandon their illicit nuclear programme and continuous support given to terrorism, and achieve peace."

The Vice-President was particularly open with Russia's representatives, whom he asked to join with the United States and NATO, not stand uncertainly on the perimeter: "We must work together. We must carry on with the good work by prolonging the Strategic Arms Treaty (START). We must control, reduce and stop the traffic in nuclear and drugs-connected substances." Afghanistan exports 90% of the world heroin market.

8ᵀᴴ MARCH

Focus on Chinese orphans

This episode is more Asiatic than European. I do not apologise for this. What happens in a country of the size and power of China affects what happens in Europe. China is the most populous state on this planet, and her government is Maoist Communist with no pretensions towards western-style democracy. China has been ruled for thousands of years by a tiny minority of immensely powerful men: women have never been welcomed into internal politics. In the 20th century a group of women (including the wife of a Great Leader) conspired for change – and were executed for treason, though their arguments were logical. The subject of this special edition of EF is in fact execution. If you have feeble digestion, read no further. It appears that statesmen from America and Europe enjoy strong digestion, because since Nixon broke the ice with Mao, the West has drawn as close to China *as the Chinese permit*. We are constantly told of the 'wonders of China', and that her 'special form of Communism' works so well. Chinese goods flood European markets. Half the interior parts of your European motor car were made in China under licence.

Should you visit China as a tourist, one of the things you might notice is the abundance of orphanages. All are filled to bursting. A conservative estimate has shown that there are every year approximately 100,000 new orphans, all under-age. Some suffer blindness or deafness. The majority of the children are however healthy. These are children born to adolescent couples who disobeyed the severe rule exerted over the Chinese masses concerning numbers of children allowed per matrimony – namely *one*. By far the largest numbers of these orphans have no parents because they have been executed by the authorities. Each year, some 400,000 persons are imprisoned. Of these, 70% are married and have, nominally anyway, one child. The Reader may ask how China manages to maintain so many millions of her people in gaol? The answer is oriental and simple. They don't, because China's laws encourage the death penalty for sixty-eight offences. These include murder of course, but also drug trafficking, rape, habitual crime, the stealing or commercial use of national treasures or cultural objects, presentation of false receipts or personal tax returns, production or sale of pornography, exploitation of prostitution, manufacture and distribution of forged coinage; 'corruption' (which can cover almost anything), speculation (especially in the construction industry), unexplained wealth and a great crowd of etcetera's. China claims to have executed less than 500 people last year. Investigators claim an actual figure of ten thousand.

Chinese people used to be executed by shooting, but this kind of killing has now been 'civilized' by the presence of vans, painted blue and white, which tour the massive country. Death by injection for 'criminals' is expensive; this is immaterial, for China has recently become very rich. The executions take place in the vans. One of the orphans the visitor might see is Hou Yu Hang (13), who shares a small room with six others. She says that she is looking forward to her mother coming to take her home again. This will not happen, sadly, because her mother is condemned to die for selling false credit cards – her only source of income. Hou Yu says she misses her mother terribly because she used to sing her gay songs and caress her before bed. A Chinese official says, "last visits by a mother or father are not allowed. News of the execution is not passed to a new orphan." Xian, the oldest city in China, and source of the original Silk Route associated with Marco Polo, has always done business with Europe, Persia and Arabia. 7.5 million people live there. Xian is also the HQ of the colourful vans, which carry doctors specialising in the execution of 'criminals', and the immediate extraction of valuable organs, such as the cornea, kidney, heart, small intestine etc. Extraction of organs sometimes happens when the 'criminal' is not clinically dead. From Xian, the medical vans work right across China. According to an investigator from the Academy of Social Sciences, the greater part of daily executions in China is still by firing squad. Only 40% of deaths are caused by the injection first of Sodium Thiopental (to make the victim unconscious), Bromide of Pancuronium (to block breathing), and Potassium Chloride (to stop the heart). In China, a kidney transplant can cost between $7,200 and $20,000, cheaper than anywhere else. Officials of criminal institutions who inform the medical services about forthcoming executions can earn around thirty-seven dollars per cadaver. Did you enjoy the Chinese Olympic Games?

The *Prestige* inquiry publishes its opinion

Everyone in Europe knows what happened; now, six years after the super-tanker *Prestige* sunk off the coast of Galicia, leaving hundreds of miles of oil slick to slime the region's rocky coast, costing millions of euros in a tremendous cleaning-up operation, the official Inquiry into causes and effect of the accident has published the results of practically six years of arduous investigation. The tragedy that (temporarily) ruined Galicia's beaches and left hundreds of thousands of seabirds and sea fauna dead took place on 13 November, 2002.

The Inquiry exonerates from all blame the ex-naval director of La Coruña, Ángel del Real, the then *Delegado del Gobierno,* Arsenio Fernández de Mesa, and the then Minister of *Fomento,* Francisco Álvarez-Cascos, who agreed with the professionals' decision to tow the already stricken tanker as far out to sea as possible, avoiding entrance to any Galician port.

Court No. 1 at Corcubión considers the investigation concluded, and has withdrawn the accusation of negligence against the principal actors in the drama. The same Court dissociates the then government of José María Aznar of any blame for the incident, or culpability in its aftermath. It will be remembered that a special 'anguished protest' group called '*Nunca Máis*' was set up to attack the then government from every angle, egged on inexorably by the chief party of the Opposition in Parliament, the PSOE. The leader of the opposition, José Luis Rodríguez Zapatero said, "nothing functioned as it should, there was a total lack of diligence, and no communication between departments. It seems impossible that none of the ministers responsible for the accident (sic) have resigned". Mr José Blanco, also of the PSOE, said that "the Aznar government acted with incompetence, negligence and lack of coordination . . ." and added that the phrase 'criminal negligence' might well be used. The action group *Nunca Máis* said that José Luis López-Sors (ex-director of the Merchant Marine) had acted negligently, thus causing the tragedy.

The fact is that 77,000 tons of crude were emptied into the Atlantic from a sinking super-tanker, and the Enquiry's difficult job was to find out who to blame. The PSOE found it easy to blame ministers and other persons of elevated position, because they are always easy targets. If a rotten tree is blown over by a hurricane, knocking down a house, blame the Ministry of Agriculture. If the notoriously dangerous seas off the coast of Galicia catch a possibly sleepy ship's captain unawares, and a cargo of nearly one hundred tons of crude shifts, it is naturally the Minister of Development's fault, especially if he was spending the weekend as a guest in someone else's house at the time. Obviously, he should have known that a tanker off the Galician coast at that moment was going to get into difficulties.

Judge Carmen Veiras Suárez reached the conclusion that the decision to tow the crippled giant away from the coasts had been 'prudent and reasonable'. Experts attending the Inquiry had told her that 'it was the best of the alternatives'. If *Prestige* had been towed into an important port like Vigo, for example, the eventual damage might have been even worse. Nor, the statement adds, are port authorities *obliged* to permit access to a port. If the opinion of experts at the time was correct (as the judge assumes it was) no option was left to the port authorities but to deny access. The statement also points out that when the salvage company appointed by the ship's owners agreed to take over the situation, according to maritime laws, they did so only if it were agreed to get the tanker to a position 120 miles away from the coast.

Thus the most important environmental legal case in the last decade enters its final phase. Accusations remain held against the ship's captain, Apostolos Mangouras; his chief engineer, Argyropoulus Nikolaos, and the first officer, Irineo Maloto. They are accused of offences committed against natural resources and the environment; and disobedience. The next move is an actual trial. Meanwhile, anyone who wishes to appeal against the findings of the Inquiry can present it in writing within five days. The action group *Nunca Máis,* which had been disbanded, has gathered itself together again quickly to appeal. The conclusions of the Inquiry cover 192,311 pages.

4TH APRIL

Bad news for Kosovo and a surprise for the Spanish contingent

Soldiers are usually known for not understanding the subtle manoeuvres of politicians more interested in protecting their seat in any Parliament than in unimportant things like Life and Risk. Carme Chacón's recent bombshell as Minister of Defence has offended plenty of military men and women serving under her in potential boiling pots like the Balkans. Whether or not the withdrawal of Spanish forces from the peacekeeping contingents in Kosovo was Chacón's idea, or she is simply obeying orders from Mr Rodríguez Zapatero is for the reader to judge

The troops know as well as any reader that being withdrawn from NATO's protective forces in Kosovo does not necessarily mean an easy regression to peaceful military life – training, drills, life in peacetime barracks etc., in their own country. In fact, it was not very long before Carme Chacón had her turn to be surprised, as Foreign Minister Moratinos suddenly announced a matter of days later that Spain's contribution to military forces trying to hold Afghanistan together will very shortly be increased. Poor María Teresa Fernández de la Vega held what must be her 1000th press conference, at which she admitted that it was quite likely that twelve 'specialists', probably police experts, would indeed be sent out to Afghanistan – to help train the Afghan police. Really, for a PSOE government that is supposedly keen on being seen as pacific, Spain does seem to be rattling the sabre rather a lot.

As it turned out, Spain's President of the Government later made it clear (at the G20 summit) that a contingent of around 450 professional soldiers would be heading for the Khyber. It is difficult these days for political commentators to write anything that does not appear to be rubbish, as

Spain's present administration is a master at the game of producing different Ministers out of a hat, each with something different to say on the same subject.

In Kosovo itself, Ardian Djini, who is vice-president of the Alliance for the Future of Kosovo lamented Spain's withdrawal, saying that this was 'no time for a joke'. Ten months ago the Alliance went into combat in the region to help protect a European state from its own government. It seems that Kosovo is treated by both the EU and NATO as their 'own special baby', and the announcement made by one of its most effective governesses that she is quitting the cradle has not been taken with the best of humour.

At KFOR HQ, in officers' messes and other places where soldiers meet, eyebrows are raised; a certain ironic acceptance of the inevitable is abroad; sometimes an angry word is said. Soldiers, one of them explained, do not understand 'diplomacy'. Nor do they understand or appreciate being left in the lurch without explanations. Ugly words like 'chickening out' are being (no doubt) unfairly bandied about.

Back home in Spain, the official explanation coming from the Moncloa Palace is that the sudden withdrawal is perfectly logical and correct, and that it will be made discreetly and gradually. But one Kosovan paper thought that Carmen Chacón's bombshell had disrupted Kosovan relations with the United States. This might well be, but Americans understand politics, and will know that Zapatero's second famous withdrawal (the first was from Iraq) is purely political and electoral in tone. Italy has complained that she had been given no warnings from Madrid, but Zapatero's administration insists that her allies on guard in Kosovo had been 'adequately informed'.

To add some piquancy to the sauce, it must be remembered that Spain has never actually recognised the independence of Kosovo, even twelve months after it was declared. Nevertheless, the latest inquiry made by the European Foundation for the Balkans reveals that Kosovo is the happiest of the seven nations in that region. Kosovans are contented with their lot, we are told. But to most observers it seems that the country is still desperately poor, ill equipped for independence, lacking in hospitals and educational institutions, and still very much a gunpowder keg waiting for someone nasty with a slow match. Serbia is always waiting to pounce, and when an important country like Spain drops the Kosovans in the manure for rather obvious electoral reasons, the reputation of Spain is harmed perhaps rather more than nice young women like Carme Chacón realise. And, do you know, one does sometimes wonder *why* this young woman was appointed to head the Ministry of Defence. One day we will be told.

20TH APRIL

Germany: the Federal Agency of Employment reckons to run out of cash by October

While in Spain the president of the national Bank has said the same thing (promptly denied by the Minister of Labour) in Germany none other than the Federal Agency of Employment has announced that they 'will have problems of cash flow' by October of this year, faced with an increase in unemployment and in consequence, a decrease in tax revenues and other deductions.

Changes approved by the German Government, and transfers of financial obligations provoked as a result have 'made a substantial hole' in the coffers, leading to requests for State credits, as explained to the press by a spokesperson for the Agency. It has been confirmed that a putting-off of payments usually supplied from revenue stemming from value-added-tax has led to the present embarrassment.

Until now, the Federal Employment Agency received every month its share of the 7,800 million euros which was annually transferred. But from this year, this payment will be made in its entirety in December, leaving an unfillable gap in liquidity in the last quarter of the year. Nevertheless, there is a silver lining, explains the Minister of Labour, Olaf Scholz; he says he can guarantee that the supply of unemployment benefits is stable until 2010, and that, in the event of there being a lack of funds, rescue will arrive in the form of an unscheduled contribution from the State budget.

The number of unemployed works has risen during the last three months. In March, the figure stood at 3.58 million workers receiving unemployment benefits. This means 8.6% of the working population. Meanwhile, the Crisis, Recession or Depression (I hope the last word is not yet appropriate), becomes worse and worse, despite Mr Zapatero's joyful declarations at the recent G20 summit, when he tried to persuade glum state leaders that the *whats its name* has reached bottom, and will now begin to vanish. Beatrice di Mauro, a member of what in Germany is called 'The Five Wise People' (who advise the European Government on finance), has admitted to the newspaper *Berliner Zeitung,* that the worst effects of the Crisis have yet to come. She, on behalf of the wise five, advises the Government to be very hard with the banks, though she reckons they (the banks) will not be able to deal with the problems to come. She says, "there have been a couple of pieces of positive news recently, which have encouraged a kind of momentary euphoria, but I am afraid that little change in the crisis is noticeable in the labour market and employment in general, which leads me to the sorry thought that what is to come will be worse".

At the same time in Tokyo, President of the European Bank M. Jean-Claude Trichet denied at a Conference that there was dissension on his Board. Nor did he deny the persistent rumours that the Bank will again lower the Bank Rate, which I suppose will soon hit zero. Trichet made it clear that the Bank was likely to lower rates 'according to what is needed'. The official cost of money at present is said to be 1.25% - not exactly a figure to encourage borrowing – but Trichet himself said that this figure was not likely to go any lower. With patience, we will soon know, because the next meeting of the Board is scheduled for May 7th.

England: Prince Philip, longest runner in the 'Consort stakes'

On 18 April, the Duke of Edinburgh beat a British record; he became the longest lasting consort of a British monarch in history. This is good going for the man who Sir Alan Lascelles, a courtier, described as 'a bad-tempered, uncultured young man who will probably be unfaithful to his wife'. The king's consort who had previously held the record was Charlotte, wife of the occasionally mad George 111. Charlotte made it to 57 years and 70 days. Philip Mountbatten began *his* royal journey on 6 February, 1952, when his princess and he were on holiday in Africa, and were told Elizabeth's father George VI had died. When the bereaved couple arrived by aeroplane in London, Philip waited inside the aircraft until his young wife had begun descending the steps that led to nearly 58 years as Sovereign. He has somehow managed to be just behind her ever since, though it is said of him that he exercises a great deal of authority *within* the royal family.

4TH MAY

The shadow of unemployment

Mariano Rajoy went to Warsaw on May 1. He was to speak to the assembled leaders of conservative hue gathered from across Europe. He preached austerity, support for merited initiative and 'structural reforms' – the latter meaning massive cuts in government spending – something most of the Twenty-Seven are already trying to do.

President of the European Community the Portuguese Manuel Barroso, hardly surprised any delegate when he mentioned that the ongoing financial crisis affecting everybody seems to be particularly affecting Spain. Rajoy agreed, explaining that that 'paradigm of Socialism', Rodríguez Zapatero, was not much help. He had persistently refused at first to accept that a recession loomed. Later, the packet of reforms presented by the now compulsorily retired Pedro Solbes were 'weak' and 'non-productive'. Public spending, according to Rajoy, was out of control. Where other members of the Union were busy excising unnecessary Ministries, ZP has increased Spanish ministries from twelve to seventeen. Rajoy asked delegates to calculate the cost of this extravagance to the public purse.

The conservative conference voted officially to denounce the 'incapacity' and 'passivity' of the PSOE administration in confronting the crisis.

In one of those ironies that we hardly notice these days Barroso, the Commissioner for New Technologies Vivianne Reading, and Secretary-General of the *Partido Popular* Antonio López met in a luxurious, supremely capitalistic hotel recently opened in Warsaw, built right opposite Stalin's Palace of Science – an exercise in aesthetic gloom. The European Elections approach rapidly, and the forces of the Central Right and the Right were assembling to discuss electoral policy and campaigns.

Rajoy lost no time in disqualifying ZP altogether, for lack of zest, self-pity; shutting himself up in the Moncloa Palace only admitting the closest of toadies, only appearing in public at rallies of his own Party (where iron socialist discipline denies barracking), and (such a change!) using his vice-presidents to confound or try to confound the Opposition's attempts to encourage direct confrontation with the ongoing crisis, instead of puffing out the usual demagoguery like an exhausted steam engine.

Spain has sadly spent the last twelve months admitting the heaviest weight of unemployed persons in Europe, and for this the seventeen delegations present at the conference decided to denounce her. Fifteen Heads of State or leaders of governments were present in Warsaw.

The delegates lost no time in revealing that unemployment in Spain has reached an average of 17.4%. They 'deplore' the failure of the administration to deal adequately with this Nineteen- Thirtieth figure, and express sympathy with the nearly four million people out of work. They also worry about the thousands of small and medium-sized businesses closing for lack of markets or failing cash-flow.

Rajoy expressed 'wonder' at the passiveness of Zapatero, who in his meeting with Manuel Barraso in Brussels the day before had put it plainly that his answer to the crisis was to throw money at it, putting the country in worse debt. Spain has a deficit of 8% as well as the seventeen percent of unemployment; PIB stands at 1.8 in the first 3 months of this year – 'the worst figure for 50 years'. Trying to be practical, Rajoy proposed extreme austerity all round, concentrated in governmental administration, and better 'cohesion between departments, supported by finer understanding between Agriculture, Dairy Farming and Fisheries. He urged the continued independence of the Central European Bank, and clarified his view that it is the smaller and medium-sized businesses that will, by their united efforts, heave Europe out of the recession.

Meanwhile, unemployment figures are there to be seen: Holland has the lowest in the European Union – 2.8%. Austria comes a good second – 4.5%. Romania and Bulgaria are among the lowest too, with 5.8 and 5.9% respectively. Great Britain stands at 6.6% and rising. Germany has 7.6%. France- 8.8%. Lithuania has 15.5%, Letonia 16.1%, and Spain holds the questionable privilege of having the largest percentage of unemployed = 17.4%. It is worth noting that the Canary Islands' disgraceful figure stands at 24% at the time of writing.

1ST JUNE

Eighteenth of June in Europe: only one candidate for the EU Presidency showing right now . . .

Elections for seats in the European Parliament will take place between 4 and 7 June. Campaigns have been bursting out all over Europe for the last three weeks, some furious, some mild and. But on 18 June, leaders of all the 27 will meet to thrash out what might be a delicate dilemma: who will preside over the European Commission for the next five years? The way things stand at present, it seems that on 19 June José Manuel Barroso will know for certain that he has been re-elected. According to the world press, this certainty will be popular with the Portuguese himself; he has made no secret of the fact that he would like to carry on. If that is, the forthcoming elections maintain the European Popular Party (José Manuel Barroso) in top position.

At the time of writing, Barroso is the only candidate, though others may pop out of the hat while this newspaper goes to print and finds its way to the newsstands. If Barroso stays the only candidate, to a certain extent it will make things easier, less suspenseful. Right now, European socialists have been unable to persuade any of their number to stand against him.

The experts have estimated, however, that following an (almost secure) poor turn-out for the election of the Euro-Deputies, anything could happen on the nineteenth. A spokesman said, "though the socialists have no candidate at present, it is quite evident that if the elections should return more socialists than members of the European conservative parties, the Left will apply all its skills in finding a way to remove Barroso".

One of the little problems with this statement is the scarcity of socialist administrations among the Twenty-Seven. The most significant are the Spanish, the British and the Portuguese Labourites, but each is backing

Barroso, however odd this may seem to those of us who do not understand politics – probably the majority of voters come into this category across Europe these days. How could the enormous population of the European Union understand politics, when the subject is hardly ever taught in ordinary schools?

The French, doubtless because they are French, don't want to make things easy for Barroso. French socialists are clamouring for a swing to the Left in the Presidency of the Commission. But again, in true Gallic manner, their un-proposed but popular candidate is Danish Poul Nyrup Rasmussen, who is the actual of the European Socialists. The French do not seem to want to push their own Madame Ségolène forward, for reasons of their own.

Even Rasmussen (not to be confused with A.F. Rasmussen, the actual Danish prime Minister who is a Liberal) is not seen as much cop by European socialists as a whole, but he is the only Labourite who might collect some of the Deputies' votes.

The personal dilemma for the actual President of the Commission is not in fact the result of the nearing election, but how political balance throughout the Twenty-Seven will be affected by it. Returning to France for a moment, Barroso is said to feel that if a Motion of Censure is put up against M. Sarkozy in France in the near future, as seems likely, he, Barroso, will be made to play the part of scapegoat. Recently, the French President appears to have passed from enthusiastic support for Barroso to a more conditional one. And then there are the Irish. And then there is the Lisbon Treaty . . . where things are not cloudy, they are muddy, and very few, if any political commentators seem anxious to predict anything concrete.

Five years ago the situation was quite distinct. Then, the Portuguese politician came to the Commission as prime minister of his own country in a bad moment of crisis, and few people thought he would be elected to the top position in Europe. Now, in June 2009, it would not be unreasonable to suppose that José Manuel Barroso will be victorious again – though the question hangs dully in the air – who cares?

14TH JUNE

The European Elections: swinging – where?

Results of the elections for the European Parliament and Commission were roughly what the press and opinion polls had predicted: the socialists lost heavily everywhere, including Great Britain and Spain. In Britain, Gordon Brown's Labour Party became the third power in Britain's sphere in Europe; the second most-voted-for group turned out to be the British National Party (BNP), which is neither Nazi nor fascist, an illusion fostered by the British press and of course the Labourites themselves. But the BNP *is* decidedly against immigration and foreign labour in the UK, and has little respect for any Labourite or Conservative.

A violent reaction set in the day after the elections in Britain. Crowds of skinheads and worse hustled, whistled, surrounded, and heckled members of the BNP. Once again there were heavy and heady reminders of Britain in the Thirties of the 20th century.

In Spain the PSOE gained twenty-one seats in Strasbourg against the PP's twenty three, not a huge difference, but most journalists considered this a major victory at last for beleaguered Mariano Rajoy, leader of the Popular Party. One of his leading spokesmen, when asked if the European results would lead to a vote of censure (no confidence) in Congress against the PSOE, said this was ridiculous and what is more, unnecessary: "The results of this European Election are in themselves a vote of censure,' he said.

Not unexpectedly, Mr Rodríguez Zapatero, much miffed by the obstreperous reaction of the Spanish public, who should know they must *always* vote for the PSOE . . . utterly refused to make any official comment whatsoever on the 23 – 21 result. In the Senate, when pressed, he sniffed: 'you had better go ahead and enjoy your little victory.' No-one really expected anything else from ZP. Losing the European Elections to the main

Opposition party is as unreal to this pathetic man as anything else in real life, such as the worst unemployment figures in the Union, and the pressing need to raise taxes yet again as apparently the only means of struggling out of the crisis. This writer is seriously beginning to doubt ZP's overall sanity. On the one hand he directs matey judges to search for and find suitable corruption cases against important members of the Popular Party (a useful and easily-made smokescreen) and on the other he takes no heed of anything happening in his own party, where corruption and construction run so closely together across Spain that we will need to invent a new composite word to describe it – '*corruption*', maybe? One of his friendliest judges, Garzón, is about to be hauled up before the most senior court in Spain on serious charges, but we cannot print a comment on this from Zapatero because he never makes one. Spain is going through a peculiar time indeed.

One of the victims of the socialist disaster, we are very glad to report, was the awful Leire Pajín. The ex-Secretary of PSOE Party Organisation has said she is eager to become a Senator. This is probably a reaction to certain words uttered by Mr José Blanco, who used to have that job before he became this week's Minister of Development (*Fomento*). After the disaster of the Election became clear, Mr Blanco blandly remarked that he would have to take over his old job again, as the socialists' campaign had obviously been badly handled. "Only a joke! (*¡es broma!)*" he said, perhaps too rapidly. Anyone who knows the Spanish people (and their subtle language) well, knows that when a Spaniard says, '*¡es broma!*' after a strong or pithy comment, he accentuates the fact that what has been said is very far from being a joke . . . that it is, in fact, entirely true.

But will Leire Pajín be allowed to become a Senator? Quite a lot of the present lot have said that if Pajín is let in they will leave; including socialists. This is not because they don't think she is good enough to enter the senior debating chamber. The reason for the Senators' animosity became painfully true during the lead-up to the European Election. *Srta.* Pajín is a bitter-eyed, bitter-tongued young woman with a bitter face and a bitter expression. She will go a thousand miles away rather than cooperate or collaborate with anybody. No Senator likes the possibility of being seated next to her, for fear her hatred might become contagious. During one of his pre-Election speeches to his own party, Mr Mariano Rajoy said, 'Spain does not need any more *Pajines*'.

14TH JULY

L'Aquila: Zetapé as second-best supporting actor

As the reader knows, the most powerful (and richest) nations on Earth have just had one of their family reunions – always graced with the letter 'G' before a number – 'G8', 'G14,' 'G20', 'G27' etc. President of the Spanish government José Luis Rodríguez Zapatero (known to most of the Spanish press as 'Zetapé' or 'ZP') managed to squiggle in and have his say in the 'G' meeting which took place in this ancient Italian cathedral town. What he said will cost the Spanish taxpayer 500 million *euritos* plus another little sum he thought he would throw in to please the Pope and Mr Berlusconi. The unemployed will be gratified that they have no income from which the Government can screw taxes to back up Mr Zapatero's words.

Though most observers thought very little of the results of the binge, the important men and women present were able to discuss infant feeding resources (there goes Spain's 500 million) and safety. Poor Zetapé's problem is that Spain, must to his chagrin, is a member neither of the G8 nor the G20, partly because of her astonishing unemployment rate, and, it must be confessed, because it is no secret that other world leaders do not pay much attention to anything promised by Spain's President of the Government. This might be because the same afore-mentioned observers think Zapatero speaks with a false tongue. His minions are at this moment negotiating a deal with the PSOE government in Cataluña which will end with that region receiving a huge sum (3,600 million euros) during the year from the national budget, while other regions (by which I mean regions not ruled by the PSOE) will have to struggle by (as far as government grants are concerned) with a couple of *céntimos* and a signed photograph. Even Andalucía, another *gran feudo* of the PSOE, will have to crawl along with a thousand million less than Cataluña, because Catalan votes are the mainstay of the present Administration.

Another nagging tooth is that what appeared to be mutual admiration between Mr Obama of the United States and ZP immediately after the former's election as President has now softened down to a vapid smile of recognition when and if the cameras flash. The reason for this might be the Spanish President's apparent confusion between reality and his own media projection – a wide smile, a quip, unanswered questions; votes, votes, votes. But the photo call in Italy with Barack Obama has also cost the Spanish taxpayer another 40 odd million euros because Zetapé grandly informed Pope Benedict (the Vatican is after all a part of Italy) during the conference that Spain would pay for the restoration of the great fortress of L'Aquila, because it was built at the orders of Carlos V. *That* gentleman was not only Holy Roman Emperor - he was the King of Spain too. So Zapatero informs the Spanish taxpayer that he and she will be paying for re-construction of a medieval building in Italy. One can only pray that the architect will not be *el señor* Calatrava. One dare not imagine what Santiago Calatrava would do to a medieval fortress, given enough cement, glass and steel. Perhaps a hundred foot beak emerging from the battlements? Meanwhile 800,000 Spaniards are being fed by the Church's Caritas organisation. Thank God for the Church, incidentally seen by the atheist administration of Spain as one of its worst enemies, despite the 800,000 grateful lunchers.

While the countries that at present really count in our global pleasures and pains go ahead, Spanish diplomacy is at its lowest ebb; a second-best supporting role indeed. But Mr Zapatero does not seem to notice. He used soundbites like 'now is the hour of Spain!' to the evident surprise of some delegates, who might have thought that a European state with nearly 20% unemployment should not be making offers of vast sums of money in food aid for children, but spending the cash on generating employment. Naturally, ZP claims this is being done, but the growing dole queue might not believe it. Mr Zapatero said, when elected by the people in 2004, that he intended to 'put Spain well and truly on the world map'. Historians found this difficult to swallow because Spain has already been present on the world map for centuries. Spain under Roman Law was one of the most important of all Roman possessions. The Moors did not own half Spain for eight centuries for nothing.

Germany: dog eats dog

It is enough to make poor Angela Merkel sweat; two of the greatest and most historical names in motor-car manufacture, hype and sales have apparently lost control of the wheel and are heading towards the precipice. They are Porsche and Volkswagen. VW is Europe's biggest car manufacturer: you can see a Volkswagen in any street in every country in the world. The 'Beetle', an example of which probably all our readers have at one time or other owned, was designed (just to make things complicated) by Ferdinand Porsche. He had to wait until Adolf Hitler agreed that a small, well-built, reliable four-seater with an engine where the boot should be was just the ticket for a new Germany – the Third Reich. At the unveiling ceremony the Führer himself presented the Beetle to an admiring crowd. With him on the podium were all the gang. It was to be a great moment for German industry. The factory and head offices were in Wolfsburg, Lower Saxony. The little car was to become emblematic of Teutonic industrial strengths: well-designed, efficient, methodical, perhaps slower than one would wish, but by no means sluggish; certainly conservative.

But VW means not only the Golf and Passat and all the other successful models today; VW owns Skoda (originally from Czechoslovakia), Seat (originally Spanish), the magnificent, super-fast and luxurious Audi (the S8 is one of the world's fastest saloon cars, with a price that only the super-rich would not gasp at), and (for God's sake how did it happen?) – Bentley, one of the world's most prestigious cars. The waiting list for your new Bentley Continental (cost: 250,000 euros and upwards) is around three full years – even in the middle of a recession.

In the upper regions of the upmarket we find Porsche. Their 911 has been the most successful of all true sports cars. From the engine comes a siren shriek that makes knowledgeable young men across the planet put their mobile telephone down and mutter, "that's a Porsche!". Based in Stuttgart, the company started out as a specialist (and expensive) sports car maker, and still is. While other specialist manufacturers were vanishing, Porsche were racking up the profits. I read that Porsche shares shot up from an average €20 in 2001 to €186 in 2007. The boss is wonder-man Wendelin Wiedeking. It is said in New York that the problem lies here; Porsche was not only selling highly priced wheels to investment bankers, but the company believed it could do business the same way. *Big* trouble. We must go back a little. The connecting link was an engineer called Ferdinand Porsche, who worked for Daimler-Benz in the 1920s. Daimler-Benz took no notice of Ferdinand's idea of a small car, preferring to continue the line of elegant limousines called Mercedes. Only Hitler, as already mentioned, would listen, and listened again a little later when Ferdinand designed the Tiger tank for the 2nd World War. After the War Ferdinand found himself in clink and spent nearly two years as a suspected 'war criminal'. After he was released he found his son Ferdinand, known (luckily) as 'Ferry', hard at work in Austria on a sports car design for something called the 356. Money was available from the royalties received by father Ferdinand for the original Beetle design, and the first Porsche sports cars began attracting the kind of attention they always have attracted since the 1950s.

It is difficult to imagine the tortuous relations between the Porsche and Volkswagen empires, but I can mention that Ferdinand's daughter married a lawyer from Vienna called Anton Piech, and that *their* son (confusingly called Ferdinand too) is now chairman of VW. Then a third generation Porsche called Ferdinand (what a surprise!) designed the world-famous 911. The majority of the shares in the company are owned by members of the Porsche and Piech families Though it seemed at the time a ridiculous ambition that could only end in ignominy, the twin families decided they would capture the Volkswagen Empire. In the year 2008, VW had sales of €100 billion, while Porsche at Stuttgart managed *only* €8 billion. Nevertheless, around four years ago Porsche bought 20% of Volkswagen. Wiedeking said this was not an offensive, but a *defensive* move at the time, as VW supplied many of the parts used in Porsche cars. Motoring correspondents said the purchase was about as defensive as Adolf's invasion of Poland.

Meanwhile, as the years crept by, Porsche kept on buying VW shares until at the beginning of this year they owned more than 50% of VW, with added options to buy another 20%.

13ᵀᴴ AUGUST

Bulgaria: an extraordinary fellow (royal too)

Simeon of Saxe-Coburg-Gotha (born in Sofía, Bulgaria in 1937 was the last King to reign in his country. He ascended the throne of this much-troubled nation in 1943 at the age of eight, in the middle of the Second War. Only three years later, thanks to the carving up of Europe and Asia by Churchill, Stalin and Roosevelt (the last-named actually dying) at the end of the War, he started an exile that lasted a little longer than the Communist regime that ruled his country under the baleful surveillance of the USSR.

There is a close connection with Spain, in that ex-King Simeon lived there for 50 years and in many ways is more Spanish than Bulgarian, but in 2001, leading his own party (the Simeon II National Movement), he drew more than enough votes in his country to become leader of the party *and* Prime Minister. The occasion was unique and historical, the first and only case of a dethroned monarch returning to direct his country's fortunes as PM.

Simeon was premier until 2005, a notable feat considering he is his nation's chief toff and carries a triple-barrelled surname shared, incidentally, with that of the husband of Queen Victoria. The other feat, apart from sheer survival, was that during his stint as premier he achieved what he set out to do, which was to get Bulgaria into the EU. Now, perhaps thankfully for his family and friends, he lives in retirement, comparatively content, surrounded by a huge family.

Simeon of Bulgaria married a Spanish lady called Margarita Gomez-Acebo in 1962, after studying at the French Lycée in Madrid. There are five children and (at the last count) eleven grandchildren. The oldest is Kardam (48), known in the family as 'K1'. Kardam married doctor/scientist Miriam Hungría, with whom he has two children, Boris and Beltrán. In August last year Kardam experienced a disastrous traffic accident which left him in a coma for several weeks. His medically expert wife (she is a haematologist) declares that he has now recovered, though there are speech difficulties.

Second son is Kyril (47), a clever man who read Physics at Princeton, but now works in the banking sector in London. Kyril married a professor of the History of Art called Rosario Nadal. They have three children, Mafalda, Olympia and Tácilo. Following the tradition of starting each of Simeon's sons' first name with the letter K, the third son is called Kubrat (45). He is a surgeon (they *are* a talented lot), and is married to Carla Royo-Villanova (the Spanish connections are ever-present), and they have three children: Mirko, Lucas and Tirso. Son number four is called Konstantin who is 46. He is a director of the Rothschild branch in Madrid. His marriage with María García de la Rasilla has produced twins, Humberto and Sophie. The youngest in the family is also the only daughter, called Kalina. She is 39 and married to explorer and adventurer Antonio Muñoz – sometimes known as *Kitín*. They have come full circle by naming their four-year old son Simeon.

Simeon and Margarita live in an uncomfortable but not unimposing villa in Vrana, a suburb of Sofía. Taken over by the Communists following the War, this near-castle was returned to the royal family in 1998. Surrounded by a small forest, the house was built by Simeon's grandfather, King Fernando 1, who planted at least 300 saplings in the immediate vicinity. Most of these have now become huge trees that dwarf even the three-storied mansion, now just over one hundred years old.

During the forced Communist regime, Vrana became a film studio used for making Bulgarian propaganda films to re-educate the people. We have the same system in Spain in this part of the 21st century. It is called the *Memoria Historica*. During Simeon's apparently interminable exile, part of the royal home was damaged or destroyed, and remains in ruins, perhaps as a not unsinister reminder to Simeon of his fifty - year stint as an ex-monarch.

Germany: Hitler as artist

It might be that the younger among our readers did not know that Adolf Hitler was not only the Chancellor of his country, a housepainter and the direct or indirect cause of more than 50 million deaths between 1939 and 1945; he was also the painter of more than seven hundred and twenty known pictures and sketches. Given the state of modern education, it is also perfectly possible that many of our younger readers do not know who Adolf Hitler was either, but that is neither here nor there. What can you do? Modern education in Britain includes no teaching of the alphabet, and so little basic grammar that most Britons born after 1980 are effectively illiterate. As far as History goes, a few memorable dates, a dozen or so kings and queens, a Reform Act or two and Charles I's head chopped off by Cromwell. That will do; which is why the modernists in education have ensured that few children know about Hitler or even the Second World War – unless their grandparents or great grandparents have been talking.

According to a report on the *Daily Telegraph*'s website recently, three watercolours By Adolf Hitler showing cottages, old mills and churches nestling in the countryside are to be auctioned today September 5 at Weidler's auction house in Nuremberg.

Kerstin Weidler of the old-established auctioneers says that they are very 'neutral' paintings, whatever that means, and adds that 'Hitler never made it into the Academy of Fine Arts'. The watercolours are dated from 1910 and the year after, and originate from Vienna (Hitler *was* Austrian by the way, children) where Adolf spent several of his younger years trying to be a successful commercial artist. In this task he did not prevail, so he joined the Army and fought in the first Wars to End all Wars, an interesting international conflict for it ended the civilised world as it was then known, and ushered in the worst century in the history of mankind. Although the precise number of works by Hitler known to be in existence is not known, Weidler tells us experts have reckoned there are 723 paintings plus sketches extant, which seems to be a pretty precise figure. The auction house expects a 5-figure sum for each of the paintings up for auction, and they are probably quite right. Paintings by Winston Churchill, more or less of the same quality as those of his arch-enemy (Churchill was Britain's PM during the 2nd War, children), sell very well when you can find an auction of his works – no easy task. Ms. Weidler says that the sort of people who buy Hitlers usually have an academic interest in the man himself, or wish to own a painting that can never lose value. Neither Churchills nor Hitlers lose value. This should jerk modern educators at ministerial level into realising that History *does* mean something after all.

If there *are,* among our younger readers, some who would like to know a bit more about Adolf Hitler, you could make a good start by buying a DVD recently released called *Valkyrie,* which will tell you what Hitler's Wehrmacht generals thought of their leader by 1944, and explain what happened to those officers when everything went wrong with their plot. In addition, try Antony Beevor's two books *Stalingrad* and *Berlin: the downfall.* For Heaven's sake, if you really are a scholar, why not trying getting through a translation (unless you are actually German, which will make the task easier) of Hitler's own book, called *Main Kampf,* composed during and after his imprisonment (in 1923) in Germany between the wars. What happened between 1939 and 1945 guaranteed the near- ruin of Britain, the vanishing of her Empire, and the triumphant ascendance of the only two world powers – the USA and Soviet Russia.

Scotland

With August came the festivals, to Scotland that is, where recessions are not usually permitted to affect the International, the Fringe, the Book, the Jazz, the Television or even the Politics Festivals. Oh and there is a Tattoo in there somewhere as well. I am not sure if this means a *military* tattoo (marching, gun-hauling by large horses, martial music etc) or the scratching of inks in an artistic manner on your shoulder, bicep or male cleavage.

Devolution for Scotland is now enjoying its tenth anniversary, and total separation from England draws nearer, much to Alex Salmond's delight. His Scottish National Party has been in a minority administration since May 2007. Does the thought of the break-up of the United Kingdom worry the English? I expect some of the latter will be tearing their hair, but not many. Might it not worry some Scots? The idea of the separation enthused members of the SNP so much that when they won by a majority of one the major part of the 129 seats in Holyrood; their first reform was to order a regiment of painters, scaffolders and sign-writers to change the words 'Scottish Executive' outside and inside all public buildings in Edinburgh to 'Scottish *Government*' (my italics). The Scottish section of the BBC in London, for instance, use the word 'government' in their daily news programmes, not bothering to clarify which government they are talking about – the government of Scotland or that collection of expense-defrauding MPs who are vulgar to each other in a neo-gothic building in Westminster. It is true that the same Scottish BBC teams occasionally make a scathing reference to 'the Westminster Government', rather as if the people from Munich were to talk of 'the Berlin Government'. "You know who I mean," the Scotsmen say, "those foreigners down there . . ." looking grimly southwards.

By 'those foreigners' they mean the Prime Minister and his Cabinet of the United Kingdom of Great Britain and Northern Ireland. Bizarrely enough the Prime Minister they refer to as a 'foreigner' is a Scot himself. Never mind. If Scottish BBC imagines Mr Salmond is grateful for this kind of appeasement, they are sadly mistaken. He recently said that he wants to do away with all London-produced programmes for Scotland, and replace them with bulletins produced in Glasgow - one presumes using announcers who speak and understand Glaswegian. This would give them a 'Scottish perspective' on the news, says Mr Salmond.

Did the reader know that Queen Elizabeth II is also 'Queen of Scots', as in 'Mary, Queen of Scots'? This title had not been used much until revived by David Steel (Lord Steel of Aikwood), the first presiding officer of the Scottish Parliament. Alex Salmond thinks this is just fine because he wants to maintain 'the Union of the Crowns', if not any political unity. Does the reader also know that a special commission has been set up to examine the actual powers of the Scottish Parliament? The Committee was slow to start work because they discovered that many Scotsmen do not, themselves, know what powers their Parliament has, and others simply did not care. Anyway, the Calman Commission recommends some 'transfers of authority' from Westminster to Holyrood, including giving Scotland increased responsibility for the raising and spending of its own tax revenue. Again, Mr Salmond, who sees himself as a reincarnation of Sir William Wallace, is, as the Daily Mail says, 'thrilled'.*

In fact Salmond is already working on the type of ballot paper he will use in the referendum on separation he has every intention of holding. The fact that his own Scottish Parliament has turned this idea down will not deter Mr Salmond. As separation is not actually on the agenda for most Scots, Mr S. will have his work cut out. He is clever enough however to word the ballot paper in such a way that the referendum does not ask for complete national approval of a separate state *outside* the United Kingdom. It merely asks for permission to open negotiations with London which might lead to independence for Scotland.

The majority of British newspapers, especially those successful London dailies that carry special Scottish editions, such as the *Times,* the *Telegraph* and the *Mail* seem to live in a world apart on the independence issue, indeed on anything that might be newsworthy that occurs in Scotland. For example, though the first swine 'flu cases were reported in Scotland, it was not considered important until someone in London caught the disease.

So the polls tell us, and everyone seems to agree, that the Union engendered by making James VI of Scotland into James I of the United Kingdom *is in no danger.* But it is also true that there are powerful forces at work (on both sides of the Border) that intend to undermine it. If there still *are* any ardent Unionists, both Scottish and English, they had better work a bit harder, and stop the constant appeasement of the separatists.

*It is devoutly to be hoped that Mr Salmond does not die in the same manner as Sir William.

15TH SEPTEMBER

Britain: Gordon Brown's Fifth Column

I believe the expression 'fifth column' was first used at the beginning of the Second World War. It meant the intentional placing or leaving of subversive elements by the enemy, in a nation with which the latter is at war. In 1939/1940, for instance, the War Cabinet considered any Italians, Germans or indeed, Russians (after the Stalin/Hitler Pact) resident in Britain or Northern Ireland potential spies. Hundreds of these unfortunates, the great majority of whom had lived in Britain peaceably and peacefully for generations, suddenly found themselves behind barbed wire; Londoners fond of Italian cooking lost their favourite spaghetti joints overnight. Japanese who had been doing their own version of Chinese laundering could not hang up their washing on any line- Siegfried or Maginot.

In Occupied France, the Wehrmacht were bothered by the Resistance, a form of fifth column. In Germany itself, a madman broadcast his fifth column efforts on the radio, greatly amusing the British population with his accent – "This is *Chairmany* calling, *Chairmany* calling; this morning the Chairman air force shot down four hundred and fifty Spitfires and Hurricanes over the English channel!" I was a very small boy then, but I remember our Mrs Mop tut-tutting "Ooh, how he do go on! We aint *got* that many 'planes anyways!" After the War the British got hold of 'Lord Haw-Haw' and strung him up as a fifth columnist of the first order.

If David Cameron wins the next general election, he will not only see Mr Brown off the premises (and about time too), but he will be forced to do something about the vast fifth column the latter has been busy installing in Britain ever since his ex-boss Mr Blair woke up one morning in 1997 at Number Ten, Downing Street.

It is estimated that Brown has arranged for between seven hundred and eight hundred thousand mates, cronies, placemen, confidants and stooges –

all card-holding members of the Labour Party – to sit on committees and quangos from end to end in the United Kingdom.

It would not be going too far to say that these invented and unelected quangos look like a list of names consisting entirely of Blairites and Brownites. Their power is formidable. They represent, as a London journalist recently said, 'Labour's stay-behind fifth column'. They must not be under-estimated by Cameron. Nor must their threat. They are totally opposed to the Tory reform programmes, and will do everything and anything to thwart them. That is their job. That is why they are there. And there are more than 1600 of them in full operation at this moment.

Mr Cameron has promised the electorate 'change'. At the last Tory Conference he used the 'ch' word twenty times in one speech. He has told Barack Obama that if elected he will start a total transformation of government in Britain. Americans, much bemused and somewhat horrified by 'modern Britain', hope he means it.

According to the papers, Britain's people are 'fed up to the back teeth' after twelve years of 'New Labour', and the 'smug, arrogant and largely unaccountable class' now in charge of everyday life in Britain: bureaucracy, the endless network of agencies, the control freaks grasping most of national life from exams to hospitals. All of this is organised down to the last infuriating detail by the committees and quangos.

In 1997 Blair, surrounded as he always been by malevolently clever *politicos*, wasted no time in shoving out the Party's yesterday men and replacing them with toadies. He effectively destroyed the only political forum ever able to control, pacify or rectify the shouts, mumblings and groans in the House of Commons; his politically-motivated destruction of the House of Lords will be one of the things Blair will be remembered for. In previous centuries he would have lost his head for it. But it gets worse: at the same time as he threw out the aristos with no axe to grind, he and Gordon created the quangos – armed with much sharper axes. There were times when London newspapers compared the two Bs' Machiavellian actions with Soviet purges. At the end of 1997, the Tories were calling for an independent enquiry into why experienced and trustworthy members of National Health Boards were being removed, only to be replaced by Labour councillors and weak parliamentary candidates.

30TH SEPTEMBER

Some views on Little Britain, an Election in Germany, Giscard and what is left of Spain

Will Mr. Cameron, should he win the next election in some seven months' time, be able actually to *do* something with what the American magazine *Newsweek* chooses to call 'Little Britain'? Will he be able to pull the country out of the mire like Margaret Thatcher did in a similar situation? Ronald Reagan did the same with an ailing United States. But the UK in 2010? After twelve years of Blair/Brown, the British people have had their morale lifted a tidge by the news that the stock market is recovering. Good, but the fact remains that 'Little Britain' has the worst public finances of any similar western economy. Unemployment spreads across the land like a stagnant pond. The Army, not long ago lauded as being the best (not the biggest) in the world will shortly be recalled from Afghanistan. Where does Britain stand among the nations of the world? Following the dreadful 'oil-for-Megrahi' mistake, the United States sees Britain as a third-rate, untrustworthy, ex-*fiancé*. The *New York Daily News* has famously said, 'Gordon Brown has given grounds to believe today's British are a cowardly, unprincipled, amoral and duplicitous lot: because he is all of those.' An exaggeration of course, but one sees what the writer means. The sadness is that, in 1997 at least, Britain stood a very good chance of becoming Great again. The Labour Party crashed into Parliament with a huge majority, the good wishes of the people, and a fine chance of staying there for at least two terms, improving everything in sight. What happened?

The two and half million on incapacity benefit were neglected, while imported immigrants were brought in to fill (almost) the three million jobs created. Savage surgery could have been performed on the cumbersome National Health Service, but instead, taxpayers' pounds were used to create a gigantic bureaucracy that now costs around £40 billion per year. The Government did nothing about the transport system, except allowing 'Pride with Prejudice' Prescott to carve his own personal empire and abandon his own promised 'integrated transport system'. Children who have spent their entire school life under Labour now join the dole queue, or their workmates if they are lucky – almost illiterate and innumerate. The country has to make do with an enormously costly public sector lapping up a fortune today and leaving £1 trillion in pension liabilities for our children to cope with tomorrow. Labour inherited a fortune and squandered it. According to the National Institute for Economic and Social Research our national debt is going to double, and the interest payments will cost more than the cost of educating the children or defending the islands.

Britain amazed the world after 1979, but the current situation is much worse. The right kind of leadership from the right kind of person will be desperately needed from early next year. Will David Cameron be able to provide it? As a prominent political magazine has it – 'Britain's future now depends on the answer'.

An Election in Germany

Chancellor of Germany Angela Merkel was re-instated by the German people, though she will have to rule by making pacts. Her party won just 33.6% of the vote, while the Liberal Party (FDP) obtained 14.7%. Merkel announced on the day of election (September 27) that she would soon be talking with the Liberal leader Guido Westervelle. They will plan what form the new coalition government will take. There is always a shock at election time, and this time round was no exception: The Social Democratic Party under the previous Foreign Minister Frank-Walter Steinmaeir sank without trace, winning under 23% of the vote. Merkel became Chancellor in 2005 (with 35.2%), but has sunk lower this time, with only 33.6%. It has already been written in the political papers that Guido Westervelle has ascended with his Liberals at Merkel's cost. A substantial number of franchised citizens did not bother to visit their polling station, a European phenomenon seen more and more as this new century painfully reveals that ordinary people are sick to death of politics and politicians.

Valery Giscard D'Estaing

He is eighty-three years old and has an appropriate place in the history of France, and the political construction of a dream called Europe. It is no secret that Giscard played a super-important part in the modernisation of France and Europe, using personal charm and decisive initiative. He was the key mover in the final change to nuclear energy. He took decisions that broke his country's ties with the current Gallic traditions, such as legalisation of abortion, and divorce through mutual agreement.

The Giscard years (1974-1981) massively collided with traditional and conservative France. Now, only seven years separating him from his ninetieth birthday, Giscard is revealed as a Great Lover in the Italian mode. Insisting that it is pure fiction, he has published a *novel* whose protagonist is a world leader who mixes summit meetings with more sensual occupations in bed with 'an English Princess'. The book's description of these two make it blindingly clear that the statesman is Giscard (thirty years ago) and that the 'Princess' is quite alarmingly like the seriously unlucky Diana, Princess of Wales. This is not what the world's press expected from the statesman who created the 'G5', 'G7', the 'SME', the ECU, universal suffrage in the elections of the European Parliament, and the successful French electro-nuclear programme. It would not be going too far to say that the French press, too, is gob struck. Could there be something in it? Giscard had the reputation of a Great Womaniser when he became the youngest ever Finance Minister under de Gaulle in 1962. In 1974, when he was President of France, he famously drove into a tree one night, blowing the horn on his car outside the flat of one of his mistresses. As President, he startled members of the international press by commenting favourably (and loudly) on the beautiful legs of one of his lady Ministers. But this was the man who (with Helmut Schmidt) invented the single monetary system, so he must have spent some time examining important papers of state, not merely ogling lovely legs. Nevertheless, the novel is written and published, and has left an astonished world wondering if there really was a coming together of a French 'emperor' and a possible future Queen of England.

Spain

At last Spain's Finance Minister and her President of the Government have officially announced that their chief weapon of defence against the current recession will be the raising of taxes. Despite Mr Zapatero's promise (watch my lips) some months ago that this would not happen - it will, and it is the Spanish middle class that will bear the brunt. IVA on vehicles and most goods will rise from 16 to 18% from 1 July. In housing and catering it will rise from 7 to 8%. If any Spaniard still has any savings, in the form of income from rented property for example, bank accounts and so on, the IVA from 1 January will make you pay 19% on your income from these investments (up to €6000) and 21% on anything above this sum. The automatic €400 reduction on your earned income tax (IRPF) has now been eliminated.

Most commentators on the current financial scene had hoped that Spain would follow the lead of other countries now emerging from the recession which had decided that the last thing you needed was an increase in taxes. They are sadly mistaken. One of the first 'improvements' made by Zapatero when he had at last admitted that 'there might be a crisis' was the invention of five more Ministries. Does anyone out there know how much a Ministry (buildings, employees' salaries, budgets etc.) costs?

16TH OCTOBER

Five little Russia's

I deal now with Europe as a continent, instead of 'Europe' as a political entity of twenty-seven states. After the collapse of Soviet Russia, five of her satellites became 'democratic' (in their fashion; remember that East Germany used to be called 'the free and independent democratic republic' though it was neither free, nor independent nor democratic). Five presidents govern more or less how they like, drenched with cash which rolls in from their substantial sources of oil and gas. These new nations are the 'Istans' – Uzbekistan, Tayikistan, Kasajistan, Turkmenistan and Kirguizistan. Have you ever noticed them, visited them?

Each republic acknowledges one 'boss', governing 'via' an unelected administration, with each president proceeding from the previous Soviet Russian establishment. An expert spokesman from the Foundation for International Relations and Foreign Dialogue (sic) says: 'they are dictatorships. They have presidencies for life, no democratic elections and the executive does not have to account for itself to 'parliament' either for its political policies or its public spending'.

The strategic position of these five nations, their richness in resources such as oil and gas, and their borders with Russia, Iran, Afghanistan and China mean that the USA, Russia and China maintain a very close watch on these 'Istans', because they have to. At the moment, the influence of Medvedev and Putin's Russia is paramount. The European Union has to keep an eagle eye open too, and intelligence gathering in this eastern zone is at a maximum, though this can prove a dangerous task.

Uzbekistan has a permanent *caudillo* in the bulky form of Islam Karimov and a population of 27 million. His daughter is the country's ambassador to UNESCO. She is distinguished for her work in education and sport, as well as her own undoubted sophistication and glamour. Her father, however, is a typical sovietised iron man, aged 71. He swam up through the Soviet Russian establishment as an economist and mechanical engineer. Despite being closely associated with Gorbachov's *perestroika,* his personal agenda never veered from ultra-Marxism. Nor has he ever allowed scruples to hinder his upward mobility. When he was made President in September, 1991, he maintained and guarded the old echelons of Communist Russia, simply by employing old colleagues in powerful (but not *too* powerful) positions. 'Re-elected' in 2000, he then ignored the rule that a president can serve three times, becoming Leader again in 2007 with the apparent support of *88%* of the 'electorate'. The election was deemed non-democratic by the United Nations' Organisation for Security and Cooperation.

Karimov's repressive, occasionally cruel rule has been excused by the nation's conflicts with Islam (that religion's political party is called Hisb and Tahrir). Harsh treatment of Islam is admired by Americans, especially since 9/11. The US obtained special permission for the establishment of an airbase at Janabad, in return for the usual fistful of dollars. Organisations in the defence of human rights are continually denouncing Uzbekistan on account of the thousands of 'dissidents' kept imprisoned, the presence in the rest of the world (but especially the Spanish islands) of citizens who have left and cannot return, and unjustified control and censorship of the media with the added plus of the widespread use of torture.

Karimov plays double games, relying on a fragile relationship with the US based on business, as well as a strong friendship with Russia, based on common sense. He is wary with the EU, because that organisation sanctioned him in 2005 for the brutal repression of dissidence in the Fergana zone. One third of the population 'live' beneath the poverty line, despite the vast reserves of hydro-carbons. Another daughter, Gulnara, is expected to be named Karimov's successor, though she is at pains to deny this. Uzbekistan, is, like the four other nations featured in this article, a 'Tsardom' in which leadership is inherited.

26TH OCTOBER

Spain: a foregone conclusion

The much heralded Budget 'debate', in the Spanish Cortes was not so much a debate as a waste of time. Spain knew before the parties started their snarling and scratching that the result was a foregone conclusion. Each party in the Congress had declared its voting intention *before* the event. Though most of the marginal, small parties had promised to vote against the PSOE administration and Elena Salgado (Minister of Finance), the Government had been told by their representatives that both PNV (the Basque Country) and CC (the Canary Islands) would vote with the Government whatever happened during the Great Debate. This would give the socialists the tiny but effective majority of six. As it turned out, three more wild cards gave the Government their vote, and the proposed total rejection of the 2010 Budget was thrown out by nine votes.

In the opinion of newspapers not dominated by the PSOE, Mariano Rajoy, president of the Popular Party effectively destroyed Elena Salgado in the Budget Debate. This should have been good news for the PP, but according to Salgado, in one of her many replies (*replicas*) after the Rajoy battering, it was just *machismo*. Thus she played the feminist card, surprising really for a senior minister in a government that insists on equality, even to the extent of having a *Ministry of Equality*. Salgado said that in his speech Rajoy had shown 'an extraordinary lack of respect'.

Perhaps one is being unfair to the lady minister, as everyone knew she had been ordered to represent her ministry and the PSOE, opposing in Parliament the leader of the *Populares,* instead of the President of the Government, who should have done so. It was common knowledge that Elena's long defence of the budget proposals was prepared by José Luis Rodríguez Zapatero and his six hundred advisors. It is also well known that

ZP prefers to delegate anything potentially tricky, or politically dangerous, to any member of his immediate *coterie,* rather than appear himself. It is always Pepe Blanco, Fernández de la Vega, Juan Antonio Alonso, Manuel Chavez, even the under-educated Leire Pajín, who is sent to the Front if the subject is contentious. What ZP likes about being prezzie is the occasional trip abroad to be a statesman. Indeed, immediately after the Budget Debate he was expected at the White House for a remarkably brief exchange of views with Barack Abama (one official dinner; one 30-minute chat in the Oval Room). *This* kind of thing, photographed internationally, is what ZP prefers to long and detailed battles in his country's parliament over small matters like four million unemployed (and rising), and actual poverty beginning to make itself ugly right across Spain. Still, on this occasion, ZP didn't have to stay in a hotel in Washington. A special house for honoured guests of the USA was provided for him near the White House. *Too* thrilling!

Salgado's accusation of *machismo* was intriguing partly because Rajoy in his speeches was not saying much more than an ex-Minister of Finance called Carlos Solchaga had said a few days before the debate. As he is a member of the socialist party one would have expected a reprimand from on high for daring to dispute with the Leader and his Advisors. If such a reprimand was made the newspapers didn't receive the leak. Solchaga actually said that Zapatero never consults his Ministers, nor listens to them. In ZP's opinion (said Solchaga) ministers are mere secretaries, useful enough, but whose opinion is valueless, because all policy is directed by ZP, and dissent is unheard of. Solchaga considers this attitude bad, because certain themes, such as the Economy, require the mind and opinions of experts in that field. No-one in Spain, not even in its reddest corner, sees Zapatero as a financial expert.

In his opening speech Rajoy absolved Elena Salgado of any blame for the appalling mess the proposed Budget reveals. He reminded the House that she was merely echoing her master's voice. It was this that led Salgado to lose control and accuse Rajoy of *machismo.* Someone in the corridors of the Cortes was heard to observe during the debate, referring to Salgado, "it's not her fault, she is inexperienced". Such an odd thing to say about a woman who has spent years in socialist politics, *and* headed other Ministries.

Happy 20th birthday! Two decades since the fall of the Berlin Wall

In 1959, just fifty years ago, I was in Berlin with the British Army. The infamous wall had not yet been built round the whole city, which was divided into four sectors, Russian, American, French and British. Berlin stood geographically to the right/centre of East Germany, or 'The People's Democratic Republic'. The rest of the country had been divided into zones by the victorious Allies following the destruction of the Nazis and suicide of Hitler.

East Berlin was like a small model of East Germany, a Soviet-controlled wilderness where the people unfortunate enough to be have been thus segregated scratched out whatever living they could, while the State erected huge blocks of ugly flats. The British Zone of Berlin was mostly residential, and included part of a navigable river-lake called the Havel, a military airport at Gatow, a very well designed and spacious barracks at Kladow, shopping in Charlottenburg and the Kurfurstendam (itself maintaining a ruined church as a memory of the fall of Berlin), and beautiful parkland. The British also had the great prison at Spandau, where survivors of the War Crimes Tribunal were locked up. The French, despite General de Gaulle's efforts not to, got most of industrialised, rather slummy West Berlin as their zone in the Reinickendorf, Wedding and Jungfernheide. Both the US Zone and their Sector in the city were southerly, residential and blessed with good weather. They also had Tempelhof Airport. The Soviet Sector was singularly larger than the rest of the Allied sectors put together. The East authorities hardly bothered to level unbelievable bomb damage, except for carparks and soviet-style apartment buildings looking as if they had been transferred brick for brick from the new suburbs of Moscow.

This grim atmosphere was somewhat lightened by the fact that soldiers serving in any of the sectors were free (more or less; you had to be in uniform and carry all necessary papers) to visit other sectors. At that time the West Mark was worth nearly three times more than the East Mark. British soldiers would take advantage of this by buying normally very expensive Leica cameras and equipment from eager shopkeepers in the Russian Sector. We could also hear and watch grand opera in the hardly damaged Opera House. Most of the singers were Russian or Polish and in fine voice.

Both Russia and East Germany were at that time anxious, because hundreds of citizens of the People's Democratic Republic wished to join their relatives living in the rapidly recovering western zones and sector, though they were not allowed to. The illusion of the modern, democratic 'good life' brought by Russians to the good burghers of East Berlin, Danzig and Dresden was just that – an illusion. This led to a constant stream of families and professionals such as doctors and architects going West. The Kremlin and Honneker, president of East Germany decided to build a massive wall, and mount guard on it with Russian and East German soldiers and police with orders to shoot to kill when they found men, women or children (sometimes pathetically accompanied by household pets), trying to climb the wall to freedom. To the horror of both sides, the great 155 kilometre wall was built, mostly in 1961.

One of the first escapees was in fact an East German soldier, who, deciding he did not like the implications of the great wall, vaulted over barbed wire on 15 August, with the athletic ease of his 19 years, seeking (and finding) freedom in the Bernaurstrasse. He was much photographed during the feat. After the Wall was finished, people like the 18-year old bricklayer Fechter were shot attempting to repeat young soldier Schumann's escapade, and the photographers were kept busy for years afterwards snapping bleeding corpses. The 'freedom' of the 'Democratic Republic' found expression in the following figures: there were 14,000 frontier guards, armed to the teeth: 3,221 would-be escapers were arrested in the act: there were five thousand successful jumps over the electric fences, guard dogs and wall. Between 239 and 800 (the difference depends on the source) person were killed trying to leave East Berlin: Twenty-seven East German soldiers or policemen died in fire-fights with escapees. Two complete families escaped using hot air balloons. Thomas Krugen flew out in a borrowed light aircraft. Many escaped hidden uncomfortably in motorcars. 70 tunnels were dug, boarded and aired for use by escapers.

Habemos Van Rompuy *and* a Baroness

The European Council is to be graced by Belgian PM Herman van Rompuy as its new president. In the European mishmash, as the alert reader will know, there is a Parliament, a Union, a Council, a Commission and God knows many more Committees, Bureaux and assorted excuses for gathering together groups of over-paid bureaucrats with chauffeurs and all-expenses-paid.

As to whom Herman van Rompuy is, there are a number of ways of seeing this consummate bureaucrat. If you are Belgian, you will be proud that your countryman has been chosen as the first permanent president of the Council, though you will be girding up your loins in expectation of a barrage of criticism oozing out from the rest of the Twenty-Seven. The British press, for instance, has been active since the news broke, demanding to know why this hardly known, grey little prime minister is to become permanent president.

This might be considered odd when at the same time, the Twenty-Seven selected a British lass, the Socialist Baroness Catherine Ashton, as High Representative, and vice-president of the European Commission with responsibilities for foreign policy. But then, the Baroness could be seen through a grey glass darkly, just as much as van Rompuy. When she is speaking publicly, she doesn't sound like a baroness. Actually, the European press finds this secondary appointment as puzzling as the first.

A private Belgian radio station (RTL) reminded us on 21 November that the election of Jacques Delors some years ago was 'unexpected when Delors was not even a grey eminence, just grey, within the ranks of French politicians . . . though the result turned out to be a triumph, as Delors was one of the best presidents of the Commission in history'. (sic) If I remember rightly, Delors got us all into the Single Market, and introduced the idea of the *euro*. Whereas the Italian Romano Prodi arrived with a halo of success as prime minister round his head, and proceeded to a mediocre performance.

Meanwhile The Times remembered that when this 'job' was first designed by Valery Giscard d'Estaing (then president of France) it is likely that he thought it out in terms of himself, which is why the appointment seemed planned for a Frenchman with French ideas and plans.

Some of our readers will be wondering what happened to the Tony Blair candidacy. Do you recall how everyone thought the permanent presidency was just made for ex-prime minister Blair? The press thinks that Blair turned out to be a no-no because he was stabbed in the back (as usual) by British PM Gordon Brown, who has every reason to hate Blair. Whatever the reasons, Mr Blair got nowhere, and will have to continue making highly paid lecture tours in the USA. But at least the loss of Blair meant the ascent of the socialist Baroness Catherine Ashton. One wonders what Catherine did to become a peer? She can't simply have inherited the title, because there aren't any 'inheriteds' in the House of Lords any more. The men and women who inherited centuries of political knowledge and experience were all turfed out by Blair, who needed a second chamber stuffed with toadies.

The dear old reactionary Daily Express howled with pain: 'the European Union should be ashamed of itself! These appointments are a bad joke!' This was a reference to the methods used by the bureaucrats to set up a protocol whereby van Rompuy and Ashton were elected. Van Rompuy himself showed a little spirit, and lost a shade of greyness, when he asked in his first press conference after the appointment if the Daily Express was suggesting his election was similar to the election of a Chinese president?

He went on to claim that the voting system had been democratically organised. Well, of course.

One point made in the press was that a large difference could be seen between the huge European press coverage of the election of Barack Obama as President of the United States, and the minute American presence at van Rompuy's election. This may be explained by the undoubted fact that most Americans, especially in the mid-western states, care little about 'Yurrup', and think 'van Rompuy' is a brand of cigarette. In fact there was more American interest in the socialist baroness, as most Americans 'dearly love a lord,' or a *lady* for that matter.

7TH DECEMBER

Spain: a terrible week for *Zetapé*

Most Spanish newspapers agreed on one thing at least this past weekend: that Mr Zapatero's administration has suffered an awful *week*, what with one thing and another. But then there are several columnists who say that Mr Zapatero's Administration over the last five *years* has been pretty awful anyway. In 2004 the PSOE, as skilful as always, managed to take advantage of a terrorist attack on commuter trains in Madrid that was perpetrated by sheer coincidence a couple of days before the date of a general election. Mr Aznar's administration, acting on advice from its own security services, told the nation the bomb attacks were the responsibility of ETA, the Basque separatist terrorists. If that had been true, nothing would have happened, but the PSOE's brilliant planners moved against the idea, and it was officially announced that the savage terrorist attack was a reprisal committed by Al-Qaeda for Aznar's alliance with George Bush. Logically, therefore, a little more than half of Spanish voters voted against the Popular Party two days after the catastrophe and very shortly afterwards an unknown lawyer from Leon became President of the Government. Typically, he gathered together a group of nonentities (with the exceptions of Solbes and Rubalcaba) to act as his Ministers in the Cabinet.

Mr Rodríguez Zapatero was immediately nicknamed ZP, or Zetapé, standing for '*Zapatero Presidente*'. His mother's surname went into general use. His newly chosen cabinet contained eight women and eight men, greatly satisfying the liberals and equality fans. His new senior vice-president, a most fashionable woman, seized the moment to publish (in *Vogue*) a number of later famous photographs of the eight ladies, dressed superbly by leading designers, posing with nonchalance on the steps of the

Moncloa Palace. Thus, in one stroke, the ideology and policy of the new administration was launched, namely, *appearances*.

Instantly, the PSOE party machine swung into action. While 'government' was left to the *hauts fonctionnaires*, the ministries and spokesmen began the principal task allotted to them by their Leader and Mr. Rubalcaba: that is, to maintain and concentrate a constant barrage of criticism and verbal assault on the largest party in parliamentary opposition (the PP), while promising anything they wanted to the many smaller parties in return for their votes. This has continued for five years, because when their first four-year mandate was over in 2008, the PSOE won again, though without a large majority. There has been a change recently, however: now the PSOE has changed its image, to that of a hard-done-by, bullied schoolchild in the playground, scorned and assaulted by the wicked Popular Party. This has happened because Mariano Rajoy, who leads the latter, suddenly became fed up with the consistent shelling of his positions by the PSOE, and decided to fight back using the same weapons. The PSOE was shocked by such treacherous behaviour.

One of the problems during these five years has been (as eminent journalist José María Carrascal pointed out), the series of highly coloured (and quickly collapsing) balloons floated by this Administration since 2004 as an attraction for voters who do not really care for any party except the PSOE, but who need something to enthuse their flagging spirits. Secret peace negotiations with ETA that led to ignominious nothing; the unjust and possibly unconstitutional Catalan Constitution; the hugely damaging economic crisis not recognised (by ZP, at least) as a crisis at all until it was too late; the inexpert and facile 'sustainable economy' only recently launched, to be demolished instantly by *The Economist* as 'unsustainable'; the impossible and slightly risible 'Alliance of Civilisations' (by which Mr Zapatero means his cuddling up to Cuba, Venezuela, Bolivia, China and of course Mr Putin's Russia); the *Memoria Histórica*, by which Zetapé meant giving his favourite historians the means to re-write History to suit the international Left. Several balloons were released that were not meant to be - surprise balloons as it were - such as the female Moroccan activist intent on starving to death in Lanzarote for political, geographical and geo-political reasons, and the cheeky chappies from Africa kidnapping Spanish fishermen and receiving uncountable and unaccountable ransom in return.

28TH DECEMBER

Socialist Croatia

Social-Democrat Ivo Josipovic has just won, in the first round at least, the presidency of his country Croatia. This Balkan country, along with Serbia, Macedonia, Montenegro, Bosnia and the former Yugoslavia, has been a centre of violence and unrest for centuries. It seems only yesterday that the Balkans were immersed in a pre-medieval battle for power between religionists so appalling that both the European Union and, finally, the United States in the form of UNO, had to intervene, not before thousands of lives were lost, and many more thousands of families were shattered. Josipovic (MP, jurist and acclaimed musician) did not manage to encourage more than 50% of the Croatian population to vote, however. It is estimated that he had convinced between 32.7 and 33% of the voters who bothered to go to the polling stations - not enough to satisfy the rules, which demand a turn-out of more than half the franchised citizens (five million voters). This means a second election or round. Whatever happens, Croatia is in urgent need of an elected President, because she is due to join the Union (much to the disappointment of some of her neighbours).

Josipovic's opponent in the second round on January 10 next year will be the mayor of Zagreb, Milan Bandic, an independent, who obtained 14% of the votes. But another candidate will be present too – Andrija Hebrang (not the easiest names, I confess, to commit to memory). He won some 12%, and represents another socialist group, the Democratic Union of Croatia (DUC). Yesterday's victory for Josipovic will not guarantee a similar victory in the second round. Anything can happen, and there were twelve candidates for the Presidency, which indicates a certain looseness of political acumen in Croatia. The problem seems to be that Josipovic is quite a nice man, moderate, patient, far-seeing, obviously cultured. Rather the same as the leader of the conservatives in Spain, Mariano Rajoy, who is a thoroughly nice chap and all that, but is seen as toothless by many of his confederates in the Popular Party. This is Josipovic's case too. The centre-right is far from being attracted by a toothless musician – however nice he is, and it is said that whoever controls the centre-right in Croatia wins. A journalist in Lubliana wrote, "Ivo has personal charisma, but no political charisma whatsoever," and this would seem to be the case.

It must also be admitted that the Social-Democratic Party rose from the ashes of the Croatian Communist Party, and citizens with long memories will find this difficult to assimilate when the time comes to cast a vote. Meanwhile, Josipovic has promised, as part of his electoral campaign, to fight corruption within and outside politics in Croatia. While almost every politican promises this with the greatest facility in all democratic countries, the new president after January 10 must certainly try. As is traditional in the Balkans, governmental corruption is massive, and will require an unswervingly tough administration to reduce it, or, if humanly possible, remove it altogether. Ivo also promised to adopt the right measures to enable his country to get out of the current depression – but this is easily said – and difficult to achieve. The method used by the president of the government in Spain – simply to ignore the recession and wish it would go away - did not work, and Josipovic would be well advised not to follow the same dreamy path.

If the January president does indeed deal successfully with the recession, Croatia is due to enter the European Community in 2012. The first Croatian democratic president was one Franjo Tudjman, leader of the mildly conservative Croatian Democratic Union. He died in 1999. Second in the job was Stjepan Mesic, an independent backed by centre-left parties. It is this fellow whose mandate is due to expire in January 2010. Each president has five years' service to perform, and most of his daily work is governed by protocol. As in so many central European states, the actual day-to-day governance of the nation is firmly in the hands of the state functionaries, including education, police, food supplies, health and traffic control. Industry is in the rather shakier hands of private individuals, many of whom are no better than they should be, and suddenly find themselves living in retirement in Monte Carlo, or dead in the back of a car; or maybe both.

The conservatives have been in power for almost eighteen years, except for a brief period of socialism between 2000 and 2003.

2010

Italy: Berlusconi puts on his immigrant hunting gear

Having partially recovered from a damaging collision between his face and a sharp object thrown at him on December 13 in Milan, Silvio Berlusconi returned to work as Prime Minister of Italy on January 11. He has spent nearly a month planning a batch of new laws, and has had his considerable energies renewed by surgeons, his family, the comfort of his billions, and, probably, a pretty female or two at his hospital bedside. High on his 2010 agenda are positive reforms in the tax system, justice, and last but not least, the Italian Constitution itself. Some reporters working for newspapers in his country can be heard murmuring 'and about time too!'

On 12 January Silvio left his home in Milan for Rome for a top-level meeting with Giulio Tremonti, his Economics Minister. Then he was off to the Palace for a long conversation with President of the Republic Giorgio Napolitano. Reports tell us that during the first encounter Silvio laid out his suggestions drastic reform of the tax system: during the second, the Prime Minister spoke at length about the *Laudo Alfano,* his amendment to the Constitution which (when passed by Parliament) will give immunity to the top four incumbents in the Government. Again, political wags have wondered aloud why Berlusconi wishes so much to change the Constitution to allow nobody, nor any Body the right to prosecute the President, the Prime Minister and two more of the most senior officials of the State. Immunity means just that. Berlusconi will be immune to prosecution or perhaps even criticism during his period of power, and after it. Might the reason be that Silvio has a bad conscience about various actions of his in the past?

Last year this important but arguable amendment to the Constitution was thrown out on grounds of unconstitutionality, but Silvio's party PDL is about to present an amended draft again – with the 'unconstitutional' bits ironed out, presumably. In this way the Prime Minister hopes to sort out the Opposition, who routed the first draft last year. Working groups within PDL have been working hard on the new draft for the amendment for months. It will be proposed to the Senate tomorrow 12 January. Another task facing *Il Cavagliere* looms large in his agenda; on January 18 he must appear in court in Milan, in connection with the Mediaset Case. The PM is not yet immune from set-backs such as this. He is accused of crooked dealings in broadcasting rights. And there is another case to answer too, as if the Mediaset affair were not serious enough; Silvio is accused in another courthouse of having bribed British barrister David Mills to bear false witness.

Il Cavagliere has got a lot on his plate, but seems enthusiastic enough to see it all through with his usual mixture of bombast and Mediterranean charm. He must deal, for example, with the recent rebellion of immigrants in Southern Italy. During the last week or two, African immigrants living in or near Rosarno (Calabria) have been moved to violent protest and manifestation. The police are supposedly busy too, investigating the whys and wherefores of the disturbance, during which there have been sixty-seven casualties. Six of the latter remain in hospital with grave wounds. In the last few days, hundreds of immigrants have actually been expelled from the region by the police, who claim to be attempting to reduce the tension by removing the 'rebels' from the scene. Local newspaper reports tell us that immigrants are leaving en masse because of threats to their safety made by Calabrian *mafiosos*. Add to this the even greater danger to the immigrants personified by their own Italian neighbours, who appear to be fed up, and manifest this disaffection by physically attacking any African immigrant they can find. Whatever the reason, immigrants are getting out- on foot, by car if they have one, by bus and train. A painful exodus, and Berlusconi is not saying on which side *he* is on, though he has in the past criticised excessive immigration. The press in Rome and other cities have exacerbated the situation by talking of 'a witch-hunt of immigrants'. And now the lady Minister of Education, Maristella Gelmini, does not greatly help Berlusconi's peace of mind by announcing a proposed 30% cut in school places for foreign students in the schools. Nevertheless, Italy is the first state in the European Union to be showing belligerence of a very real nature in the thorny and potentially explosive area of immigration.

24TH JANUARY

Strasbourg: Zapatero speaks to the Euro Camera

Newly installed in his turn as President of the European Union, Spain's José Luis Rodríguez Zapatero, accompanied by his Foreign Minister Moratinos, rose to propose 'A Great Social Pact'. This grandiose idea envisages a coming-together of the Unions and the Corporations, to confront the ongoing crisis and strive towards a more common political policy, helped by what he described as 'a serious and exiguous government'. Zapatero was appearing for the first time in his six-month presidency, with a Plan. His speech was, remarkably for him, noticeably economic in tone. Under normal circumstances, he leaves economics, which he does not understand, to qualified persons. He promised 'an energetic impulse' in common with the other nations of the EU, a 'digital' European market (I don't know quite what that means by that but I have no doubt Mr Moratinos does), new strategies regarding the design and production of electric cars, plus the expansion of European university education, by a process of building construction, the training of more teachers and professors, and the search for renewable energies.

The great majority of European deputies, including the conservative delegation from Spain led by Mayor Oreja, supported Mr Zapatero in his predications and promises; perhaps because they are accustomed (after five years of his presidency of the Spanish government) to his tremendous capacity for making promises. This has always been his style; making unsustainable promises in his role as Great Orator. They are always good soundbites. Nothing ever happens afterwards, but conditions are so pathetic in Spanish politics no-one expects anything else. The deputies pronounced Zapatero's speech 'ambitious', though some more conservative deputies expressed their doubts as to the efficacy of the proposals.

After being criticised in the Euro Camera for Spain's extremely high rate of unemployment (almost 20% of the working population), and therefore his own inappropriateness as President of the EU, Zapatero replied to the offending deputy: "If tomorrow the unemployment rate descends in your country, whoever governs it, my reaction as President of my Government and Europhile would be to support the initiative and provide solidarity – not recriminate as you are recriminating'. We can see no change in Zapatero then; always the viper's lunge, vituperation being his *forte*. We have seen this in Spain all the five years of his presidency, and now European deputies will see it for themselves. In this case Zapatero directed his bile directly against German conservative deputy Werner Langen.

Zapatero went on in Churchillian mode; "If we do not take advantage of the energies bursting to break out within our 500 million citizens in the economic zone, our tens of thousands of businesses, large and small, our millions of workers, and our great capacity for work and study, we cannot become authentic protagonists in any scenario, made urgent by ever-expanding globalisation: indeed, we will become spectators, not protagonists." He clarified that he is backing 'more common economic targets', and promoting the idea of 'breaking down the barriers' – his aim with his 'objectives for 2020'. He also made it clear that he intends during these six months to challenge what he calls 'the Lisbon Strategy', as well as promising 'growing prosperity' in the years that will follow his semester as President.

Talking of the responsibility of each of the Twenty-Seven, Zapatero said he would opt for new methods of preventing economic crises within countries, such as those from which most states are now emerging. Spain, 'the moaners' point out, is not among them. The new European president did not talk of sanctions – those sanctions publicly refused by the German minister of finance – but he did wish to record that applied sanctions already exist in the Union, and that will need to be properly coordinated. He also warned of the growing economic might of countries like India and China.

Angela convinces nobody in Germany

Shortly after celebrating her first hundred days in the re-elected government on Germany, Angela Merkel has discovered that the people do not much admire her new coalition. On this occasion she chose to form a pact with the Young Liberals, under their not very young leader Wolfgang Schäuble. The press in general thinks the coalition unpredictable and unsure of what it is doing. In Zurich, an infantile but popular 'Wanted' poster has appeared accusing Merkel and Schäuble of 'bank robbery and concealment of stolen goods'

In the year 2005, Merkel's Democratic Christian Union linked arms with the Bavarian Christian Socialists *and* the Social Democratic Party (all socialist in creed and intention) – and together they found success, if not true love. The leadership was tranquil, social stability and sustainable economic reforms abounded, and a firm and admired international stance was adopted.

Above all, *that* coalition was able to unburden Germany of the obstinate left-wing and bright green legacy left by both Schröder and Fischer. In fact things were going so well that Angela was able, to a certain extent, to go it alone. Her 'friends' in the SDP began to howl that she was taking all the credit, but they cannot have shouted loud enough. In politics, once empowered by the people's vote, many leaders, if not all, become strangely deaf. In present day Spain, for instance, the only Spaniard in the whole country who doesn't know that Mr Zapatero is inept and floundering is Mr Zapatero – but that is only because he cannot hear, and he makes sure he is encircled by toadies.

In Germany now, 100 days after the elections which maintained Merkel in the seat of power but with a different coalition, not one single medium of communication can be heard (or seen) uttering a single word of praise for the government. The media has actually examined Merkel's coalition and found it sadly wanting. Political analysts are frustrated and angry with this 'adolescent' coalition. They claim it contradicts itself. They find that the first of these coalitions worked better 'from the first month' than the actual example.

Perhaps this is true, but the great reformist zeal of the post 2005 government functioned well because the Great Recession had not yet appeared. It is perfectly possible that no government or coalition government could function well under the conditions of 2010, with darkening clouds of inflation, unemployment and social unease looming over Europe and the rest of the Western world. The actual coalition has discovered that grand promises made by its predecessor cannot be fulfilled. Taxes have not been reduced, and the German Treasury demands stronger discipline in terms of salary and bonus; this imposition is hardly likely to make the new coalition popular. The people are told that the National Deficit (the all-important difference between national income and national expenditure) this year is 5%. The Government says the Opposition is 'neo-liberal' and 'uncooperative'.

During the German recession of 2002 and 2003 Germans felt insecure and pre-occupied by their country's apparent decline – and that is how, according to newspapers like the *Frankfurter Rundschau*, citizens are feeling again – after these first 100 days. The Munich paper *Abendzeitung*, concentrating on Bavaria, reckons that the coalition's 'married' parties 'only function properly at regional level. Internal criticism within Merkel's party (UDC) claims lack of purpose or direction, after only sixty days of Merkel's government. She has been invited not very cordially to explain her purpose before the whole party.

The unacceptable budgetary equations, and the confusing and contentious German military presence in Afghanistan are producing stress for Angela Merkel, though fortunately employment stays comparatively stable thanks to a sensible reduction in working hours, which economists claim has saved more than a million jobs. Even so, concerted opinion in Germany seems to indicate failure, at least in these first hundred days.

22ND FEBRUARY

Spain: a nervous week for the Spanish

In an attempt to show solidarity with his fellow Premier Gordon Brown, Spain's President of the Government, also temporary President of the EC, José Luis Rodríguez Zapatero, flew off to Downing Street. Brown is also flailing in deep and dangerous waters for his party, but Zetapé read a speech (delivered in Spanish) to an assembly of the best financial brains in the UK, even if the assembled suits could understand a word of it. which might be seen as little help for Gordon Brown, or for the future economic condition of either country. In the city considered by many as the financial capital of the world, Mr Zapatero delivered a stinging reprimand to British bankers and stockbrokers, blaming them for the worldwide recession, and all the ills that affect Greece, Portugal, Ireland and of course Spain. The speech did not go down well, but Mr Zapatero probably thought it did, because it had been prepared by several of his hundreds of highly paid personal advisors, who obviously know best.

Then it was discovered by an aggressive press that a video had been made of some Government-appointed munitions and explosives experts examining and analysing remains of the trains and stations blown on March 11, 2004 in Madrid. The film was made a week or two before the opening of the Tribunal which would investigate the whole tragic affair, in which nearly two hundred people on their way to work died as a result of the terrorist attack. In several startling scenes, the experts are filmed, their comments clearly heard, as they discover to their amazement ("Huf!" said one, "this is going to make us famous!") that the explosive used to wreck the trains and kill 193 people, and badly hurt hundreds more was not, as had been declared officially by the Government, Goma 2 stolen from mines in Asturias, but standard old TNT, a favourite weapon of the Basque terrorist organisation ETA. Judge Gomez-Bermúdez did not allow the showing of this video during the hearings. He did however send two foreigners and one schizophrenic Spaniard to jail for hundreds of years, for their involvement in the planning of the outrage. As readers will remember, three days later a General Election took place. During these three days the masterful organisation of the Spanish Workers' Socialist Party orchestrated nationwide demonstrations, persuading half the Spanish population that the '11M' was the fault of Aznar and his Popular Party. There was just enough time to ensure a not very resounding victory of the PSOE, and Mr Zapatero became President of the Government, thanks to pacts made with small, suitably sweetened Nationalist parties across the country.

With the findings of the Tribunal made public, plus the blowing up of other terrorists 'involved' in the destruction of the trains - in a 'watched' flat in Leganés - the case was closed, by both the PSOE and the Opposition. But the victims and their mourning families were left. Silence on this subject was dutifully observed, until the extraordinary revelations of this last week. Now Spaniards have learnt that the material weapon declared responsible for the deaths was *not* what tribunal witnesses from the police forces swore it was. It is as if the police, after finding a murdered person, swear he died of stabbing. The alleged murderer is punished on this basis, and some time afterwards, evidence is brought that the victim died of gunshot wounds in the head. Now where does that leave the police, officials and judge?

Meanwhile Mr Aznar went to make a speech to the assembled students at Oviedo University. The ex-Premier of Spain was loudly heckled and interrupted throughout his lecture by a small group of students, all of whom were aged around twelve when Mr Aznar was President of the Government. They had been well primed however, and the barracking irritated José María Aznar, as well it should. Campus officials made no attempt to stop the caterwauling, but as he approached the end of his thwarted speech, Aznar's patience left him, and he showed a derisive middle finger to the barrackers; as the cries of 'terrorist!', 'Nazi!', 'Fascist!' 'Warmonger!' continued, Aznar made his gesture. He was much photographed doing it.

9TH MARCH

Profitable skull and crossbones: 21st century buccaneers proliferate

Since 2007, Spanish vessels have been attacked eleven times by pirates in Somali waters. Six assaults have been successfully repelled by security forces sailing with the fishermen on their boats. But it took until the last 3 months of 2009 for the Spanish government even to permit armed bodyguards on board to help defend the fishing boats. In 2008, a piratical offence of great importance happened: the assault on the Basque tuna vessel *Playa de Bakio.* In 2009 a fishing craft was actually captured, and the crew kidnapped for ransom; this was the case of the *Alakrana.*

In both cases the ships and crews were released only after the payment of a huge sum in ransom. This annoyed the Spanish people a great deal, because their taxpayers' money was being used, but it pleased the happy corsairs no end, because they were able to use the cash to re-arm themselves, and re-fit their pirate ships. Many Spanish people, among them a lot of ex-seamen, asked each other how the Somali pirates could get away with their crimes so easily, when Spain has a small, but effective and well-disciplined navy.

The pirates have not gone away. The aggression continues in the Indian Ocean, concentrated mainly on Spanish shipping, for a good reason: the pirates know it is easy to negotiate huge sums with the Government ruled by Mr Zapatero, whereas French, Italian or Portuguese fishing boats will fight tooth and claw to defend themselves and their catch. Their leaders have also declared they will pay no ransom to pirates. The great Spanish captains and navigators of history must be churning up the sand that lies around Davy Jones' Locker.

Only forty-eight hours ago three more boats were assaulted; the good ship *Albacán* was attacked using a missile launcher! From where, I wonder, did almost naked pirates get a deadly weapon like this? Luckily no member of the crew was hurt. On Thursday 4th February the 'fellowship' of the skull and crossbones started the *jornada* prompt at 9 am, with an attack on refrigerator boat *Intertuna Dos*. The assault was launched from three high powered launches packed to the gunwales with laughing, singing buccaneers, waving Kalashnikovs. The freezer-boat was then about 70 nautical miles (130 kms.) distant from the exact position of *Albacán*. The Spanish crew saw the attack coming and prepared the ship against boarding, while the security men aboard took up positions for aggressive defence against potential boarders. There followed a period of about thirty minutes in which pirates and bodyguards exchanged sporadic fire. Surprised, perhaps complaining about their rights to international piracy, the buccaneers withdrew in their battered launches. No doubt their lawyers will have prepared a complaint to be placed before some European court or other.

Meanwhile the radio operator on *Intertuna Dos* had alerted his colleagues on board *Artza* and *Alakrana*. The two ships raced towards *Intertuna Dos'* position. At this precise moment, with their usual accurate timing, yet another attack was launched by pirates, this time against the good ship *Artxanda*, busy fishing in the international zone. Now that all Spanish fishing fleets are allowed arms, the latter craft responded to the shooting, and the pirates withdrew to lick their wounds. No-one, on board a Spanish ship at least, was hurt, and no doubt a spot of celebratory rum was issued by skippers; while toasts were being made on deck, yet another assault formation was speeding towards *Intertuna Tres*, a sister ship. On this occasion there was no exchange of fire, however, because the ship's captain spotted the launches when they were four miles astern, and immediately rang down for full speed. He soon outran the slower launches, and shooting was avoided.

During these pirate attacks, not one member of any of the three crews was injured. The skipper *of Intertuna Dos* opted for changing course to hold up in Puerto Victoria, Seychelles, where repairs could be made, fresh ammunition bought for the protecting gunmen, and interviews with the press arranged. Other Spanish vessels on their lawful fishing tasks in the zone remained on 'maximum alert'. In one of the press interviews with a crew member, it was reported that 'the whole zone is buzzing with pirates'

23RD MARCH

France: Sarkozy denies everything

It has often been said that French democratic presidents live in greater pomp than any hereditary monarchy. In the case of France, this is undeniably true.   French Presidents live in the midst of Byzantine splendour in one of Europe's finest palaces, surrounded by fawning ministers and anxious advisers. The present incumbent, dwarfish but determined Nicholas Sarkozy cannot be said to be an exception. And while we talk of 'denial' the President has just (yesterday) scotched the latest attempts by an international press to announce an imminent separation between himself and First Lady Carla Bruni.

"C'est fini? Jamais!" We are pleased to declare that all the recent column inches imprudently employed by the press and media to publicise the unhappiness of Bruni and the melancholy of Nicholas have been a waste of paper. The rumours started, of course, on Twitter, a not very attractive online engine devoted to frivolity. *Le Journal du Dimanche* is supposed to be a better class of medium, and its journalists decided recently to divulge what it called 'the story of the year'. The presidential marriage was 'taking its last breath' (sic).

Well, said Europe, this is not entirely unexpected. Nicholas has already been married thrice, and Carla Bruni (a very beautiful woman's woman, ex-professional singer and model) has been heard not to deny that she is not much given to monogamy. Once, she recorded an album called '*no promises*', which, to the Gallic mind anyway, is suggestive to say the least. Then one must point out the crucial difference in height between the President and his First Lady: four inches. This means that at least in public, the President must wear lifts while his glamorous wife slops about in flatties. Rumour has it that Carla has been dallying in the close presence of a well-built singer called Benjamin. Photographs have been illicitly and unfairly taken. Some press reports insist that M. le President has been finding comfort in the strong arms of his *karate* champion lady Minister Chantal Jouanno. But yesterday Nicholas Sarkozy trashed the rumours by savagely putting the skids under a British journalist who dared to ask him if such rumours of an impending break-up were true. Sarkozy was furious, blankly denied the rumours, and added that he found it difficult to believe that the journalist could possibly have used the moment of his permitted question to offer such stupid impertinence. So now we know. The President has spoken. All is well between Nicholas and Carla, who have been appearing together hand in hand a lot in the last week.

One supposes this means that, Nicholas being a politician after all, announcements of his imminent separation and subsequent divorce cannot be lingering far away.

Britain

Beleagured and besieged Mr. Brown appeared before the Chilcot Inquiry into the Iraq War. Questioned by the inquiry board, he denied that when he was Chancellor of the Exchequer he had manipulated or in any way 'squeezed' British defence budgets. Several officers have published reports stating that the British expedition was woefully handled economically, and added that no army, however brilliant its reputation, can operate successfully without adequate resources. Mr Brown said, 'At any point, commanders were able to ask for equipment that they needed and I know of no occasion when they were turned down.'

Lord Craigie, Chief of the Defence Staff (1997 – 2001) and Lord Boyce, Chief of the Defence Staff (2001 – 2003) agreed that Mr Brown, in saying this, 'was being disingenuous'. My dictionary says this latest cant word means 'not sincere, lacking candour', but let us not be euphemistic . . . the ex-Chiefs are saying Mr Brown is lying. After his grilling at the Chilcot Inquiry., Mr. Brown flew off to Afghanistan, where the latest British soldier killed on active duty there brings the total of British dead in someone else's war to 272 since 2001.

The trade deficit in services and goods in Britain did not surprise many experts when it widened to £3.8 *billion* last January. In December it had stood at £2.6 billion. At the same time as members of parliament were given a thousand pound *raise* in pay by the Senior Salaries Review Body, the PM confirmed a pay *freeze* for senior public sector employees. This anomaly cannot be said to have pleased the latter. News of the Post Office (or whatever the service is called this week): under a new contract for postmen (and women of course), most rural areas in Britain will not now see any post delivered until after 4 pm.

News of the banking sector: The Financial Services Authority has licensed the Metro Bank (a new high street venture) to welcome dogs into its branches. It is not known if this generosity includes permitting the dogs to open an account with the Metro Bank. Around the same time as this important new reform was announced, the Government of Mr. Brown also proposed an amendment to the 1991 Dangerous Dogs Act. All dog owners must now insure their pets (however small) against biting people.

The sparrowhawk (a small hunting bird running into danger of extinction in Britain, thanks to the insecticides used by farmers on grain which reduced the population of the sparrowhawks' principal source of food) has been accused of being responsible for the sudden downturn in the life expectancy of 'songbirds'. These are sparrows, robins, wild canaries, chaffinches, greenfinches, bull finches and other finches; they make up most of the Summer's dawn chorus that awaken one in English gardens at unearthly hours. Well, according to the 'experts', the sparrowhawk, one of the more ancient species of predatory birds in Europe, is responsible. They must therefore be punished by the lifting of equally ancient rustic laws that prevent them from being slaughtered. So take a last look from your English garden at those circling brown and grey birds with the sharp eyes, watching for the innocent pigeon, the scurrying vole, the rat which has been bothering your hens for so long. Bang! Bang! There goes the sparrowhawk.

The British Trust for Ornithology has spoken; the song birds have suffered a decline as a result of the sparrowhawks. We are now waiting for the announcement of a 'cull' in the sparrowhawk population. We will probably remember what happened to our magpies when the same organisation accused them of not only being thieves, but acting with murderous intent towards the sweet songbirds. Countrymen of course know that if there is a healthy population of sparrowhawks, there will be a healthy population of songbirds, as sparrowhawks are far more dependent upon their prey than their prey are dependent on sparrowhawks. You see what I mean of course.

There are a number of oddities here. The songbird is not the usual prey for sparrowhawks, which prefer a nice fat pigeon. *Cats* kill songbirds in your garden (or out of it) at an estimated rate of 100 million a year. But this fact will not impress bodies like the British Trust for Ornithology, and many others like it, because bird charities depend for their money on owners of cats, who provide them with huge amounts of cash every year. It is logic therefore that you will not find cats included in any Government-inspired cull, and the finger of blame must be pointed at something easy (and lawyerless, unlike cat-owners) such as the sparrowhawk. There are those in Britain who compare giving money to bird charities to giving money to Amnesty International though your knife-wielding teenage children go Paki-hunting every weekend.

No-one has asked the opinion of the condemned sparrow hawks, nor of any other species that our masters the conservationists might decide to exterminate for their own twisted reasons. The common mink, for instance (high up on the list of disapproved animals that likes a meal occasionally, and whom God irrationally made carnivorous); also the coypu, or grey squirrel, or ducks that make such a mess in the parks you know, or rats and mice. Fingered by the conservationists, who tend to have a policing nature, we try to police Mother Nature, and of course we make a hash of it, with the usual appalling unintended consequences.

Alike as two peas . . .
(Seventy-two years ago, a distinguished novelist and travel writer wrote this:)

"The constitutional opposition to which the opponents of Fascism aspired, has never come into existence. There is still one political party in (   ); seats and offices are appointed at parliamentary headquarters as in all totalitarian states. . . The nation has sacrificed its political liberties without getting internal security or foreign prestige in exchange. Thus it is not surprising that a political career has now few attractions for persons of decent principle. It is difficult to say where the fault lies when the government of a country gets into the hands of its worst elements; there is a natural trend of all political forms in this direction. Those who have wearied of democratic forms forget that history is full of instances of legitimate royalty being ruled by corrupt courtiers; English Whigs in the eighteenth century enriched themselves from the public purse; it is not only in France and the United States that the worst men may get to the top. What is certain, however, is that there is a Gresham's Law active in public life: bad rulers drive out good. In France and the United States it is unusual for respectable citizens to go into politics.

"The lawyers are an able and influential class. Apart from endless litigation, which is a feature of life, they occupy themselves prominently with political controversy in the Press. There are many prominent socialists among them…the judges, as has been mentioned above, are now political nominees.

"The priesthood…has been driven into the life of the catacombs . . . They are, of course, opposed to their persecutors but it is generally believed that their political power is completely broken.

"At present time there is no opposition of the kind that flourishes in a democratic country, and when one questions those who are most bitter in their complaints of the regime as to how they hope to see it altered, the answer nearly always comes back to the Army.

"As legitimate trading ceases to offer sensational profits the taste for gambling in fictitious values grows on the part of the rich with consequent sudden fluctuations of prosperity and employment, while the demands of the workmen cease to be temperate, are political in character instead of economic, and become frivolous and vindictive, that is what is popularly known as the class war. The middle class suffers from both sides and sees itself threatened by extinction while at the same time those whose interests and not exclusively economic and class-conscious, are ashamed at the ignominious aspect their country has in the world at large . . . Then the devil comes into that too; cranks and criminals get into power."

(The writer is Evelyn Waugh: he wrote this after a protracted visit to Mexico in 1938. I had no idea he was a prophet. If the Reader fills in the gaps in brackets with 'Spain', or' Spanish', she will see that an account written about Mexico in 1938 or Spain in 2010 can be identical.

Germany: forgetting heroes

The family of one of the chief conspirators in the July 1944 plot to kill Hitler and thus shorten the War now finds itself in a new and acrimonious struggle. This time it is with the Government of Angela Merkel. The grandson of Prince Solms-Baruth, heavily involved in the failed bomb plot, is making himself a thorn in Merkel's flesh. The problem is that the Government refuses to indemnify his family, which was deported, and all their lands and property confiscated, by the Nazi Party, after von Stauffenberg failed to assassinate Adolf Hitler in what is known as the 'Valkirie'. As is generally known, Stauffenberg and hundreds of other officers and men involved in the desperate attempt to shorten the War were summarily executed at the orders of General Fromm, though the latter knew everything about the plot, but refused to come down off his fence. Among the very few that escaped execution was Prince Solms-Baruth, arrested but not shot.

Poland before and after the death of a President

An unfair burden of tragedies and melancholy has assailed this beautiful European country throughout most of its history. Poland is a north-European country with a Baltic Sea coast. Its boundaries have been the basic cause of most of Poland's miseries: Germany to the west, Russia, Lithuania, Belarus and Ukraine on the east, and the Czech Republic and Slovakia (the former Czechoslovakia) to the south.

Geography

Poland lies on the north European Plain, sandy in places, marshes and bogs in others. The countryside requires meticulous cultivation, though inland it is drained by the River Oder (now Odra), the Vistula and others. Small to medium-sized forests lie everywhere, gradually increasing in size as the land rises through undulating hills and richer soils towards the Carpathian Mountains in the south-east. Trees are mostly spruce and fir.

Economy

Following the (limited) collapse of communism, Poland managed the transition to an open market economy, but this liberalisation led to economic problems which included high inflation, large budget deficits, and high foreign debt. In 1989, an economic reform package was introduced in order to gain International Monetary Fund support. Wages were reduced (unpopular) as well as price subsidies (equally unpopular). The Polish Stock Exchange was re-opened (popular). By now most of the arable land was again in private hands, descendants of those families dispossessed first by the Nazis and then by Soviet Russia, having returned from exile to claim their property. Wheat, rye, barley, oats potatoes and sugar beet are the main crops. Poland has huge stocks of coal ready to be mined (in case coal becomes popular or necessary again). In fact the country possesses some of the greatest bituminous and lignite coal fields in the world. There is also copper, iron, silver, sulphur, lead and natural gas, but efficient industry is often hampered by power shortages and high fuel prices. Financial difficulties have delayed the nuclear energy programme.

History

Slavic tribes inhabited the zone from before 2000 BC, though Poland did not become an independent kingdom until the 9th century. The country became Christian with Miezko (962 – 992). Greater unity was imposed by Ladislas (1305 – 1333), and then Casimir the Great, who improved administration, logistics and defence, as well as encouraging trade and industry. By 1572 Protestantism was well established, and arts and sciences were flourishing. Poland was probably most important in the 16th century, after Lithuania had been incorporated (a process that required two acts –

one in 1447, the next in 1569). Now at last Poland stretched from the Baltic to the Black Sea.

The hereditary monarchy was weak, however, and though both Casimir (1648 – 1468) and John Sobieski (1674 – 1696) won victories, internal decline and foreign attack effectively undermined independence. Much territory was lost to Sweden and Russia. Savaged by the Northern War and the War of the Polish Succession, Poland lost her independence in the 18th century. Starting in 1697 the Electors of Saxony took the title of King, and Poland, not for the last time, found herself partitioned in 1772 between Russia, Austria and Prussia in 1772. This was the beginning of many sorrows for the beleaguered Polish people. Sadly, Kosciusko tried brief resistance, but the only result was a further partitioning in 1793 and 1795, greatly to the benefit of Catherine II (the Great)'s Russia, because Poland was now effectively a 'protectorate' of that huge country.

In 1807, after the Treaty of Tilsit, Napoleon Bonaparte created the Grand Duchy of Warsaw (under the King of Saxony), and introduced his Gallic system of Law, the Code Napoléon. But he also maintained semi-slavedom in the countryside, and the feudal nobility. The new Duchy collapsed however, after the battle of Leipzig. Later the Congress of Vienna returned parts of the Duchy to Prussia and Austria, but the bulk of the country became the Kingdom of Poland, having its own administration, but with the Russian emperor Alexander I, as King. Naturally, being Poland under the conditions of serfdom, there were revolutions in 1830, 1846 – 49 and 1863.

18TH MAY

Britain and Spain

In 1940 Churchill agreed with Attlee to 'share' management of the Second World War. The labour leader became Deputy Prime Minister, with Winston as PM and generalissimo of the armed forces' three arms. Throughout the long years of war these two elderly men worked together, with hardly a harsh word. Clement did a splendid job, frequently smoothing tempers irritated by Churchill's authoritative ways. At the end of the War the British people turned against Churchill, and voted Clement Attlee in with the Labour Party, ousting Winston. The dreadful years of maximum austerity began in 1946. Things were so bad in 1948 that Britons rich enough to do so would climb on the ferry to Calais or Ostend simply to buy some decent food – yet France, Belgium and Holland had been occupied by the Nazis for most of the war years. No-one in Britain understood it, and voted again in 1951 for the Conservatives and Churchill, now an aging memory, as PM.

The 2010 General Election, seventy years later, provided no majority for the Tories under David Cameron. In order to govern, he has decided to invite the Liberal Democrats to govern with him, which means that the grand surprise of these elections, LibDem Nicholas Clegg, rises to become Deputy Prime Minister. Gordon Brown has resigned from politics. Some admittedly awful people might think about time too.

Cameron/Clegg have not wasted time. A cascade of relevant proposals and revolutionary ideas has issued from Downing Street. The object is to reduce governmental costs drastically, reduce the deficit, not raise taxes for the moment anyway, continue with the 50p in the pound tax on 'the rich', introduce special taxes which will affect the banking sector, especially the monstrous bonuses the banks like giving their directors – recession or no recession. Reduction of costs in such areas as education, health or security will not in fact materially affect these three sectors.

After thirteen years of Labour the deficit is nearly 13%, more than Greece's, though it must be seen that Britain's international credit rating is in a different league. Cameron and Clegg have decided, and will carry out, significant cuts in public spending; they have not chosen the strange path chosen by Mr Rodríguez Zapatero of Spain, who chooses instead to start recessional reform by reducing salaries of the civil service by 5%, and freezing pensions. (In Spain, one should note, these two 'reforms' have proved most unpopular, especially with State functionaries and pensioners, whose representatives complain that no cuts in salaries paid to members of the Congress and the Senate have been announced, and that at least five completely redundant Ministries are not to be touched. One of these, the 'Ministry for Equality' is a clear case for suspected lunacy – but its Minister, Bibaino Aida, remains unscathed.

With Brown retiring back to the misty glens on the other side of Hadrian's Wall, the question remains in Britain's Labour Party: who will replace him? Perhaps the new Labour chief will be one (or indeed both) of 'the Miliboys'? David Miliband is 44. He recently announced his candidature, to be followed two days later by a similar announcement from his brother Ed (Edward? Edwin? Edgy? Edelweiss?) who is just 40.

David Miliband was one of the inner circle surrounding Tony Blair, and is equally conservative, though a radical member of the Labour Party. One must remember that during Blair's premiership many commentators found him more conservative than any Tory or LibDem. Ed Miliband supported (and tolerated) Brown, and is politically more left-wing than his brother. It is said that David is the more articulate, whereas Ed punches his message to the people better, David is probably better looking and more pragmatic; Ed cleverer by half. David is married with two children; Ed is half of an unmarried couple, with one baby.

"David is my best friend in the world!" declares Ed, and continues, "there is no way I could be treacherous towards him, off the record, on the record, or behind the scenes." "Brotherly love is much more important than politics," states David in his turn.

In 2007 both Milibands had a seat in the Cabinet – the first time this had happened since the brothers Chamberlain in 1931. That, and fraternal love, are all very well, but will the Brothers Miliband be able to control their two distinct (and perhaps uncontrollable) groups of supporters, more than capable of digging the knife in and then revolving it in the wound?

David Miliband made an admirable Foreign Minister, despite his youth, and is certainly better known by the British public. His brother was Minister for Energy and Climate Change, and gained much prestige while occupying a ministerial seat. It is said that various important members of the Party are in favour of the younger brother in the leadership stakes.

It is also rumoured that the Lord of Darkness himself, Peter Mandelson, has been the greatest pusher behind David's candidacy, Judging by the questionable success of Mandelson's odd career in politics – he has failed in everything he has done, except for an undoubted success in making him the most feared in the Party – one would imagine David Miliband would prefer not to be pushed or promoted by Peter Mandelson. If Peter has always promoted David in the leadership race, he will have done so to spite Gordon Brown, a mortal enemy.

The boys' father, Ralf, came from Belgium in 1940. They had escaped to Belgium from Poland, harried by the Nazis. Ralf married fellow Pole Marion Kozak, and the couple soon became known for polemical debates within the family and outside it. It would not be going too far to say that Ralf and Marion were communists. The boys' father died in 1994. Marion has survived, and says she will not vote for either son. Her vote will go to Jon Cruddas. Marion explains this by saying she cannot possibly cast a vote for this son or that son, thus provoking the possibility of family friction and unrest.

Both boys studied at Oxford and in the United States, David became a Member of Parliament in 2001, and was a Minister in 2005, the same year that his younger brother entered Parliament. Within two years Ed was a Minister.

Spain again

At the moment of writing, this country is bewildered (as usual) by the customary obtuseness of the *Consejo de Ministros* and the President of the Government, José Luis Rodríguez Zapatero. No-one seems to know what is happening. The President announced desperate measures to reduce Spain's deficit, both cuts affecting the people, but neither central government nor the *Autonomías*. When Spain's chief trade unions, *CC.OO* and *UGT* made it plain they would oppose freezing of pensions or cutting into civil servants' pay, and the latter's own union announced a personal strike (which would paralyse the country), Zapatero backed off and postponed the cabinet meeting which would have ratified the proposal.

In a speech in Congress, Rosa Diez leader of her own party UpyD asked the President of the Government to stand down, and convoke a general election. The leader of CiU (Cataluña) demanded the resignation of Zapatero, and asked his fellow members of the PSOE to name a new leader, as (he claims) Zapatero inspires no confidence in either parties or people.

The President of Congress, José Bono, is the subject of a furious media onslaught on the usual grounds of alleged political and financial corruption. Bono has said that he has become the subject of a violent attack directed by the 'Extreme Right', because he is 'a socialist and a Christian'. It is clear that for the socialists, anyone not actually voting socialist is an extreme right winger, fascist and traitor; also irresponsible and anti-progress.

Bono's wife has told the press that the immense Bono fortunes come not from her husband's admirable work as a politician, but from *her* labours as an impresario and businesswoman. The couple recently bought their son a large apartment in Madrid costing nearly two million euros.

2ND JUNE

Germany: Horst Köhler resigns suddenly

A Member of the same political party as his Chancellor (Angela Merkel), the Democratic Christian Union, Kohler (67) was an unobtrusive president of The Federal Republic of Germany from 2004 until the last day of May, 2010. By origin he was Germano/Rumanian, born at Skierbieszow, East Poland in 1943. His family was known to tolerate Hitler's III Reich. Köhler was Director of the International Monetary Fund from 2000 to 2004. Before that he lived in London, where he presided over the Reconstruction and Development Banking Corporation. Under Helmut Kohl, he had been Secretary of State for Finance, and played an integral part in the re-introduction of a solvent Mark at the time of re-union with the former East Germany. He was also one of the pillars of Monetary Union at the Treaty of Maastricht, creating the Euro.

Few things seem to be going right for Angela Merkel during her second mandate as Chancellor, and one of these is Köhler, who precipitously announced his irrevocable resignation 'in order not to damage consensus'. Actually he resigned because of several rather incautious words he uttered during a radio interview: he had told his audience that Germany's presence in Afghanistan was due to economic (if not commercial) reasons, not humanitarian ones. In more brutal terms, he meant that Germany was in the war-torn country for economic betterment of an already prosperous state, not for any more altruistic motives. The *Frankfurter Allgemeine* states that Köhler was 'an unknown quantity' when he came from the IMF five years ago, and that 'not much has changed'. *Der Spiegel* says that his resignation meant 'running away'. *Die Welt* claims the resignation is 'humiliating', especially as on his inauguration he announced he would be 'a President for everyone'.

The general opinion is that Köhler's curiosity, loquacity, and self-opinion has done him in, and that he has made things more and uncomfortable for himself since becoming President. Apparently his opinion that Germany's 'strategic obligations' had nothing or very little to do with her sending troops to Afghanistan is nothing new – it is just that no-one expected him to declare himself so openly in the media. Of course he could not have made a greater gaffe, as Germany tends to be filled to bursting with persuasive (and sometimes bullying) pacifists. Certainly Angela Merkel has been terribly shocked, because the sudden resignation of her President has left an embarrassing gap. Really, the resignation should not have come as a surprise, as commentators report that things have not been at all easy between Merkel and Köhler for months. She says she is 'terribly moved', and that she had tried to dissuade Köhler from resignation but that 'it proved impossible'. She adds that she has been 'profoundly moved'. 'Köhler,' Merkel adds, 'is a very important advisor economically and financially during this period of uncertainty and crisis'. Some columnists have found this sudden sympathy rather cynical.

The Vice-Chancellor, not to be outdone, admits that when he heard the news he found himself 'lamenting the sad decision with all his heart' , though he of course respects the decision, and wants to show how he appreciates the work Köhler had completed before his exit.

The First Minister of Baden and Württemberg underlines the 'inconvenience of it all', now that 'the greatest country in Europe (sic) finds itself headless in the middle of a financial crisis'. The Minister of the Economy points out that 'a huge hole' has now been found in ongoing attempts to solve the financial crisis, and begs for 'extra-cooperation' from the Opposition. And that Opposition's leader, Sigmar Gabriel, replies that he 'valued very much' Köhler's presidency, and adds that 'he never hid the fact that he would make an uncomfortable President'. He would like to add that all this 'upset' is the fault of the coalition parties in power.

Leader of the Left Gregor Gysi considers the resignation 'exaggerated', and that 'a President should learn to accept criticism' (this refers to the huge outpourings of tears and horror in Germany after the ex-President had given his opinion about Germany's presence in Afghanistan).

One wonders where all this leaves Spain, where the current Government has made hundreds of mistakes and gaffes during the last six years, but is rather one-eyed about it all: no-one resigns in Spain, honour or no honour. There have been enough major errors made here only in the last two years to provide for a dozen resignations, but one must not expect too much. As was to be predicted, the harshest criticism has come from 'The Greens', who have always found Köhler 'superfluous'. And what does Herr Köhler himself have to say? Accompanied only by his wife on the podium, he explained to the rapidly convened journos that he had become the subject of unacceptably vociferous criticism after his words on Afghanistan were published. He 'laments' that his words on such an important subject should have been 'misunderstood'. Some reporters present say the ex-President was tearful when he complained that his critics have been 'disrespectful' towards a Head of State.

And what did he actually say? Roughly this: "We all know that for a country of the size of ours, with its dependence on foreign trade, military intervention is necessary for the defence of our interests, like having free commercial channels, and in order to prevent the instability of our regions, which in turn could negatively affect our commercial opportunities, jobs and incomes".

Köhler made this remark during an interview with journalists on the radio station *Deutchlandfunk* at the end of April. The ex-President was attempting to provide reason for German military presence in Afghanistan, something that has always been heavily opposed by many of not most of the German people. Instead of merely mouthing platitudes, such as those uttered by so many other leaders, about 'defending the ordinary people' and 'combating terrorism' etc., Köhler was blunt enough to be honest – and has had to resign (he claims) as a result. Who will become President? The German Constitution states that in such cases the successor to the presidency must be the President of the *Bundesrat,* and Köhler has already communicated with Jens Böhrnsen. Still, the Federal Assembly must announce a definite nomination before 30th June.

14TH JUNE

Spain: speaking of labour reforms and taxing 'The Rich'

There are 17 autonomous communities in Spain, plus two autonomous cities – Ceuta and Melilla. Andalucía heads the list in terms of the quantity of highly paid civil servants, presidents of this, general-secretary of that etc. These VIPs move about in 1,200 expensive official cars, mostly Audis.

In neighbouring Extremadura, there are more state functionaries per head of population than in any other region. Andalucía and Extremadura also boast between them the largest number of 'subsidized workers'. It is difficult if not impossible to explain that modish phrase *'subsidized workers'*. My suspicion is that it means hundreds and hundreds of men and women who receive government money (our money) to 'work' in NGOs, committees, associations, think tanks, family planning offices, and official 'advisors'. In Extremadura one in every five workers actually works for the administration of Extremadura.

These top-heavy administrations govern the two most under-developed, poorest and most politically miserable regions in Spain. They are both governed by the PSOE, have been for years, thirty in fact. In the present parlous financial state, with national bankruptcy staring us all in the face, Andalucía and Extremadura and all other PSOE- held regions are pressing central government hard to increase the percentage we must all pay in our annual Income Tax Declaration *(IRPF)*. This nineteenth century Fabian reform is called 'taxing' or 'soaking' the rich. But can we define 'the rich'? Are there any 'rich' left? Are not 'the rich' defined by the PSOE as gloating moguls who became rich by 'stamping on the faces of the poor'? Do the rich still keep their riches in Spain? How rich is rich?

The PSOE has decided, fear not, who the rich are: if you come into this category, I am sorry, but there it is. You are rich if you earn €60,000 to €80,000 per annum (€4285 and €5714 per month with 2 *pagos extra)* and if you earn more than that you are 'super rich' and you will be 'super-taxed'. It does not matter a jot if these stupendous riches are gained from properties you may own and rent, or you earn them by working as an architect, auctioneer, accountant, lawyer, dentist, surgeon, business manager etc. In other words, you work in a professional capacity after appropriate study and the passing of qualifying examinations at the university.

There will be exceptions of course. No-one in Government has yet suggested super-taxing professional footballers, some of whom get a million or two euros per month. Nor has the Minister of Justice yet brought any kind of investigative action against the present President of the Congress, whose actual declared wealth has been revealed as impossible to account for given the total of his official incomes plus generous expenses.

It should be mentioned in passing that those in Spain who do indeed earn more than 60 or 80 thousand a year number around 30,000 out of a population of more than 40 million inhabitants. These, plus the pensioners (whose pension has been frozen where it is), and the state functionaries (doctors, engineers, university professors, police, judges, prison officers, social workers, air traffic controllers etc. are the social groups chosen to bear the weight of this Government's last-ditch attempt to avoid the deadly *quiebra* now assailing both Greece and Portugal. A few days ago the chief Spanish trade unions *Comisiones* and *UGT* called for a strike of one day by all state functionaries. The latters' own Union was not consulted, and the strike was a dismal failure, with barely 11% of functionaries going on strike.

'The rich' used to be landowners, or chairmen of banks and corporations. It is useless to try to get their money because it is already outside Spain. Does anyone in the PSOE imagine Mr Botín, president of Banco Santander, keeps his billions in Spain? It is the salaried middle class who will become the victims in just two days' time, at a Cabinet Meeting on June 16th. No-one in the PSOE has dared suggest that a little cash might be saved by reducing the quantity of 'special advisors' (more than 400) kept on salary by Mr Rodríguez Zapatero, or the more than 1000 advisors paid by the (PP) Mayor and Corporation of the City of Madrid.

Squeezing the rich – a politically attractive proposition

The thing is, how do you do it, if you are a lady like Elena Salgado (Minister of Finance) in Mr Zapatero's cabinet. How do you keep walking down the thinnest of thin lines that separate huge and unpayable deficits and the possibility of losing votes? How do you raise the revenues needed, and still appear fair to the poor, the needy (2½ million Spanish people are living without any visible means of support, income, subsidy or dole) or the disenfranchised?

The PSOE thinks the answer to this thorny question is as easy as pie. All you do is 'tax the rich'. You do this by raising the capital gains tax rate, along with other new upper rates. But any decent economist will be cautious about this; he will explain that this is one of the greatest fallacies in economics.

The ominous premise is that the rich, because they own so much of the country's wealth, won't find it difficult to pay higher taxes. Also, simply because they form such a minute part of the community, no one will hear their shouts as someone else tightens their belt for them. How super this would be if only it were true. But is it? When you threaten a citizen who has worked like stink to build up a respectable business which makes money, implying you are about to confiscate half their wealth because 'the rich must be forced to pay up in order to save the country', the private sector's counter-offensive will move into rapid action. It is a basic rule of economics that if you increase taxes, especially in time of high crisis, you will never get greater revenue. You will get reduced revenue. This has been known since bankers existed in Venice and Egypt. But one must not expect Mr Zapatero to know this, because he is distinguished by the fact that he never listens to anybody – even his most ardent fans in his own Cabinet.

Someone might casually mention to him, when he is in a relaxed mood (you can tell by the eyebrows) that people and businesses respond to incentives. The rich can *change* how much work they do, where they do it, how they earn money, and where they *keep* it. Reagan realised that reducing the burden which government places on the economy, through taxation, in the surest way to ensure growth. Who has ever heard of a country that taxed itself into prosperity and managed to reduce a monstrous and crippling deficit? Could not some of those four hundred 'advisors' whisper in the Presidential ear that if Spain raises capital gains and other taxes, people and businesses will find good reasons for removing themselves (but not their employees), their businesses and their assets to somewhere else, which means even more unemployment (nearly five million out-of-work in Spain), and much less revenue.

Raising taxes 'on the rich' will increase the need for more welfare payments to the poor, the unemployed, and the underemployed. It is about as bad an idea as any other one could imagine, but Zapatero, Blanco, Salgado, Alonso, the appalling Pajín and the rest of the crew are determined to do it.

If one wants poor people to do better, find jobs etc., *create jobs for them*, as Aznar's government did, whether the PSOE likes it or not. Create jobs, not welfare. Cut ridiculous public spending by more than 50%. Sell those black Audis. Don't have three chauffeurs to each official car. Tell the outrageous autonomous communities to fend for themselves. There aren't enough bridges, even in Spain, for *all* of us to live under when the roof caves in.

3RD AUGUST

Italy

As if recent high temperatures in Italy were not bad enough, the political atmosphere is getting uncomfortably warm too. The President of Congress, and co-founder of the party in power, Gianfranco Fini, has just announced the formation of a new parliamentary party following Silvio Berlusconi's decision to expel him from the party he helped to found (PDL).

At a hastily prepared and very well attended press conference, Fini said: "I have been thrown out of my party without being given the opportunity of defending myself." He added that he had no intention of resigning his crucially important position as President of the Italian parliament. "Asking me to resign as President is typical of the way politics in Italy is presented as just another form of business, which is the stamp of this government. It has nothing to do with democratic institutions. Obviously I shall not resign because the president must guarantee respect for our laws, as well as the impartiality of the chamber." Fini was visibly annoyed as he spoke to the journalists and political columnists about the ridiculous accusations made by PDL in its document of expulsion.

'It is the first time' (the document claims) 'a president of the Congress has assumed such a pronounced political role, renouncing all institutional partiality.' It seems that Fini's offence was that he criticised Berlusconi. This is not permitted by Berlusconi, in exactly the same way as Zapatero in Spain (another hot country) will not accept criticism, or even advice. Though their politics are of a different colour, the two men share a creed – that they are right, that everybody else is wrong (unless they show complete and unswerving loyalty), and that the best way to deal with party dissidents is to sack them. Allies and friends of Fini have already announced the formation of their new party, named *Future Liberty for*

Italy. It comprises at least 32 members of parliament in support of Gianfranco Fini. "Our group is formed by free men and women who will always support the government when it takes measures included in its electoral promises, just as the group will oppose an measures taken which it considers will damage the national interest, " says Fini

With the apparition of the new party, Mr Berlusconi will have to take stock of his position, as it most likely he will lose his absolute majority. Before the storm, his party held 344 of the 630 seats, but he will not have only 310, which means six votes less than the absolute majority. The situation will be repeated in the Senate, where he had 174 votes, but can now count only on 160. He will have to seek support from minority parties in a centre-right position, merely to be able to continue his mandate and complete his ample programme of reforms. But he will have to do so under the furious gaze of an increasingly hostile Chamber, angered by the expulsion and attempted humiliation of Gianfranco Fini. A prominent member of the opposition said, "he (Berlusconi) cannot just carry on as if nothing has happened."

The Berlusconi/Fini 'marriage' had lasted seventeen years, though it had its ups and downs. The couple first met in 1993, when *il Cavagliere* burst into politics as a billionaire businessman. Their first success took place within a year of their meeting. Their 'coalition' won the 1994 elections. The mutual understanding seemed perfect, until the eruption on the political scene of Umberto Bossi's 'North League', a federalist declaration of intent. Fini annoyed Berlusconi with a declared mistrust of Bossi; he made it clear he would not concede anything or hand over any power of any kind to the 'North League'.

Since 2009 the Berlusconi/Fini axis has been sorely strained, over immigration, telephone tapping on behalf of the State etc. More than once Fini has clearly shown his frustration and disagreement, just as Berlusconi has shown his impatience and irritability with his 'partner'.

Things rose rapidly to a head in a sad show of bad manners on public television. Harsh words were spoken by both leaders during a party conference. On that memorable occasion Fini shouted, "What are you going to do, kick me out or what?" To his great surprise, that is exactly what Berlusconi has done. Fini has been kicked out, and is expected to resign as Leader of the Congress.

17ᵀᴴ AUGUST

Great Britain: No-one reads Gordon Brown

Poor Mr. Brown; an unelected prime minister for two years following Mr Blair's triumphs, Brown rather quickly published a book called *The Change we Choose* and much to the publisher's and the author's chagrin, nobody seems anxious to read it. The book is a hastily made collation of Brown's speeches delivered mostly in Parliament from 2007 to 2009. It emerged on April 1ˢᵗ, which turns out to have been an unfortunate date, given the British public's propensity to a sense of humour. By May 1st only 32 people had bought the book. Not even the electoral campaign raging during this period helped Mr. Brown in his quest for best-seller status. If you click on to Amazon, you will find *The Change we Choose* listed at no. 262,956 in popularity, which must be quite a blow to the Scotsman's pride. He has, by the way, retired to Scotland to lick his wounds, only visiting London occasionally.

On September 8ᵗʰ Tony Blair's book *A Journey* will be released to voracious readers around the English speaking world, with translations already nearly finished. Publishers have reckoned Blair's tome will sell in millions, though one wonders why, since there cannot be a word of truth in it, as indeed we never heard a word of truth from Mr Blair during his peculiar years as Premier. Perhaps his book will be published as fiction?

We learn that Mr Brown's opus was originally priced at £20. This proved optimistic so the booksellers reduced the cost price to around £6. No, it did not work. Some bookshops tried giving the work away, but that did not work either. Poor author. One feels so sorry for him. Not even the fact that Brown's duologues with the famous are reproduced in the book has helped sales. Conversations with persons such as Kofi Annan and Barack Obama should have boosted sales. The *Daily Telegraph* in an ironic article suggests that many of the 32 buyers might indeed be the subjects of those interviews with Mr. Brown.

Meanwhile, what has become of the man who has been placed at third from the bottom in a recent poll of prime ministers' popularity (or the opposite) since the War; beneath him are Alec Douglas-Home and Anthony Eden (how unfair to both these men, who 'did their best' I am sure). Eden had Suez and his own failing health to deal with, and Douglas-Home should have stood by to allow Butler into No. 10, though many Conservatives still think that Butler had too much intellect for the job, something that the 14th Earl could hardly boast, though intelligent and painfully honest he certainly was. Brown is thinking of looking for a job in the International Monetary Fund, though perhaps that august body might be barring its doors to the Man from the Manse. We do not know yet who will succeed Brown as Leader of the Labourites in September. It might be a Miliband, David or 'Ed', and then again it might be a Balls . . . whoever the winner is, they will have to work mightily to restore the popularity of the Labour Party. Six years of Blair and Brown have diminished both the UK and any bright image Labour might once have enjoyed.

Brown is also having problems with Cameron, Clegg, and the offices at No. 10 Downing Street. Up to the time of writing, it appears that Mr Brown's attempts to extract certain data concerning the financial crisis and his bungled attempts to alleviate it have failed. The offices have been ordered not to hand over sheaf's of notes made by Brown so that he can include the data in another book he is writing, precisely about the lead-up to the depression. Colleagues of Brown have been heard criticising this draconian decision. They cannot understand the deliberate obstruction, and are saying so. But the people responsible at No. 10 reply that they would be delighted to lend Mr. Brown the documents, given that he makes a proper written request for them. Apparently he thought that a simple telephone call would expedite their release, but a spokesman said Mr. Brown was behaving as if he were still prime minister. It is rumoured that in his new book, Brown makes all kinds of suggestions as to how to get out of the depression, which Conservatives find a bit risible, since it was Brown's inactivity and bad judgment that got Britain into the mess in the first place.

Russia: the 'Curse of the *Kursk*' pursues poor Putin

K-141 *Kursk* was the pride of the Russian Navy. Launched in 1994, the nuclear-powered super-submarine was probably the most sophisticated warship on (and under) the seas, but ended its days in the icy waters of the

Barents Sea on 12th August, 2000. With her to the bottom of the ocean went 24 *Granite* missiles, and a dozen torpedoes of the latest type and design.

The submarine's experienced captain was Liachin, a bit of a legend in the Navy. The shipwreck took him and 118 crew members to a slow, agonizing death. Why did it happen? The tragedy placed in perspective the fact that despite its fearsome reputation, the Russian Navy was in lamentable condition, due mainly to excessively low budgeting. Even today there are senior naval men who claim that the *Kursk* was in fact sunk by the US submarine *Memphis,* and that the sinking was a 'warning' from America that Russian sea power had become too strong to be unnoticed. There had also been the Russian threat to sell *Shkval* torpedoes to China. These were at the time the fastest and most destructive naval weapons on earth. It seems certain that that August 12 put the world at risk just as much as had John Kennedy's missile crisis with Kruschev in the Sixties.

An account of the end of the *Kursk* is to be found in a book written by the sea captain and historian Vitali Dotsenko called unambiguously *Who killed the Kursk?*

It seems that the naval exercise called by the Northern Fleet in that fateful August was the largest seen since the disintegration of the Soviet Empire. The object of the exercise was to test the *Shkval* torpedo to the utmost, as well as to convince the Chinese of its superiority, and, in passing, to cock a snook at the US Navy. The latter was doubtless Putin's idea, and the shock of what happened will stay with him.

At 11.18 on August 12, a resounding explosion beneath the waves was recorded, and two minutes later another, even more powerful radio contact with *Kursk* was lost. No messages were heard again. That day Mr. Putin had begun his summer holiday at Sochi on the shores of the Black Sea. First news of the explosions and loss of contact came through on the fourteenth, but apparently there was no mention of the *Kursk.* Nor was there a mention of the fact that she was carrying nuclear arms, which she was. It was only two years later, when the submarine was at last salvaged, that an admission was made that the Granite missiles were indeed nuclear.

On the 12th, divers reported hearing hammerings from inside the hull of the stricken vessel. The Russians tried seven times, using bathyscaphes, to enable rescuers to break into the submarines and save members of the crew. But they had to report that the bow of the submarine, containing the missiles, had been almost completely destroyed, and that a huge crack in the submarine's flank had been detected.

Naval authorities reached the conclusion that *Kursk* had collided with another submarine, though they did not discount possibilities of an enemy attack. Author Dotsenko claims she had been hit by an American torpedo, type Mark-48, but the official version eventually released states that the tragedy was caused by the accidental inflammation of one of the torpedoes, which provided for a chain reaction.

Putin stayed on holiday, and accepted the official version. He also accepted an international offer of help. Norwegian and British vessels especially equipped for salvage arrived with a team of divers. The combined effort managed to open the hull, and shortly afterwards news of the death of all hands was confirmed; Putin now cancelled his holiday and went to the naval port of Vidiayevo, where he had a stormy confrontation with the crew's families.

In October, 2000, the first twelve bodies were extracted from the wreck. Among their effects were notes written in total darkness, therefore almost illegible, but one of the notes had been written by the First Lieutenant, Dmitry Kolesnikov. Experts deciphered the news that men from compartments 6, 7 and 8 managed to join with the 9th in the end compartment in the stern; in all twenty-three persons. These had died in appalling circumstances, no electricity, finally no air. One year later the vessel was re-floated, all except the severely damaged bow. The bodies of the entire crew were brought home, along with the missiles, and the two reactors. The rest of the hull was broken up. Putin survives to this day as Prime Minister of Russia, but accusations of his negligence and inactivity have also survived.

1ST SEPTEMBER

Spain: what happened to the Cabinet?

The Spanish Government has disappeared for the holidays. Spanish people not actually following the iron discipline of the PSOE are wondering if there is in fact any government at all. The actual cabinet lacks coherence, and as a working group has ceased to exist. During the August break, with the President absent, the few decisions made by only two in the cabinet – José Blanco and Alfredo de Rubalcaba, have only echoed a spectral voice from the Moncloa Palace. This is nothing unusual, as everybody in the PSOE must toe the Zapatero line faithfully – or they find themselves bewitched, bothered, bewildered – and out. Each phantom minister contradicts another in every speech they made throughout the 'holiday' The ministers' lack of direction and coordination leaves me breathless. Unlike the Tories in Britain, the ministers have not yet unsheathed the knives, but it is only a matter of time. Meanwhile, where is Fernández de la Vega, the Senior Vice-President of the Government, you know, the woman who looks like a close run between Cruella deVille and Chiang Kai Shek? Has she, as Nancy Mitford used to write, b...d off? Perhaps she is circling with the hot air currents above Madrid, awaiting her Leader's call to take a seat with the *Consejo de Estado.*

The useless and ineffable Moratinos, Foreign Minister, has also disappeared. Half Morocco is busy assaulting Spanish citizens, including women police officers; the King of Spain feels impelled to telephone fellow King Mohammed to chide him for his country's attacks on Melilla; ex-President Aznar feels equally impelled (as an ordinary Spanish citizen) to rush off to Melilla to find out for himself what is happening; Spain has no Moroccan ambassador in Madrid; Morocco has no Spanish ambassador in Rabat; a message comes from the Foreign Ministry – "everything is simply divine in international relations between Spain and Morocco, we cannot think what all the newspapers are going on about". Zapatero is said to be seriously considering replacing Moratinos and shoving him forward as potential mayoral candidate for Córdoba.

Carme Chacón (a Minister of Defence invented by Lewis Carroll) and Celestino Corbacho (Minister of Labour) are up to something in Cataluña, while Spanish troops and policemen are murdered regularly in Afghanistan and Iraq, and at home the unemployed figure approaches five million. One must never forget that governing, as such, is of secondary importance to the PSOE. Electioneering and its concomitant games come first. And now the latest news is that Carme Chacón and her spouse are involved in the buying of a large chalet somewhere in the Caribbean. So much to occupy the poor woman! It is obviously too much to spend time on the care of her servicemen and women in far off places.

Pathetic Elena Salgado (Economics) has to keep a wary eye on what other ministers are implying about the Spanish economy and possible pension and labour reform shocks. Very often what is said is wrong, and Salgado has to sally out to rectify the situation with yet more questionable half-truths.

Trinidad Jiménez (Health) is not seen at her Ministry because she is locking horns with another obstinate PSOE candidate for the forthcoming Madrid Community elections. Tomas Gómez thinks he is the ideal candidate, and is ready to argue with Zapatero, who has promised this juicy morsel to Trinidad. Both candidates appear regularly on TV saying through clenched teeth how much they like and admire *everybody else,* even Esperanza Aguirre (actual President of the Community).

Manuel Chavez, who just escaped with his political career dangling on a thread in Andalucía, and was made a sort of twelfth-man Vice-President for his pains, is kept around the PSOE though very few people like him, with a hangdog expression, no competence, nothing to do except await his doubtless luxurious pension. You surely remember Chavez; he's the one who after presiding over Andalucía for years gave ten million euros *of public money* to his daughter's business.

13TH SEPTEMBER

Turkey: Erdogan strengthened

Yesterday that difficult country Turkey held a referendum; the people had to decide whether or not they wanted Prime Minister Recep Tayyip Erdogan to enjoy much more power, via proposed constitutional reforms. The people democratically voted Yes.

Yesterday by coincidence was the thirtieth anniversary of a military coup d'Etat, which unleashed a wave of political repression unprecedented even in Turkish history. That unhappy period ended in the signing of a Magna Carta under whose more benevolent jurisdiction the country has been governed to this day.

The question in everybody's mind is – will Erdogan use his greatly extended powers in a reforming or a repressive way? His detractors were predicting during the lead-up to the referendum that he would follow the second path. Erdogan himself repeated at every public meeting the slogan: "Those who vote NO in this referendum will be implicitly approving the supporters of the 1980 Coup."

Not to be undone, the opposition printed and published cartoons showing the 1980s dissident general Kennan Evren as a forerunner of Erdogan himself. "They are as alike as cheese and cheese!"

Erdogan's promised reforms once he is firmly in the saddle (and with constitutional backing), are seen by the opposition as an attempt to remove any potential barriers that might impede the upward mobility of Erdogan's 'moderately Islamist' AKP party. Or, in other words, they see Turkey in the future forming up with other Islamist states as a firm front to the West and any other religion but Islam. Naturally the West is bothered by this, as (nuclear) Pakistan, Afghanistan, Iraq and (nearly nuclear) Iran, financed and supported behind the diplomatic smiles by Saudi Arabia, are already enough of a thorn in the flesh.

One of the most debated articles to be found in the text of the newly proposed Constitution is a proposal radically to reform judicial structures; another is the expressed wish to bring to proper justice those involved in the 1980 Coup. This has particularly angered the ultra-nationalists.

As of now, the judiciary is the firmest bastion against Erdogan's AKP. If the reforms go through, and following the referendum there seems no reason why they shouldn't, the Government may appoint judges in all the highest courts in the land, which the opposition sees, probably rightly, as an assault on the independence of the judiciary. Turkey only needs to study Spain to see what happens when judges become 'politicised'. Imagine the havoc caused by a dozen Turkish versions of Judge Balthazar Garzón.

Notwithstanding, many thinking Turks, principally a group calling itself *Yetmez Ama Evet* ("it's not enough, but it will do . . .") consider the proposed reforms as an advance in modern Turkish history, and the gradual democratisation of their country. Merve Alkici, a young activist serving with a militant group of young people, has said: "this will be the first civil Constitution since 1921." He went on: "this must go through, because it is only the commencement of many other essential reforms!"

Of course the Kurdish population of the country have demonstrated very little, because the proposed reforms do not affect the Kurds in any way. They made the normal fuss, but in a half-hearted way, and have been bashed by the Turkish police for their pains.

England: Ed before Dave

In the not very likely case of the League of British Loyalists questioning my title, my answer is that since Scotland and Wales achieved their devolution and acquired their own parliaments, I consider anything that happens in London (capital city of England, goddit?) is a matter for England. In Scotland, they have a parliament where no Englishman or woman can sit; in Wales, they have a parliament where no Englishman or woman wants to sit. But the odd thing is that Scots and Welsh members abound in England's House of Commons. Maybe many Scots and Welshmen prefer to live in London than Perth or Carnarvon.

Perhaps even odder is that the Scottish referendum was pushed through by Mr Alex Salmond, the Great Scottish Nationalist, though only 60% of the Scots bothered to vote for or against their own devolution. In Wales, led patriotically by a gentleman called Davies, only 50% of the 50% having the right to vote in the referendum bothered to vote, so it was a quarter of the enfranchised who brought devolution to dear sad Wales. Mr. Davies did not last long governing Wales, however, because he was one of those who chose to live in London, and went by night to a dark park inhabited by men only. Davies had his wallet stolen by a knife-wielding young man. He resigned immediately, which is right, especially when they are seen by society as wrong, all right?

Well, that is all as it may be, but in England 40-year old Ed Miliband (we must call him 'Ed', not Edward) has beaten his own brother over leadership of the demoralized Labour Party ('New Labourites, Old Labour men, New Social Democrats, Old Blairites?). The brother is the slightly older, but equally experienced David Miliband (we must call him *David*, remember? Not Dave). We used to have a Prime Minister whose name at a very snooty school was Anthony Blair, but we had to call him Tony. These names! I suppose forty years back we would have had to make do with Harry Macmillan and Al Home pronounced *Hume*. W.H. Auden the poet had for thirty years a lover called Chester Kallman. I quote Alan Bennett: 'his grandmother's name was Bobby. His stepmother's name was Syd; in their choice of names the Americans have always been more eclectic that we are: a girl in *Dynasty*, for instance, is called Kirby, a name hitherto confined to a grip. These Kallman names can't have helped. With a grandmother called Bobby, and a stepmother called Syd, it's not surprising Chester turned out to be a Nancy'.

On 26 September Ed Miliband won 50.65% of the votes in the primaries; brother David won 49.35% - a hair's breadth of difference in the brothers' battle to lead the New Old Labour Party. It was a splendid beginning to this year's Old New Labour Party's Conference in Manchester. The Miliband brothers embraced each other, as good brothers (and comrades) should, but journalists fear the New (but really Old) Labour Party is divided by schism and misunderstood dogma.

As usual in England, the voting system is complex – not always understood completely – even by those who must vote in it. Throughout all the preliminary primaries, if you see what I mean, it was brother David who shone, aided by the militant socialists and the parliamentary party group, but the last of the preliminaries was won by brother Ed because of unfailing support by the trade unions, who see in Ed a re-manifestation of brother mineworkers' and boiler-makers' union leaders. The New Old New Labour Party will head right back to the good old days of strikes and pickets and Art Scargill. Old New Socialists believe that with their election of Ed, they can return to grassroots, to Leninism; to real Marxism.

What a scuffle! David is the Leonidas of the militants, and brother Ed the Alcibiades of the unions. David is the heir to Blairism, while brother Ed was always a thorn in Blair's tender flesh. Still, both brothers in their speeches urge renovation as the only way to scupper Cameron (Dave) and

Clegg (Nick). We admit that David is the more pragmatic and moderate, while young bro is more energetic and visionary, positively impetuous sometimes.

England: the ups and downs of Socialism

England's Labour Party has elected a new party leader, Ed Miliband. It must have been a good choice, because the opinion polls held *since* the leadership contest show that Labourites have been distinctly encouraged by Ed's push to the top. It would be difficult to describe the politics of the last two Labour prime ministers. Tony Blair showed disdain for typical socialist dogma, and was probably more to the right than Margaret Thatcher or John Major. Gordon Brown (never elected by the people) should have been a true blooded socialist, as the relatively poor son of the manse, but wasn't.

It is time to take a much closer look at Socialism with a capital C: how did it come about? What was it? What is it now? What has it achieved? It started at the end of the 18th century with the Jacobins, Girondins and the French Revolution, which was more about greed, envy and pride than about Liberty, Fraternity or Equality. In the 19th century, phrases and ideas can be traced in the writings of Saint-Simon and others in France, and Robert Owen's experiments in his Scottish works, in the co-operative control of industry. Socialism covers a multiple of positions – communism at the totalitarian end, and liberal democracy at the other, gentler but perhaps more insidious. Nothing could be more difficult to define with accuracy.

It would be easier to count what Socialists are against, rather than what they stand for: capitalism in any form of course; a defining of the social classes that eight centuries of European development had clarified; Capitalism in socialist eyes (which tend to be firmly fixed by socialist dogma) enriches the owners of capital at the expense of the employee or worker. It provides no security for the poor, and sacrifices the welfare of society to private gain. This is what socialists teach socialists, through the writings of Victorian reformers, and gatherings such as the Fabian Society (G.B. Shaw comes to mind) - members of the latter tended to be highly intellectual members of the English and German upper classes - and thus was born the unanswerable question that has taxed our minds since we began to think, namely why is it that so many prominent socialists came and come from the very class they are supposed to despise and deprecate?

Socialists you know will argue that the community as a whole must *own* and *control* the means of production, distribution and exchange in order to capture a more equal division of a nation's wealth. This can be done by creating state ownership, or ownership of industry by the workers themselves. The instrument to be used to achieve this was, and is, the trade union. But the trade union has become an antediluvian instrument only useful in that it provides an income for people who prefer not to work for a living. This has just been demonstrated in unmistakeable fashion by the ignominious failure of the General Strike in Spain. Socialists recommend a replacement of the market economy by some kind of vaguely defined planned economy. Fine, but the aim of these measures was to make industry socially responsible, viz. the name 'Socialism'. It should bring about a much larger degree of equality in living standards. Not satisfied with this, socialists have fought for special provision for those in need, in the form of an organised welfare state. But in England it is engorged and essentially blind welfare that has partially infected an efficient, modern and industrialised state.

Karl Marx wanted to demonstrate scientifically how capital profit was derived from exploitation of the worker. He argues (in *Das Kapital)* that a truly socialist society could only be achieved by a mass movement of the workers themselves. This is where the troubles began, and pure theory became impure force of a kind never seen before in History, for the *methods* by which the transformation was to be reached, and the manner in which the new society was to be managed remained the subject of massive disagreement, producing a wide variety of socialist parties (different in each country), ranging from moderate reformers, Sweden for instance, to the ultra-left wing communists dedicated to social upheaval by violent revolution (Russia, Cuba, China etc.).

25TH OCTOBER

Spain: the significance of the cabinet re-shuffle

On a recent Sunday the President of the Government was asked at a meeting if he intended to remodel his government, by making changes among the ministers. Rodríguez Zapatero replied briefly to the effect that the only change considered at the time was a new post for the retiring Minister of Labour, Celestino Corbacho. Sr. Corbacho had announced his intention of returning to the normal (?) everyday debate in Catalan politics. As writers in all the Spanish newspapers correctly predicted, this meant that on the day after, a Monday, the *El Pais* website duly 'leaked' the news that there was about to be a positively volcanic re-shuffle of responsibilities in the Cabinet, in which only Mr Zapatero himself would be untouched, one way or the other.

First, Zapatero has removed three of his most stalwart fans and supporters. María Teresa Fernández de la Vega, senior vice-president and ZP's staunchest admirer; Miguel Angel Moratinos, Foreign Minister, and Elena Espinosa, Minister for the Environment, are all *out*. They will be given sinecures for their pains. Moratinos learnt about his abrupt dismissal while occupying his seat in Congress, and was seen to weep.

Zapatero has elevated his 'Rasputin', Alfredo de Rubalcaba, to the position of First Vice-President. He stays at the head of the Ministry of the Interior too. His powers are almost unlimited. He will certainly make himself President of the Government soon. Elena Salgado stays as Second Vice-President and Minister of Finance. Manuel Chavez stays as Third Vice-President and Minister in charge of Territorial Politics. Ramon Jauregi (one of the formerly great barons of the Party) has been rescued from his post at the European Union, and reinstated in the Cabinet as *Ministry de la Presidencia,* in charge of most matters connected with the present incumbent of the Moncloa Palace. This had been another post held by De la Vega before the Great Re-shuffle. Trinidad Jiménez, fresh from her humiliating defeat in the Madrid candidacy battle, has been moved to *Exteriores,* replacing tearful Moratinos. The female Minister of Defence, one Carme Chacon, stays put, much to the chagrin of certain senior army officers, who strangely think (but keep quiet about it) that a country's Ministry of Defence should ideally be headed by a man with some military experience. Chacon is a lawyer, like so many politicians of today. The new Minister of Labour, who must face the nearly five million unemployed in Spain, is a trade unionist who was much photographed demonstrating with other workers during the recent rather unsuccessful general strike. His name is Valeriano Gómez. He will now have to negotiate with his fellow strikers, which could prove difficult, and amusing for some. Francisco Camaño stays in the hot seat as Minister of Justice. Leire Pajín has been lifted out of her job as Party Organiser, and dropped into the chair at the head of the Ministry of Health. There is a difference of opinion in various newspapers about Srta. Pajín's qualifications for high office. Some say this young lady (34) has a Degree in Sociology. I do hope so. Other organs claim she left school young with no examinations of her knowledge having taken place. Who knows? Spain has had six years of Zetapé's government, and has experienced a remarkable indifference to the truth throughout those years.

The dumb Ministry of Equality invented by Zapatero under the leadership of one Bibiana Aído has vanished. The repulsive José Blanco still has his Ministry of Development (*Fomento*), but he isn't often seen there. He leads the rabid spokesmen who on a daily basis (especially at weekends) gather to insult and assault the only important political party in Opposition, the *Partido Popular.* Both the Ministry and the Minister of Housing (*Vivienda)* have gone like a puff of smoke, and ex-Minister Beatriz Corredor will become a secretary of state, which is a sad comedown for this hard-working young lady (42). Angel Gabilondo is a good Minister of Education, and will be relieved to know he has not been relieved. The Ministry of Culture (Angela González-Sinde) is untouched. So is the Ministry of Science under Cristina Garmendia.

Zapatero surprised not a few of his many supporters by plucking Rosa Aguilar (another lawyer) from the ranks of the Communist Party and making her the new Minister for the Environment, replacing Elena Espinosa. The Minister for Industry, Miguel Sebastián, one of ZP's oldest friends and advisers, stays at the helm, though the seas are very rough indeed, and he will need all his undoubted talents to avoid the rocks. Thus the total number of ministries is reduced from 17 to 15, but it has also been announced that *each* ministry will form a department working for a Spokeperson (*Portavoz)*. This means there will be no change in the cost of government. No cuts are expected. In fact not a single newspaper or political website has missed the fact that the cabinet re-shuffle has brought no new plans to deal with unemployment, rising inflation or reckless public spending in the Autonomies. It is a wholly political game of musical chairs, designed with one purpose in mind; an unending and determined assault on the Popular Party, which has started already. The significance of all this drama is to reduce the Opposition by systematic propaganda. Under the genius of Rubalcaba, who has just become the effective ruler of the country (he controls justice, the police forces, and communications), each serving member of the Opposition will be singled out for scrutiny. Character destruction via the PSOE-controlled media will be rife. Woe betide any *Popular* foolish enough to accept a bribe in the form of a box of chocolates. He or she will be dragged up before the courts as a champion of corruption. I don't need to point out that such microscopic meddling by government departments will *not* be applied to members of the PSOE. That would be stretching things a bit.

THE END OF 2010

Spain: the Emergency and some comparisons between European health ministers

I have not mentioned the air traffic controllers 'strike' because the media has talked of nothing else since the dreadful weekend at the beginning of December, when *all* air traffic over Spanish territory was cancelled at the orders, apparently, of AENA, the government-controlled body that manages Spain's only too numerous airports.

Now, however, the case is altered because our Government declared a state of emergency (called in Spain *estado de alarma*), and called in the armed forces to force the controllers back to their desks. This group of very highly paid but desperately overworked men and women had decided to 'walk-out' on 3 December, the first day of the *puente de la Constitución* holiday – a long one in which most Spaniards go somewhere else, very often by aeroplane. The airports at Madrid and Barcelona rapidly became rather like Dante's Inferno. No aircraft was allowed to take-off, fly or land in Spain. Tourism lost millions of euros.

Now putting a democratic European state under what amounts to martial law is a serious step, and it appears to have been taken not by Zapatero, who is the President of the Government, but by Rubalcaba and Blanco, the first being First Vice-President and the second the Minister for Development (*Fomento*). The airports are José Blanco's responsibility. This gentleman began calling the controllers, and of course the Popular Party, every kind of name. They were 'unpatriotic' and 'blackmailers' and 'traitors' and so on. Some of the controllers did not help their situation by calling these two politicians 'manipulators'.

The problems, according to the air traffic controllers, are that their very high salaries are paid to them following mutual agreement with AENA;

that they are expected to carry out their profession, which is maintaining the life and security of airline passengers and crew with far too few of them at the airports, and under constant pressure; they are expected to work a colossal number of extra hours; if the controller is female and has a baby, the total number of days in her maternity leave are later added on to her compulsory working hours. Now, it seems, Spain's government is bringing charges of sedition against the controllers who 'walked away'. Some of them, the ringleaders I suppose, might have to go to prison for up to eight years, if the *Fiscal General* Sr. Candido Pumpido is to be believed. This seems a little illogical, when there are too few controllers anyway, and each one cost a lot of time and money to train for this essential job.

It is one of the eccentricities of our strange modern life that an air traffic controller, in whose hands thousands upon thousands of citizens place their lives every time they catch a 'plane, is in actual fact paid far less than a youth who kicks a football for a living in a first division club.

The Government announced a state of emergency, which they said would last over a short period, during which relations between AENA and the controllers would be stabilized. This task has been patchily done, but the government has *not* raised martial law. It intends to continue it *for an unspecified time*. When asked about this, Zapatero replied in Parliament that it would last "not a moment longer or shorter than was needed".

This State of Alarm is the first since Franco. It was not declared after the atrocious attack on the passenger trains at Atocha in 2004; nor after the sinking of the oil tanker *Prestige;* nor during the almost equally disastrous Metro strike in Madrid. Many editors of national newspapers are asking why. At the same time the conspiracy merchants are having a field day on the Internet, Facebook and Twitter.

One thing is certain: Mr Rodríguez Zapatero seems to have vanished into history, though he is still alive, grinning, and 'chairing' meetings of what we must obviously call his 'War Cabinet'. *Actual* power has been grabbed by Alfredo Pérez Rubalcaba and his sidekick José Blanco. Both are wily and not really very nice. In their hands, God knows what will happen if the condition of martial law is, as we must expect, lengthened until January 15 or thereabouts. In case the Reader wonders what I am getting at, I must tell her that under martial law, the government is legally entitled to enter any field of endeavour it likes and start leaving armed colonels in offices to ensure the staff does what it is told. This includes the world of communications.

www.ingramcontent.com/pod-product-compliance
Lightning Source LLC
Chambersburg PA
CBHW070830310526
45788CB00017B/82